The Fallacies of
Cold War Deterrence
and a
New Direction

Keith B. Payne

The University Press of Kentucky

Copyright © 2001 by The University Press of Kentucky

Scholarly publisher for the Commonwealth,
serving Bellarmine University, Berea College, Centre
College of Kentucky, Eastern Kentucky University,
The Filson Historical Society, Georgetown College,
Kentucky Historical Society, Kentucky State University,
Morehead State University, Transylvania University,
University of Kentucky, University of Louisville,
and Western Kentucky University.
All rights reserved.

Editorial and Sales Offices: The University Press of Kentucky
663 South Limestone Street, Lexington, Kentucky 40508<n>4008

06 05 03 02 01   5 4 3 2 1

Cataloging-in-Publication Data
available from the Library of Congress

ISBN 0-8131-2207-4 (cloth)
ISBN 0-8131-9015-0 (pbk.)

This book is printed on acid-free recycled paper meeting
the requirements of the American National Standard
for Permanence in Paper for Printed Library Materials.

Manufactured in the United States of America.

For T.P., Birdie, Posy, and Moots.

And in memory of Dr. Holland Payne.

CONTENTS

Preface

The renowned American political commentator Walter Lippmann once observed, "If we cannot fully understand the acts of other people, until we know what they think they know, then in order to do justice we have to appraise not only the information which has been at their disposal, but the minds through which they have filtered it."[1] Lippmann's observation is unassailable: to understand others' behavior, we must first understand what and how they think. Three millennia earlier, Solomon, the third king of Israel, elegantly stated the point, "For as one that hath reckoned within himself, so is he."[2]

This truth may at first appear prosaic; but its implications are profound. It identifies thought, and the particular "filters" that define an individual's thinking, as the wellspring of behavior. To understand or anticipate behavior, you must first examine and understand the particular thought process that leads to behavior. This book represents an attempt to consider some of the implications of this truth for international relations; those implications are not trivial.

For example, in crises and war the policies directed toward a challenger frequently are shaped by expectations of how that challenger will behave in response. How a foe is expected to behave can be the fundamental dynamic behind policy. On what should those expectations be based? Intuition? Hope? Or, as Lippmann suggests, an understanding of a challenger's beliefs and thoughts? The answer to this question is critical because if expectations of an opponent's behavior are dramatically wrong, the

---

1. *Public Opinion* (New York: The MacMillan Co., 1927), p. 85.

2. *Proverbs*: Chapter 23, Verse 7 (English translation from the Hebrew Tanach).

policies based on those expectations also are likely to be mistaken. Policies built on ill-founded expectations of the opponent can be extraordinarily dangerous.

In 1938, for example, British Prime Minister Neville Chamberlain hoped a policy of appeasement would satisfy Adolf Hitler's territorial appetite, and structured British policy accordingly. An immediate result of Chamberlain's appeasement policy was the passive ceding to Hitler of the Czech Sudetenland during negotiations in Munich. In doing so Chamberlain possibly forestalled a coup against Hitler by the German military, and convinced der Führer that the West would not respond forcefully to his 1939 offensive against Poland: "Our enemies are little worms; I got to know them in Munich."[3] The broader effect of Chamberlain's policy was to facilitate a severe threat to civilization. This is not overstatement. At the beginning of the 21st century it is easy to forget how bleak the future of democracy looked in 1939 and 1940, as two bestial dictatorships, one Communist and one National Socialist, coexisted and conspired to dominate Eurasia.

What was the basis for Chamberlain's desperately mistaken policy toward the Third Reich? He and his colleagues little understood the ugliness and brutality of Hitler's beliefs and thought. They appear to have placed little value on the examination of what the leaders of National Socialism thought and, as Lippmann puts it, "the minds through which they filtered" information. Chamberlain and much of the British political elite preferred the ease and comfort of viewing Hitler as ultimately likeminded and reasonable, at heart a traditional European statesman. Chamberlain's policy prescription was doomed because

---

3.   Quoted in, Max Domarus, *Hitler: Speeches and Proclamations 1932-1945, Vol III, The Chronicle Of A Dictatorship, 1939-1940* (Wauconda, IL: Bolchazy-Carducci Publishers, 1997), p. 1663.

he greatly misjudged Hitler's basic beliefs and thus also his behavior.

Hitler was not reasonable; his fundamental goals included the defeat of France, an internal "reckoning" and "blood cleansing" of grotesque proportions, and a war of conquest and annihilation against the East. For the Western political elite to mistake Hitler and National Socialism so profoundly was not inevitable; it was a choice because Hitler was not discrete or coy in public expressions of his beliefs and thoughts. He had presented his views and goals with considerable clarity and consistency for over a decade. Indeed, rarely do leaders expose their beliefs and thought life as publicly as did Adolf Hitler.

Unfortunately, few in the West bothered to examine those thoughts and beliefs, and fewer still took seriously the warnings of those who did bother to look: Hitler's ranting was beyond the pale of reason, too outlandish to be taken seriously by political sophisticates.[4] Because Hitler's beliefs and thought processes were ignored or dismissed, expectations of his behavior—built on hope instead of evidence—were far out of line with reality. An incalculable price was paid because the seemingly prosaic truth that behavior will follow from particular beliefs and "filters" was ignored. Chamberlain chose to view Hitler as basically reasonable not for a lack of information to the contrary, but possibly because the evidence about Hitler's thinking promised behavior too dreadful to face.

U.S. policies toward challengers frequently have been shaped by the same easy and comfortable expectation that their behavior

---

4. There were some exceptions. For example, prior to the outbreak of war in 1939, R.C.K. Ensor, a Fellow of Corpus Christi College, Oxford, began a frank and concise series of monographs that described Hitler and his policy directions quite accurately. See, R.C.K. Ensor, *Herr Hitler's Self-Disclosure In Mein Kampf*, Oxford Pamphlets On World Affairs, No. 3 (Oxford: Clarendon Press, July 6, 1939); and, *Who Hitler Is*, Oxford Pamphlets On World Affairs, No. 20 (Oxford: Clarendon Press, 1939).

ultimately would prove reasonable. On occasion, those policies, based on little more than hope and wishful thinking, have proved to be dangerously misguided. Most prominently, U.S. nuclear deterrence policy, and particularly its Cold War application to NATO's nuclear deterrence strategy, was based on the assumption that the Soviet leadership would be reasonable by Washington's standards, and thus view nuclear weapons in the same fashion that U.S. leaders viewed nuclear weapons. As with Chamberlain, this expectation was contrary to much of the evidence available at the time. And, from the evidence now available it is clear that Soviet leaders, based on their own particular beliefs and filters, viewed nuclear weapons far differently from their American counterparts; as a result, Soviet war plans for Europe included the early and heavy use of nuclear weapons. We were very fortunate that those war plans were never put into operation despite the fact that NATO's policies for nuclear deterrence were far removed from the realities of Soviet planning. Some now believe this good fortune and our survival of the Cold War to be the result of our mastery of nuclear deterrence policy, and therefore advocate extending that policy into the post-Cold War period.

The question upon which this book focuses is how should the United States plan its policies of deterrence in the post-Cold War period? Are Cold War approaches adequate, or do we need a new framework? The beginning of wisdom in addressing this question is to apply seriously the observations by Solomon and Lippmann noted above, and recognize that challengers' behavior in response to U.S. deterrence policies will depend on the particular beliefs and filters that define their thinking. As the cases of Hitler and many others presented in this book demonstrate, those beliefs and filters may be extremely diverse, and well beyond anything anticipated in Washington.

This beginning point in considering future U.S deterrence policy is a sharp departure from the past. The U.S. Cold War deterrence framework truly was established on the confident assumption that foreign leaderships would behave "sensibly" when presented with severe U.S. threats. Their behavior in response to U.S. deterrence policy was expected to fall within familiar and predictable boundaries: because U.S. nuclear threats were so lethal, any sane opponent by definition would be deterred from extreme provocations. This confident expectation was not based on the close examination of any challenger's particular beliefs and filters. Rather, it reflected the heroically optimistic assumption that rationality and reason, *as understood in Washington*, would overcome any particular or unique beliefs and modes of thought that might otherwise lead a challenger away from predictably bowing to severe U.S. nuclear threats.

This book argues that if such an approach to deterrence is extended into the post-Cold War period, it will set the stage for unexpected failures in U.S. deterrence policy. On occasion, a challenger's particular beliefs and modes of thought will lead it to an assertive response to U.S. deterrence threats, a response that will astonish U.S. leaders wedded to the confident expectation that rational opponents ultimately will be guided by familiar, reasonable behavioral norms. Overconfidence in Washington about deterrence, built on apparent U.S. mastery of the subject during the Cold War, will be laid low by an opponent who unexpectedly marches to a different drummer and responds to U.S. policies in very surprising ways. Whether such a policy failure will prove disastrous for the United States will depend on the details. With the proliferation of nuclear, biological, and chemical weapons of mass destruction placing great lethality in the hands of many potential challengers, however, the prospects are increasing that a future surprise failure of deterrence will result in an unprecedented catastrophe.

Admittedly this book offers an initial and only partial solution to this question of post-Cold War deterrence. That solution is to examine as closely as possible the particular opponent's thinking—its beliefs and thought filters—to better anticipate its likely behavior in response to U.S. deterrence policies, and structure those policies accordingly. It is to avoid repeating Chamberlain's error wherever possible. It is to move away from the image of comfortably predictable opponents that remains at the core of the U.S. Cold War deterrence framework.

To determine whether this approach can lead to different conclusions about deterrence than those suggested by the Cold War framework, a case study is explored in these pages that involves a U.S.-Chinese crisis over Taiwan. (This case study scenario was selected and its examination well underway prior to the furor in Sino-American relations sparked in July 1999 by Taiwan's expressed leanings toward greater independence). A yearlong effort by my colleagues and me at the National Institute for Public Policy was the basis for some tentative suggestions offered here as to how Chinese leaders in particular would view U.S. deterrence efforts in this crisis. I have summarized the conclusions we reached; they stand in sharp contrast to the relatively easy confidence in U.S. nuclear deterrence expressed by many U.S. officials and commentators in general, and with regard to nuclear deterrence of China in particular. This book demonstrates that an examination of the particular beliefs and thinking of a challenger involved in a crisis with the United States can yield strikingly different expectations of the opponent's behavior than does the assumption that a foe will be reasonable by Washington's standards, behave predictably, and be deterred; Solomon's observation stands.

As noted above, however, pursuing an approach to deterrence that takes into account the specific opponent's beliefs and modes of thought can provide only a partial solution. It may improve U.S. deterrence policies. Nothing, however, can "ensure" the functioning of deterrence, despite the hundreds of confident claims by prominent American officials and commentators. With sufficient work and available evidence, we should be able to reduce our ignorance about how a specific opponent thinks, and thus improve our chances of anticipating how it will behave in response to U.S. deterrence policies. But the hubris regarding our mastery of nuclear deterrence "stability" that was common during the Cold War, and extended by many into the post-Cold War period, is built on the demonstrably false assumption that Washington's interpretation of what is rational and sensible behavior also will be the basis of our opponents' behavior. In truth, no matter how lethal the U.S. deterrent threat, no matter how "rational" we regard an opponent's choice to bow to U.S. demands, there remains an irreducible level of uncertainty concerning how an opponent will behave in response to U.S. threats. And in no prospective case will we even be able to define that level of uncertainty with precision. In the future, the United States will face crises in which there can be no confident expectation that its deterrence threats will control the opponent's behavior. The prospects for deterrence success may be known only after the fact.

A question raised by this finding is, what should be the U.S. response to the inherent uncertainty of deterrence? The answer offered here is to prepare simultaneously for deterrence and the possibility of its failure or irrelevance. This answer stands again in sharp contrast to Cold War thinking. For example, in a world increasingly characterized by the proliferation of missiles and weapons of mass destruction, the preparation for deterrence failure must include capabilities to defend against ballistic missiles. During the Cold War, such capabilities were rejected as incompatible with deterrence "stability" and as unnecessary because deterrence assuredly would "work." The discussion in these pages, and particularly the China case study, suggest strongly that continued rejection of missile defense on these grounds is a remnant of Cold War thinking. In the future, defenses may contribute significantly to the prospects for deterrence, and to preparation for the unavoidable possibility that deterrence will fail or be irrelevant.

I would like to thank my colleagues at the National Institute for Public Policy and others who contributed at various stages to the preparation of this book. Dr. Marin Strmecki helped in early efforts to scope the study. Kurt Guthe did his typically outstanding work on much of the original background research and writing that is reflected in Chapter Six. In fact, he fully deserves to be listed as co-author of that chapter, but modestly declined the offer. John Kohout provided several helpful reviews of the entire manuscript as it evolved. Bernie Victory, and Willis Stanley contributed thoughtfully to the China case study. Lieutenant General William Odom (USA, ret.) provided a constructive critique of the manuscript for which I am grateful, and I have benefited from discussing the major ideas and themes of the book with Dr. Fred Iklé and Amb. Robert Joseph. And, as always, Professor Colin Gray has contributed generously to my education and understanding of the complexities of international politics and power. Amy Joseph provided her usual outstanding touch in preparing and managing many versions of the manuscript, including the final pages for publication, and Dr. C. Dale Walton helped to keep track of the numerous references. I also would like to express my great appreciation to my wife Beth, not only for enduring a long research and writing process, but for patiently and meticulously editing the final proof pages. Finally, the Smith Richardson Foundation and the Lawrence Livermore National Laboratory sponsored research that contributed directly and indirectly, respectively, to making this book possible. I am grateful for their support.

In completing this book I have drawn from several of my previously published works and appreciate the permission to do so granted by the publishers of the following: *Deterrence In The Second Nuclear Age* (Lexington, KY: University Press of Kentucky, 1996); "Post-Cold War Deterrence and Missile Defense," *Orbis*, Vol. 39, No. 2, Spring 1995; "Proliferation, Deterrence, Stability and Missile Defense," *Comparative Strategy*, Vol. 13, No. 1; "Deterrence and U.S. Strategic Force Requirements After the Cold War," *Comparative Strategy*, Vol. 11, No. 3; and (co-authored with Lawrence Fink) "Deterrence Without Defense: Gambling on Perfection," *Strategic Review*, Vol. 16, No. 1, Winter 1989.

Chapter 1

INTRODUCTION

Surprise, Surprise

Surprises can be pleasant; but they are particularly unwelcome when it comes to questions of war and peace. Unfortunately, such surprises are fairly common in international relations.

In August 1941, for example, Assistant Secretary of State Dean Acheson reassured President Roosevelt that war with Japan was unlikely because "no rational Japanese could believe an attack on us could result in anything but disaster for his country."[1] Four months later Japan launched a surprise attack against the United States at Pearl Harbor. Despite Acheson's confident prediction that Japanese leaders would never dare to strike the United States, they did exactly that, believing they were "doomed" if they did not.[2] Japanese leaders calculated that they had no acceptable alternative to war with the United States.

In November 1950, U.S. forces were fighting in North Korea. At the time the CIA and Gen. Douglas MacArthur advised President Truman that China would not intervene in the Korean War, in part because they believed that Mao Zedong and, more importantly, Mao's Soviet patrons would fear igniting a global conflict. Indeed, the CIA's Daily Summaries (intelligence summaries for the civilian leadership)

---

1. Quoted in, Scott Sagan, "The Origins of the Pacific War," *Journal of Interdisciplinary History*, Vol. 18, No. 4 (Spring 1988), p. 906.

2. See, for example, Louis Morton, "Japan's Decision for War," *Command Decisions* (New York: Harcourt, Brace, 1959). See also, Richard Betts, *Surprise Attack* (Washington, D.C.: Brookings Institution, 1982), pp. 133-137.

continued until November 17, 1950, to claim that China would not intervene or, if it did, would not intervene on a large scale.[3]

Nevertheless, days later, on November 25, 1950, China hurled 170,000 troops against the U.S. Eighth Army in North Korea, signaling a massive surprise intervention that ultimately cost China a million casualties. Instead of being deterred by the prospect of war with the United States Stalin expressed support for Chinese intervention. He stated to Mao, "If a war [with the U.S.] is inevitable, then let it be waged now."[4] Mao, in turn, saw no acceptable alternative to war because he believed U.S. intervention in Korea was part of a larger U.S. plan to encircle and ultimately attack China on three fronts, from the Korean Peninsula, across the Taiwan Strait, and from French Indochina.

As Shu Guang Zhang has observed with regard to Chinese perceptions, "The PRC leadership obviously exaggerated the U.S. threat. Having long suspected American hostility toward a Communist China, it quickly concluded that U.S. intervention in Korea and the interposition of the U.S. Seventh Fleet in the Taiwan Strait was part of a long-planned U.S. offensive. The Chinese leaders were therefore unable to understand that U.S. actions in Korea were generally defensive and reflected only limited aims."[5] American leaders clearly misunderstood Chinese expectations and fears, and were taken by lethal surprise as a result.

On September 19, 1962, less than one month before photographic evidence proved that the Soviets had placed missiles in Cuba, Special National Intelligence Estimate 85-3-62, *The Military Buildup in Cuba*,

---

3.   See, Woodrow J. Kuhns, ed., *Assessing Soviet Threat: The Early Cold War Years* (Center for the Study of Intelligence, Central Intelligence Agency, 1997), pp. 16-19.

4.   Alexandre Mansourov, "Stalin, Mao, Kim, and China's Decision to Enter the Korean War, September 16-October 15, 1950: New Evidence from the Russian Archives," *Cold War International History Project Bulletin*, Nos. 6-7 (Winter 1995-1996), p. 101.

5.   Shu Guang Zhang, *Deterrence and Strategic Culture: Chinese-American Confrontations, 1949-1958* (Ithaca, N.Y.: Cornell University Press, 1992), pp. 89, 96, 115; also, see the discussion in, Thomas Christensen, "Threats, Assurances, and the Last Chance for Peace," *International Security* Vol. 17, No. 1 (Summer 1992), pp. 135-136.

essentially stated that the Soviet Union would not place missiles in Cuba because doing so "would be incompatible with Soviet practice to date and with Soviet policy as we presently estimate it. It would indicate a far greater willingness to increase the level of risk in US-Soviet relations than the USSR has displayed thus far, and consequently would have important policy implications with respect to other areas and other problems in East-West relations."[6] Sherman Kent, then-head of the National Board of Estimates, stated of this mistake regarding missiles in Cuba, "There is no blinking the fact that we came down on the wrong side." Upon reflection, Kent concluded, that "We missed the Soviet decision to put the missiles into Cuba because we could not believe that Khrushchev could make a mistake."[7]

During the war in Vietnam, Washington's civilian leaders ultimately were surprised by their general misjudgment of North Vietnam's "breaking point." Washington gradually escalated the conflict in hopes of finding that "breaking point." Yet North Vietnam essentially was able to withstand far greater loss than ever thought possible by American leaders.[8] Former Secretary of Defense Robert McNamara has described this surprise as the failure of the United States to anticipate North Vietnam's willingness to absorb loss: "The North Vietnamese were prepared to absorb far greater punishment than was ever delivered by the American bombing."[9]

In January 1979, Washington was shocked by the fall of the Shah of Iran. Indeed, only a year earlier President Jimmy Carter had praised Iran under the Shah as "an island of stability in one of the most troubled

---

6.   Sherman Kent, "A Crucial Estimate Relived," in, *Sherman Kent and the Board of National Estimates, Collected Essays* (Washington, D.C.: Center for the Study of Intelligence, Central Intelligence Agency, 1994), accessed at <www.cia.gov/csi/books/shermankent/toc.html> on August 9, 2000.

7.   Ibid.

8.   John Mueller, "The Search for the 'Breaking Point' in Vietnam," *International Studies Quarterly*, Vol. 24, No. 4 (December 1980), pp. 497–519.

9.   Robert McNamara, "Misreading the Enemy," *The New York Times*, April 21, 1999, p. A-27.

areas of the world."[10] Then-Director of the Central Intelligence Agency Stansfeld Turner has acknowledged that: "We didn't adequately predict the fall of the Shah. One reason was that while we saw the Shah declining in popularity and influence in his country, we were unwilling to believe that he would not call out the troops when the crisis came and spill blood in the streets if necessary. We had pretty good data on what was happening, but we didn't make the right assumption."[11]

On August 2, 1990, Iraqi forces invaded Kuwait; this time the U.S. intelligence community ultimately had forewarned Washington of an imminent threat. Nevertheless, the prospect for an attack was discounted by senior Bush Administration officials. They were confident that Saddam Hussein would not attack Kuwait: an Iraqi invasion simply seemed too unreasonable so soon after Iraq's long and bloody war with Iran.[12] Illustrative of U.S. expectations was Ambassador April Glaspie's reply when asked after the war why Saddam Hussein had moved against Kuwait, "We foolishly did not realize he was stupid."[13]

In November 1995 the U.S. intelligence community reported that "no country, other than the major declared nuclear powers, will develop or otherwise acquire a ballistic missile in the next 15 years that could threaten the contiguous 48 states or Canada."[14] On August 31, 1998,

---

10. Quoted in, James Bill, "Iran and the Crisis of '78," *Foreign Affairs,* Vol. 57, No. 2 (Winter 1978/79), p. 339.

11. Gary Bertsch and Suzette Grillot, editors, *Russell Symposium Proceedings, U.S. Security Interests in the 1990s* (Athens, GA: University of Georgia, 1993), p. 19.

12. Senior Bush Administration officials "assumed that Saddam would not invade Kuwait because he was a rational actor and had learned from Iraq's war with Iran how costly another major war would be." See the extensive discussion in Alex Hybel, *Power Over Rationality* (Albany: State University of New York Press, 1993), pp. 7, 51–52; see also Alexander George, *Forceful Persuasion* (Washington, D.C.: U.S. Institute of Peace, 1991), pp. 61–63; and, Douglas MacEachin, *The Tradecraft of Analysis: Challenge and Change in the CIA* (Washington, D.C.: Consortium for the Study of Intelligence, 1994), pp. 12-13.

13. Quoted in, Don Oberdorfer, "Glaspie Says Saddam Is Guilty of Deception," *The Washington Post,* March 21, 1991, p. A-23.

14. See the testimony of Richard Davis, Director of National Security Analysis, GAO in, *Foreign Missile Threats: Analytic Soundness of National*

North Korea surprised Washington with the flight-test of its three-stage *Taepo-Dong I*, a missile with potential ICBM range. Only following that test, and the sobering review of the emerging missile threat by the "Rumsfeld Commission,"[15] did the intelligence community conclude that during the next fifteen years the United States would "most likely" face unprecedented ICBM threats from North Korea, probably Iran, and possibly even Iraq.[16]

Congress mandated a review of the assumptions driving the original, now-discredited 1995 prediction of a fifteen-year window of safety. That review concluded that the 1995 intelligence estimate was "politically naive," failed to address "the motives and objectives" and possible unexpected approaches of those countries developing missiles, and placed too much weight on declared Russian and Chinese commitments not to spread missile technology.[17]

Finally, the Clinton Administration was shocked on May 11 and 13, 1998, when India conducted five nuclear tests. Despite considerable evidence of India's intentions in this regard, the CIA apparently learned of the tests from a CNN broadcast and was "as shocked as anybody."[18]

Clinton Administration officials were dismayed that India had so violated Washington's norms against nuclear testing, and fumed, "We made the mistake of assuming [India] would act rationally."[19] President

---

Intelligence Estimate 95-19, Senate Select Committee on Intelligence, Hearings, December 4, 1996, p. 1 (mimeo).

15. See *Executive Summary of the Report of the Commission to Assess the Ballistic Missile Threat to the United States*, July 15, 1998.

16. National Intelligence Council, *Foreign Missile Developments and the Ballistic Missile Threat to the United States Through 2015*, September 1999.

17. See, testimony of Robert Gates in, U.S. Senate, Select Committee On Intelligence, *Intelligence Analysis Of The Long Range Missile Threat To The United States*, Hearings (Washington, D.C.: U.S. Government Printing Office, 1997), pp. 16-18.

18. See, "India's Nuclear Irresponsibility," *The Washington Post,* May 13, 1998, p. A-16; and R. Jeffrey Smith, "India Sets Off Nuclear Devices," *The Washington Post,* May 12, 1998, pp. A-1, A-5.

19. Quoted in, Tim Weiner, "U.S. Blundered On Intelligence, Officials Admit," *New York Times*, May 13, 1998, p. A-1.

Clinton struck a moral tone by saying of India's decision to test, "It is just wrong."[20] Secretary of State Madeleine Albright admonished India and Pakistan: "Don't rush to embrace what the rest of the planet is racing to leave behind."[21]

The planet is hardly racing to leave nuclear weapons behind. But, for many officials in Washington, moving away from nuclear weapons seems the only reasonable course. The fact that other leaders could be "rational" and come to the opposite conclusion was surprising. A subsequent investigation of this "intelligence failure of the decade," led by Admiral David Jeremiah, concluded that the U.S. intelligence community had failed to see beyond its own assumptions and understand that the Indian government could place a very high value on nuclear testing.[22]

This brief survey of recent surprises is meant only to illustrate the fact that expectations of foreign thinking and behavior frequently are grossly inaccurate, and that such mistakes can have terrible consequences.[23] Armed with hindsight, it is easy to suggest that no thinking, well-informed person should have been surprised by any of these developments that so shocked Washington at the time. Attempting to project the future in real time, however, is difficult business. Mistakes that appear obvious after the fact may not be so easily seen before the event. One must be cautious when commenting on those who were surprised by the way the future ultimately unfolded.

---

20. Quoted in, Thomas W. Lippman, "Nuclear Powers Condemn Tests, Urge Restraint on India, Pakistan," *The Washington Post*, June 5, 1998, p. A-35. President Clinton criticized India's leadership, and attributed India's nuclear testing to a lack of "self-esteem" on India's part. Quoted in, James Bennet, "Clinton Calls Tests Mistake and Announces Sanctions Against India," *New York Times*, May 14, 1998, p. A-13.

21. Quoted in, Thomas Lippman, "Nuclear Powers Condemn Tests, Urge Restraint on India, Pakistan," *The Washington Post*, June 5, 1998, p. A-35.

22. Admiral David Jeremiah, News Conference, CIA Headquarters, June 2, 1998 (mimeo).

23. The classic study of such surprises is, Richard Betts, *Surprise Attack* (Washington, D.C.: Brookings Institution, 1982).

EXPECTING AND DEFINING RATIONALITY

A common thread runs through the above brief survey of dramatic and in some cases lethal surprises. The U.S. expectation was that foreign leaders would make decisions rationally, and that this rationality would move them toward understandable, predictable behavior. U.S. leaders failed to take seriously the prospect for, and thus to prepare for, what seemed in Washington to be highly unreasonable foreign behavior. In several cases, despite considerable evidence, they failed to anticipate "out of the box" decision-making, and thus were surprised.

When attempting to anticipate a foreign leadership's decision-making it is important to understand the difference between rational and reasonable behavior. All too frequently, the assumption that challengers will behave rationally, which typically they do, at least in a limited sense, leads to an expectation that they will also behave reasonably, which often they do not.

Rational and reasonable in this sense are not the same: rationality is a mode of decision-making that logically links desired goals with decisions about how to realize those goals.[24] For the rational decision-maker, a particular course of action is chosen because, based on available information, that course is calculated to be most suitable for achieving the preferred goal. A rational decision-maker also is expected to prioritize goals—some being more important than others—and recognize that trade-offs among goals may be necessary. That is, the pursuit of one goal may come only at the expense of another.

The judgment that another's decision-making and behavior is "reasonable" typically implies much more than its "rationality." Pronouncing another's decision-making or behavior to be "reasonable" suggests that the observer understands that decision-making and judges it to be sensible based on some shared or understood set of values and standards. To assume rationality, however, and on that basis to expect

---

24. The literature on rational decision-making is rich. Two useful discussions of rationality in leadership decision-making are, Stephen Maxwell, *Rationality in Deterrence*, Adelphi Papers, No. 50 (London: Institute for Strategic Studies, August 1968); and, Frank Zagare, "Rationality and Deterrence," *World Politics*, Vol. 42, No. 2 (January 1990), pp. 238-260.

behavior that is reasonable, that is behavior predictably driven by familiar, understandable norms and goals, is to risk lethal surprise.

Rationality does not imply that the decision-makers' prioritization of goals and values will be shared or considered "sensible" to any outside observer. The goals and values underlying decision-making do not need to be shared, understood or judged acceptable by any observer for the decision-making to be rational. Nor does "rational" imply that any particular moral standards guide the route chosen to realize preferred goals and values.

A familiar example may help here. An informed, rational shopper recognizes that, given a fixed amount of money, the purchase of one item means that there will be less to spend on another item. Therefore the shopper must consciously calculate the cost versus the benefit of the desired items, decide which items are of greatest value given his or her particular wants and needs, and spend money accordingly. Rationality in this limited sense has nothing to do with the wisdom or foolishness of the shopper's priority of values; it is enough that the shopper does the conscious calculations and logically links whatever the purchases might be to the appropriate expenditure of money. Rational decision-making will reflect at least a rough prioritization of wants and needs, and link choices to that hierarchy of priorities. It does not suggest that others will agree with, or understand, that particular hierarchy of wants and needs.

As applied to international relations, a rational leadership will likely pursue a variety of goals, prioritize those goals according to a particular set of values, and logically link its decision-making and behavior to the pursuit of those goals. Again, a rational decision-maker will recognize that trade-offs may be required; a leadership may have to prioritize among competing goals since it may not be able to serve all goals simultaneously. A rational leadership will link its policy choices logically to its particular hierarchy of goals and values.

The rationality of a leader's decision-making process is not related to the question of whether the desired goals, or chosen routes to those goals, will be compatible with accepted norms, customs, and values. The goals and/or actions of a rational decision-maker may seem unreasonable to an outside observer, even bizarre, without compromising the rationality of the decision-making process.

Adolf Hitler, for example, held fairly consistently to a set of goals from at least the early 1920s until his suicide in 1945, and he initiated policies logically linked to the realization of those goals. The goals and policies themselves reflected a combination of Hitler's intense hatreds and hubris, his aggressive rejection of "bourgeois" moral norms, his fanatical belief in racial myths, in his own role as the Führer of Germany, and in his race-centered version of Social Darwinism. Nevertheless, Hitler could be rational in the sense that he was capable of calculated decision-making that logically linked his policy choices to his ghastly goals.[25]

Hitler knew that the expectations of him held by domestic and foreign opponents would be conditioned by what they considered to be basic customs and norms. He reveled in the fact that his behavior would take others by surprise because he vehemently rejected those customs and norms. Following the path of Friedrich Nietzsche, he was particularly explicit about his disdain for Judeo-Christian norms,[26] which he believed were intended to inhibit great artistic geniuses such as himself from rising as they should.

Indeed, Hitler fancied himself to be a political revolutionary and a progressive scientific thinker who should not be limited by traditional customs and standards. He believed that his capacity to act far outside of

---

25. Trevor-Roper, for example, describes Hitler as violent, cruel, crude and vulgar, but also as philosophical, and "a systematic thinker," possessing a "powerful mind." See, H.R. Trevor-Roper, "The Mind of Adolf Hitler," in, *Adolf Hitler, Hitler's Secret Conversations*, 1941-1944, Normai Cameron and R.H Stevens, translators (New York: Farrar, Straus, and Young, 1953), pp. vii, xviii. Robert Waite, in a detailed psychological profile of Hitler concludes that both rational and irrational factors drove Hitler's decision making. "His mind, to the very end, was no more irrational—or rational—than it had ever been." Robert Waite, *The Psychopathic God* (New York: Da Capo Press, 1993), pp. 400, 414. Waite also observes that, "Hitler could act with high rationality and paralyzing effectiveness," in, "Afterward," in, Walter Langer, *The Mind of Adolf Hitler* (New York, Basic Books, 1972), p. 260.

26. See, for example, Hitler's discussion of science and the church in, *Hitler's Secret Conversations*, 1941-1944, Normai Cameron and R.H Stevens, translators (New York: Farrar, Straus, and Young, 1953), October 14, 1941, pp. 49-51.

"bourgeois" norms and expectations without compunction, and thus surprise those anticipating reasonable behavior, provided him with a great advantage over his domestic and foreign foes. On that score, he was in fact correct for far too long. The West's general misjudgment of Hitler illustrates the importance of understanding the distinction between rational and reasonable; the latter does not necessarily follow from the former.

In short, rational decision-making can underlie behavior that is judged to be "unreasonable," shocking, and even criminal by an observer because that behavior is so far removed from any shared norms and standards. Historically, relatively few leaders have, in fact, been functionally irrational.[27] Many, however, have been quite unreasonable. Those commonly labeled irrational, such as Adolf Hitler and Saddam Hussein, appear on closer examination to have been capable of rational decision-making. The goals and values underlying their decision-making, however, were far outside familiar norms. As a result, their behavior surprised observers.

If rationality alone fostered reasonable behavior, then only in the rare cases of manifestly irrational leaderships would we likely be greatly surprised. Assuming challengers to be pragmatic and rational, and therefore reasonable, facilitates prediction of their behavior simply by reference to what we would consider the most reasonable course under their circumstances; the hard work of attempting to understand the opponent's particular beliefs and thought can be avoided. Such an opponent will behave predictably because, by definition, it will view the world in familiar terms and will respond to various pushes and pulls in ways that are understandable and predictable. Contrary and surprising behavior would be senseless, "irrational."

More important yet, an assumed-rational and pragmatic opponent is one Washington can control by creating those pressures, the "pushes and pulls," that will guide its behavior. Its decision-making can be controlled

---

27. See, for example, Robert Noland, "Presidential Disability and the Proposed Constitutional Amendment," *American Psychologist,* No. 21 (March 1966), p. 232; and, Jonathan M. Roberts, *Decision-Making during International Crises* (New York: St. Martin's Press, 1988), p. 186.

by rendering its alternative courses more or less painful. We will not be surprised by an opponent we define as pragmatic and rational; and, with suitable levers, we can control its behavior. What could be more comforting?

Unfortunately, the convenient assumption that any rational leader ultimately will share our view of what is reasonable and therefore behave predictably, sets up the observer to discount the prospects for an opponent's conscious and purposeful moves that are outside expected norms. Consequently, when "unthinkable" behavior does emerge, it is viewed with dismay, and evidence of it initially is resisted. When the actuality of such behavior can no longer be dismissed, it typically is rationalized as an anomaly, a momentary lapse of judgment, a mistake.

In 1941 Dean Acheson believed that no "rational" Japanese would attack the United States because he judged such an attack to be too risky for the Japanese; attacking the United States must, he reasoned, also appear too risky to any Japanese leadership. But rational Japanese leaders ultimately concluded it to be the only acceptable option, and, in doing so, surprised Washington.

Washington deemed unlikely the Chinese and Iraqi attacks in 1950 and 1990, respectively, because they were judged as being too risky for the Chinese (and their Soviet allies) and for the Iraqis; when the attacks occurred they came as surprises. The Chinese and Iraqi leaderships ultimately calculated that military attack was the only reasonable option. And, Stalin, rather than restraining Mao at the time, demonstrated a surprising willingness, "for high-stakes gambling which was fraught with the potential for global disaster."[28] In each case, aggressive behavior that seemed unreasonable in Washington was viewed by the challenger as necessary.

In 1962 the Kennedy Administration considered outlandish the possibility that Moscow would, in the words of then-National Security Advisor McGeorge Bundy, "do anything as crazy from our standpoint as

---

28. Mansourov, "Stalin, Mao, Kim, and China's Decision to Enter the Korean War," p. 101.

placement of Soviet nuclear weapons in Cuba."[29] Abram Chayes, a senior State Department official close to President Kennedy at the time, later acknowledged that he, and presumably much of Washington, did not believe initial reports about missiles in Cuba, "because I didn't *want* to believe them."[30] Until the evidence was overwhelming, the possibility that Khrushchev would take the risk of installing missiles in Cuba was dismissed as unreasonable.

Secretary of Defense McNamara planned coercive U.S. bombing campaigns against North Vietnam with an expectation that Ho Chi Minh would respond as McNamara believed logic dictated. He assumed that North Vietnam would rationally seek an accommodation when the cost of continuing the war outweighed potential benefits. Douglas Pike, one of America's foremost scholars on North Vietnam, observes that McNamara's logic was "flawless," except for the devastating fact that, "they don't think like we do."[31] Accurately anticipating North Vietnam's cost-benefit calculus may have been difficult: during the war senior American officials acknowledged that they knew "very little" about Hanoi's leaders and "virtually nothing" about North Vietnamese decision-making.[32]

In October 1973, Israeli and American leaders were surprised by the Egyptian and Syrian Yom Kippur offensive even though they were aware of the movement of Arab military units and their general plan of attack. Then-U.S. Secretary of State, Henry Kissinger, has observed that American and Israeli leaders were surprised because "no one believed" the Arabs actually would strike: "Our definition of rationality did not take seriously the notion of [Egypt and Syria] starting an unwinnable

29. Quoted in, Donald Kagan, *On The Origins Of War* (New York: Doubleday, 1995), p. 503.

30. Ibid, p. 507.

31. Lewis Sorley, *Thunderbolt: General Creighton Abrams and the Army of His Times* (New York: Simon and Schuster, 1992), p. 266.

32. See Wallace Thies, *When Governments Collide: Coercion and Diplomacy in the Vietnam Conflict 1964-1968* (Berkeley, CA: University of California Press, 1980), pp. 219-220; and Joseph McMillan, "Talking to the Enemy: Negotiations in Wartime," *Comparative Strategy*, Vol. 11, No. 4, p. 455.

war to restore self-respect. There was no defense against our own preconceptions."[33]

The Clinton Administration and U.S. intelligence was surprised by India's nuclear tests because they deviated from what many U.S. leaders at the time believed were internationally accepted, "antinuclear" norms. The Clinton Administration's shock and finger-wagging in response to the Indian tests reflected the general view in Washington that moving away from nuclear weapons should be self-evidently sensible for the world.

Pakistan and India decided differently; at extreme cost they chose to develop and test nuclear weapons, and additional countries still aspire to become nuclear armed. The unavoidable fact that others were willing to pay a significant price to embrace nuclear weapons shocked Washington, given its belief of what constitutes "rational" behavior with regard to nuclear weapons. A senior U.S. Department of State official has acknowledged that Washington failed to anticipate the Indian nuclear test because "of our mindset."[34]

Similarly, the intelligence community's 1995 projection of no new missile threats for fifteen years, offered publicly and with such certainty, was based in part on the assumption that foreign behavior would be bounded by norms that seem rational in Washington. One such constraining norm, for example, was that no country that currently has ICBMs "would show blatant disregard" for the Missile Technology Control Regime, an international agreement to limit the marketing of missile technology.[35]

Unfortunately, both China and Russia have demonstrated repeatedly that they are quite willing blatantly to violate the Missile Technology

---

33. Henry Kissinger, *Years of Upheaval* (Boston: Little Brown & Co., 1982), p. 465. See also, Betts, pp. 68-80; and *CIA: The Pike Report* (Nottingham, England: Spokesman Books, 1977), pp. 141-148.

34. National Defense University, Center for Counterproliferation Research, *Symposium on Deterrence*, October 28, 1998.

35. John E. McLaughlin, Vice Chairman, National Intelligence Council, *Emerging Missile Threats to North America During the Next 15 Years*, Statement for the Record, U.S. Senate, Select Committee on Intelligence, Hearings, December 4, 1996, p. 4 (mimeo).

Control Regime in pursuit of higher economic and political goals.[36] Washington viewed adherence to such nonproliferation norms as self-evidently logical and reasonable; those same norms were disdained in Moscow and Beijing—leaving the U.S. particularly vulnerable to surprise.

There are numerous additional past examples of how the convenient assumption that a rational opponent would also prove reasonable—as defined by the observer—contributed to surprises.[37] From Japan's decision to attack Imperial Russia in 1904,[38] to Washington's underestimation of Serbia's tenacity under NATO's 1999 bombing campaign,[39] the mistaken expectation that foreign leaders would be reasonable, according to familiar norms, appears to have played a significant role in lethal surprises and costly mistakes. In the latter case, Yugoslav President Slobodan Milosevic did not intend to be reasonable by Washington's standards, and considered this to be an advantage: "I am ready to walk on corpses, and the West is not. That is why I shall win."[40]

The expectation that foreign leaders will behave predictably fits well with the theory, particularly prevalent in the study of international relations, that national decision-making should be viewed as that of a

---

36. See the summary of Chinese and Russian proliferation activities in, U.S. Senate, Committee on Governmental Affairs, Subcommittee on International Security, Proliferation, and Federal Services, *The Proliferation Primer* (January 1998), pp. 3-26.

37. See, for example, the discussion in, Richard W. Shryock, "The Intelligence Community Post Mortem Program, 1973-1975," *Studies in Intelligence* (Fall 1977), pp. 15-28.

38. Tsar Nicholas was contemptuous of the Japanese and denied the possibility that Japan would dare attack a European great power. See, Count Sergei Witte, *The Memoirs of Count Witte*, ed. and translated by Abraham Yarmolinsky (Garden City, N.Y.: Doubleday, Page, 1921), p. 125.

39. See, for example, Bill Sammon, "Clinton Misread Yugoslav Resolve," *The Washington Times*, June 21, 1999, p. A-11.

40. Milosevic's statement to German Foreign Minister Joschka Fischer quoted in, Josef Joffe, "A Peacenik Goes to War," *The New York Times Magazine*, May 30, 1999, *The New York Times on the Web*, "Archives," p. 1.

rational and pragmatic, and thus presumably predictable, individual.[41] The historical anecdotes noted above, however, illustrate well that decision-making and behavior considered scarcely plausible in Washington can appear entirely reasonable to a foreign leadership, not because foreign leaders are irrational, but because the definition of what constitutes "reasonable" can differ so dramatically. Consequently, surprises frequently are in store for those who believe that a foe's basic rationality permits confident prediction of its behavior.

---

41. As one political scientist who has studied the subject observes, "The assumption of rationality is ubiquitous in international relations theory." Neta Crawford, "The Passion of World Politics," *International Security*, Vol. 24, No. 4 (Spring 2000), pp. 116-117.

Chapter 2

COLD WAR DETERRENCE THEORY AND PRACTICE

Belief that a foe will be rational cum reasonable, and thus ultimately predictable and controllable, has been most apparent, and potentially most dangerous, in the U.S. approach to nuclear deterrence. During the Cold War confident conclusions about the reliability of nuclear deterrence were the norm. Such conclusions typically were based on extrapolations from the implicit assumption of Soviet reasonableness, occasionally dressed up with quantitative modeling of a nuclear force exchange.[1]

If the modeling demonstrated that both sides possessed a manifest and secure capability for devastating nuclear retaliation, "mutual deterrence" generally was judged to be "stable." The underlying assumption was that neither side, being rational and reasonable, would intentionally initiate a war if the end result could be widespread mutual destruction. In the context of mutual vulnerability confidence in deterrence became a tautology: any rational leader would be deterred from severe provocation by the

---

1. The classic case is the analysis of strategic deterrence stability and its requirements that supported Secretary McNamara's definitions of "assured destruction." See, Alain Enthoven and K. Wayne Smith, *How Much Is Enough?* (New York: Harper and Row, 1971), pp. 207-210. Colin Gray's concise review of U.S. schools of thought regarding strategic deterrence remains the best single treatment of the subject, and demonstrates comprehensively the pervasive reliance on the implicit assumption of a rational/reasonable opponent. See Colin S. Gray, *Nuclear Strategy and Strategic Planning* (Philadelphia: Foreign Policy Research Institute, 1984).

fear of mutual nuclear destruction; national leaders are rational (how else could they climb to positions of responsibility?); thus, nuclear weapons would deter. In short, rational leaders would be deterred via mutual nuclear threats because, by definition, they would be irrational if they were not so deterred.

This basic tautology was fully behind U.S. nuclear deterrence policy. It was assumed that any Soviet leadership, indeed "any sane political authority," would share in the basic features and logic underlying U.S. deterrence policy. This assumption overpowered suggestions that the unique characteristics of Soviet leadership and ideology could decisively shape the Soviet approach to nuclear weapons and deterrence, possibly moving Soviet leaders quite rationally in significantly heretical directions. The possible value of examining and understanding the particular beliefs of the Soviet leadership in establishing the U.S. deterrence policies intended to control the Soviet Union generally was dismissed in favor of simply assuming that "sane" Soviet leaders basically would think and behave as U.S. leaders ("mirror imaging"); they would, by definition, be deterrable because they would be rational. The deterrence tautology was firmly in play.

In commenting on Soviet nuclear doctrine, for example, Jerome Weisner, Science Advisor to the President from 1961 to 1964, demonstrated this penchant for mirror-imaging by referring to declared U.S. nuclear doctrine and forces, and observing that "they [Soviet leaders] undoubtedly have some such doctrine with numbers too."[2]

Borrowing from economics, Thomas Schelling, the brilliant author of much U.S. Cold War thinking regarding nuclear deterrence, explicitly identified a "mirror-imaging" methodology

---

2. Quoted in, U.S. Senate, Committee on Foreign Relations, Subcommittee on International Organization and Disarmament, *Strategic and Foreign Policy Implications of ABM Systems, Part II*, Hearings, 91st Congress, 1st Session (Washington, D.C.: U.S. Government Printing Office, 1969), p. 495.

as useful for anticipating an opponent's views in the nuclear deterrence realm. According to Schelling, "you can sit in your armchair and try to predict how people will behave by asking how you would behave if you had your wits about you. You get, free of charge, a lot of vicarious, empirical behavior."[3]

This methodology was taken to the extreme in the United States. With little or no reference to the specific thought, goals, and values of the Soviet leadership, numerous officials and academic commentators assumed that they knew how any "sane" Soviet leader would view nuclear weapons, and how deterrence would therefore operate. Glen Snyder, one of the early pioneers of U.S. strategic deterrence theory, demonstrated early in the Cold War how this "intuitive" basis for identifying Soviet views worked: "Perhaps the most uncertain factor for the U.S. is the degree of prospective damage which would be sufficient to deter the Soviet Union from attacking. Would the Soviets be deterred by the prospect of losing ten cities? Or two cities? Or fifty cities? No one knows, although one might intuitively guess that the threshold is closer to ten than to either two or fifty."[4] Notice here how easily self-described intuition leads to conclusions that an effective U.S. deterrence threat is "damage," defined as the Soviet Union "losing" cities, and that the number of cities to be so threatened for deterrence purposes is "closer to ten" than to two or fifty. Because "No one knows" the prospective damage necessary to deter the Soviet leadership, U.S. values and norms are ascribed to the Soviet leadership, and these then drive important and specific conclusions about how to deter the Soviet Union.

---

3. Quoted in, Kathleen Archibald, ed., *Strategic Interaction and Conflict: Original Papers and Discussion* (Berkeley, CA: Institute of International Studies, University of California, Berkeley, 1966), p. 150.

4. Glen Snyder, *Deterrence and Defense: Toward a Theory of National Security* (Princeton, NJ: Princeton University Press, 1961), p. 57.

The absolute lack of empiricism involved in such mirror-imaging and reliance on intuition helped to ensure that the Soviet leadership would be considered predictably deterrable. Actual U.S. nuclear targeting policy evolved over time, but for much of the Cold War deterrence analyses simply posited that the Soviet Union would be the rational, pragmatic, and reasonable (and hence predictable) image of the United States, and proceeded to model the outcome of large-scale nuclear wars. If some form of mutual destruction was the outcome, then deterrence was deemed "stable." It would continue to provide safety against nuclear attack.

With this methodology, analysts and commentators offered highly confident and precise answers to questions such as, would deployment of accurate ICBM warheads, missile defense, or single-warhead mobile ICBMs "stabilize" or "destabilize" deterrence? The center of attention in this approach to deterrence was on U.S. and Soviet strategic nuclear forces, including ICBMs, long-range bombers, and submarine-launched ballistic missiles (SLBMs). Indeed, because mutual vulnerability to retaliation came to be regarded as the guarantee of mutual deterrence, whether deterrence was judged to be "stable" or not was thought to depend almost exclusively on whether the number and character of U.S. and Soviet strategic forces promised mutual destruction.

Those strategic forces thought to help perpetuate the condition of mutual vulnerability were considered "stabilizing," while those that might challenge that condition were judged "destabilizing." Strategic systems thought to help preserve mutual vulnerability included: inaccurate, at-sea SLBMs; inaccurate ICBMs in protective hardened silos; and bombers on a high alert status. When inaccurate (early ICBMs/SLBMs) or slow-to-target (bombers), they could not pose a preemptive, "first-strike" threat to the other side's capability to retaliate. They could survive an attack and threaten retaliation, but they would be too slow or inaccurate to destroy Moscow's capability to retaliate; they could not "threaten the Soviet deterrent." In short, mutual vulnerability to retaliation was considered the engine for mutual deterrence, and those types of strategic forces thought most suited for preserving mutual capabilities for retaliation were lauded as stabilizing.

Those strategic forces thought to threaten the other side's deterrent were vilified as "destabilizing." These included, most prominently, active defenses such as ballistic missile defense (BMD) intended to defend against Soviet missiles after their launch, and ICBMs carrying multiple, highly accurate warheads. U.S. BMD, it was said, might undermine Soviet confidence in its capability to retaliate, and highly accurate U.S. ICBM or SLBM warheads might threaten to destroy Soviet retaliatory forces in a "first-strike" before they could be launched. Consequently, these systems were typed as "destabilizing" because they might deny the Soviet Union confidence in its retaliatory threat, and thus upset mutual deterrence. Harold Brown, as Secretary of Defense in 1979, succinctly characterized both this U.S. theory and policy: "In the interests of stability, we avoid the capability of eliminating the other side's deterrent, insofar as we might be able to do so. In short, we must be quite willing—as we have been for some time— to accept the principle of mutual deterrence, and design our defense posture in light of that principle."[5]

U.S. strategic arms control goals, reflecting this U.S. deterrence thinking, were designed to codify deterrence stability by limiting or eliminating BMD and ICBMs with multiple, accurate warheads. Strategic ballistic missile defense was essentially banned by the U.S.-Soviet 1972 ABM Treaty, and for more than two decades the United States pursued strategic offensive arms control (SALT and START) for the purpose of reducing or eliminating the Soviet Union's large, MIRVed ICBMs.[6]

---

5. *Department of Defense Annual Report Fiscal Year 1980* (Washington, D.C.: U.S. Government Printing Office, January 25, 1979), p. 61.

6. As Brent Scrowcroft, John Deutch, and R. James Woolsey observed in 1986, "Our major effort over 17 years of arms control negotiations on strategic offensive systems has been dedicated to preserving the survivability of our own silo-based ICBMs. To this end we have used, and wasted, much negotiating

The point here is not to argue for or against BMD or multi-warheaded ICBMs. Rather, it is to note that the Cold War deterrence framework promised to deliver "stability" based near-exclusively on a condition of the nuclear balance: stable deterrence was deemed to be the near-certain result of mutual, secure, retaliatory threats of nuclear annihilation. Mutual vulnerability to nuclear retaliation came to be seen as the guarantee of mutual deterrence in most cases, and all but eliminated the prospects for deliberate, large-scale war. And, because the condition of mutual vulnerability was the result of the types and numbers of offensive and defensive forces deployed by the U.S. and Soviet Union, purposefully manipulating deterrence stability came to be seen as a relatively straightforward matter of making "stabilizing" changes in U.S. and Soviet strategic forces.

On this basis, policies of deterrence enjoyed great confidence, and little serious preparation was made for their possible failure or irrelevance. Indeed, embracing the concept of mutual deterrence through mutual vulnerability helped to guarantee that if nuclear deterrence failed, the resulting losses would be beyond measure. Many in Washington claimed that preparation for deterrence failure was neither practicable nor necessary because deterrence stability could be manipulated predictably, that is it could be ensured, by adjusting the nuclear arsenals appropriately. "Stability" came to be defined in terms of a particular condition of the strategic nuclear "balance." As noted, the 1972 ABM Treaty and Washington's focus in the SALT/START process are a reflection of this deterrence theory.

The strength of this deterrence framework was its comfort and convenience. By simply assuming a rational, pragmatic, and thus reasonable opponent, great predictability could be attributed to

---

leverage in trying to get the Soviets to agree to restrictions on their large MIRVed ICBMs." See, "A Small, Survivable, Mobile ICBM," *The Washington Post*, December 26, 1986, p. A-23.

deterrence policies and hard-to-address questions of how the opponent's thought and political beliefs might shape the practice of deterrence could be avoided. Instead, discussions of deterrence could focus on those items that are relatively easy to count and predict—the number and types of nuclear warheads and their destructive potential. The downside of this methodology was that by essentially ignoring particular leadership beliefs and thought processes in favor of "mirror-imaging," it could easily be dangerously misleading if such factors influenced Soviet decision-making.[7]

The weakness of the assumption that the Soviet leadership would be rational, reasonable (as defined in Washington), and thus predictable in considerations of nuclear deterrence is demonstrated by the now-apparent lethal mismatch between Western deterrence theory and Soviet war planning for Western Europe. Western deterrence policies avoided notions of "nuclear war-fighting" as "unthinkable." This aversion is understandable given the West's commitment to mutual vulnerability as the engine for nuclear deterrence "stability." NATO policy sought to maintain a lid on the potential for nuclear escalation via sophisticated "intra-war deterrence" concepts of rational wartime bargaining and "limited nuclear war." These U.S. deterrence concepts mistakenly assumed a similarly minded, "rational" opponent, and thus were wholly incompatible with Soviet war plans. The latter called for very

---

7. Confidence in this general methodology of strategic analysis has been so firm that official documents and unofficial commentary from the mid-1960s on have been filled with claims that one particular course or another in the strategic arms arena assuredly would lead to greater strategic stability or instability. For a full treatment of this subject see, Keith B. Payne, *Deterrence In The Second Nuclear Age* (Lexington, KY: The University Press of Kentucky, 1996).

heavy and very early nuclear and chemical strikes throughout Western Europe in the event of war.[8]

As a consequence, had large-scale war occurred in Western Europe, it is likely that Western civilian leaders would have looked to their Soviet counterparts for a "rational" mutual deterrence contest of limited war, bargaining and escalation control, while the Soviets planned for large-scale nuclear and chemical strikes throughout Western Europe. The West's expectations of Soviet "rationality" could hardly have been more ill-fitting with apparent Soviet war plans.

Nuclear "war-fighting" had been judged unreasonable and even "irrational" in Washington because, as the saying went, "no one can win a nuclear war." The possibility that the Soviets might steadfastly resist Washington's logic of mutual nuclear stalemate was, against considerable evidence, dismissed by most of Washington's cognoscente. Soviet leaders, being rational, certainly would shed any "primitive" views that nuclear weapons were useable as they were schooled by Washington's more sophisticated experts and as they better understood modern technology.

Paul Warnke, a senior official in the Carter Administration, observed of Soviet nuclear "war-fighting" concepts, "This kind of thinking is on a level of abstraction which is unrealistic. It seems to me that instead of talking in these terms, which would indulge what I regard as the primitive aspects of Soviet nuclear doctrine,

---

8.   It should be noted that evidence now available out of the former East Germany indicates that had war in Europe occurred, the Soviet Union would have *begun* with nuclear and chemical strikes. See Lothar Rühl, "Noch 1990 Zielte die NVA Richtung Westdeutschland und Benelux," *Die Welt*, July 31, 1991, p. 1; Rühl, "Angriffskrieger Markus Wolf," *Die Welt*, August 9, 1991; and Rühl, "Offensive Defence in the Warsaw Pact," *Survival* 33, no. 5 (September–October 1991), pp. 442–50. See also Beatrice Heuser, "Warsaw Pact Military Doctrines in the 1970s and 1980s: Findings in the East German Archives," *Comparative Strategy*, Vol. 12, No. 4 (Winter 1994), pp. 437–58.

we ought to be trying to educate them into the real world of strategic nuclear weapons."[9]

Perhaps so, but the fact that the Soviets continued to resist U.S. tutorials on such matters hardly penetrated U.S. policies. Rather, "unthinkable" Soviet views were dismissed as unreal or correctable with sufficient enlightenment. A leading U.S. academic "Sovietologist" presented the then-popular view that nuclear weapons technology itself would compel Soviet views to "converge" with Washington's: "Soviet strategic doctrine and capabilities appear to have lagged behind those of the U.S. by about five years.... Modern defense technology determines to a large extent the kind of strategic doctrines and policies that will be adopted by the superpowers. Thus, technology seems to have a leveling effect which subsumes political, ideological, and social differences in various political systems."[10]

The notion that a unique political world view, and in particular, Marxist-Leninist ideology, could move Soviet views about nuclear weapons in a direction dramatically different from those held in Washington typically was disdained by those who assumed a reasonable, predictable opponent. Only recently, courtesy of greater access to past Soviet decision-making practices, has it become virtually unarguable that the Soviet leadership never accepted the West's definition of rationality with regard to nuclear weapons, and that Soviet expectations of U.S. behavior, largely derived from the dogma of Marxist-Leninist ideology, appear to

---

9. Cited in Richard Pipes, "Why the Soviet Union Thinks It Could Fight and Win a Nuclear War," *Commentary*, Vol. 64, No. 1 (July 1977), p. 21.

10. Roman Kolkowicz, *The Soviet Union and Arms Control: A Superpower Dilemma* (Baltimore: Johns Hopkins University Press, 1970), pp. 35-37; see also, Kolkowicz, "Strategic Parity and Beyond: Soviet Perspectives," *World Politics*, Vol. 23, No. 3 (April 1971), p. 451; and, Kolkowicz, "Strategic Elites and Politics of Superpower," *Journal of International Affairs*, Vol. 26, No. 1 (1972), p. 53.

have been a significant factor in Soviet nuclear war planning.[11] Indeed, greater access to Soviet archives demonstrates how consistently Soviet decision-making appears to have been shaped more by ideological vision than by pragmatic, *realpolitik*.[12]

William Odom, one of the West's foremost experts on the Soviet Union reports with regard to the thinking of Soviet leaders on the subject, "the notion of winning a nuclear war was both ideologically and psychologically rooted in the views of the [Soviet] 'political-military leadership.'" And, "[Western] Deterrence theory and concepts of stability were never part of Soviet thinking in these circles." [13]

Until the middle of the Cold War there was little apparent effort to structure the U.S. deterrent so that it would speak to the particular character of the Soviet leadership, including its particular ideologically-derived perceptions, goals, and values. Such tailoring, of course, was not considered necessary as Moscow simply was assumed to be the rational, pragmatic, and reasonable mirror-image of Washington. As is noted in one account of how senior civilian officials under Secretary McNamara thought about basic deterrence calculations, "It all appeared scientific and precise, but in fact it had little to do with any formulation of how much would be enough to deter the Soviets. It was the output of a computer program designed by Alain Enthoven 'laying down' 1-megaton bombs against Soviet cities and calculating, at various

---

11. See the detailed discussion of this issue in, Peter Pry, *War Scare* (Westport, CT: Praeger, 1999).

12. See the discussion in, William Wohlforth, "A Certain Idea of Science: How International Relations Theory Avoids the New Cold War History," *Journal of Cold War Studies*, Vol. 1, No. 2 (Spring 1999), pp. 51-53; and Nigel Gould-Davies, "Rethinking the Role of Ideology in International Politics During the Cold War," *Journal of Cold War Studies*, Vol. 1, No. 1 (Winter 1999); pp. 90-109.

13. William E. Odom, *The Collapse of the Soviet Military* (New Haven: Yale University Press, 1998), p. 71, and p. 436 (reference 25).

points, how much additional damage one additional bomb would do."[14] Not until the Nixon Administration's so-called Schlesinger Doctrine of 1974 did Washington even seriously claim to have made moves toward tailoring its nuclear deterrent to the specific character of the Soviet leadership.

Over the course of Cold War decades, numerous official U.S. statements, and most unofficial academic commentary, expressed great confidence that deterrence of the Soviet Union was "ensured" by secure mutual *retaliatory* threats, the "balance of terror." There was considerable debate over exactly how the Soviet Union could best be held hostage, and the nuclear forces necessary to do so. But there was little debate over the governing principle that mutual vulnerability to retaliation provided mutual deterrence. As noted above, the logic behind this confidence was tautological: any rational leader would be deterred by severe nuclear threats, because any leader not so deterred would, by definition, be irrational. Therefore, nuclear deterrence as described would "work" reliably vis-à-vis any "rational" challenger. With few exceptions, extreme confidence in this basic proposition was reflected in U.S. official and academic treatments of the subject.[15]

In 1969, for example, McGeorge Bundy, National Security Advisor to Presidents Kennedy and Johnson, set out with ample clarity the transcendent confidence inspired by this deterrence tautology: "In light of the certain prospect of retaliation there has been literally no chance at all that *any sane political authority*, in either the United States or the Soviet Union, would consciously choose to start a nuclear war. This proposition is true for the past,

---

14. Fred Kaplan, *The Wizards of Armageddon* (New York: Simon and Schuster, 1983), p. 317.

15. A prominent scholar on the subject of deterrence observed more cautiously and accurately that in the context of mutual nuclear threats, "if decisionmakers are 'sensible,' peace is the most likely outcome." Robert Jervis, "The Political Effects of Nuclear Weapons: A Comment," *International Security*, Vol. 13, No. 2 (Fall 1988), p. 81.

the present and the foreseeable future."[16] Many of those in prestigious academic positions, frequently moving in and out of senior government positions, shared this confidence. As Harvard academics Graham Allison, Albert Carnesale, and Joseph Nye observed, "In U.S.-Soviet relations, the current nuclear postures have substantially solved the problem of deterring deliberate nuclear attack."[17]

In 1973 the leading U.S. journal on international relations, *Foreign Affairs*, published a synopsis of accepted wisdom on the subject by a former senior U.S. State Department official, Louis Halle. Halle expressed similar confidence in the understanding of, and practice of, nuclear deterrence: "Our conclusion, in its narrowest terms, must be that the deliberate resort to war by a nuclear power against a power capable of effective retaliation is permanently ruled out...the deliberate resort to major nonnuclear warfare between such powers is also ruled out. And the resort to even such limited warfare as border skirmishes between them is notably inhibited by the danger that it would escalate out of control, ending in nuclear war."[18]

Over two decades later, Deputy Secretary of Defense John Deutch expressed continuing overwhelming confidence in Washington's understanding and practice of deterrence: "Deterrence is *ensured* by having a survivable [nuclear] capability to hold at risk what potentially hostile leaders value, and we will

---

16. McGeorge Bundy, "To Cap the Volcano," *Foreign Affairs*, Vol. 48, No. 1 (October 1969), p. 9 (emphasis added).

17. "Defusing The Nuclear Menace," *The Washington Post*, September 4, 1988, p. C-1 and C-2. For another such confident claim see, Sir Michael Howard, "Lessons of the Cold War," *Survival*, Vol. 43, No. 4 (Winter 1994-1995), pp. 161; 164.

18. "Does War Have A Future?" *Foreign Affairs*, Vol. 52, No. 1 (October 1973), p. 23.

maintain that capability."[19] It should be noted here that Deputy Secretary Deutch claimed the functioning of deterrence to be wholly predictable; it could be "ensured" by maintaining a particular type of nuclear threat.

These types of claims do not reflect the views of a few isolated academics and officials. They have been standard fare for decades, reflecting accepted wisdom about the nature of deterrence by "hawks" and "doves" in Republican and Democrat administrations. Deterrence, based on mutual vulnerability to nuclear threats, ultimately came to be viewed as a given: effective deterrence was judged near-inevitable in the context of secure, mutual, nuclear, retaliatory threats. As noted, a debate raged over how many, and what type of, offensive nuclear weapons were necessary to provide a sufficient retaliatory nuclear threat. But there was general confidence in the proposition, based on the tautology of the Cold War deterrence framework, that we could reliably "ensure" deterrence stability by adjusting nuclear arsenals.

Those who claimed very low numbers of nuclear weapons would be adequate for deterrence, even created a term of art, "existential deterrence." This term reflected a widely shared view that maintaining even a very small number of nuclear weapons would readily "ensure" deterrence: if nuclear weapons exist, they will deter.[20]

---

19. See, testimony of John Deutch in, U.S. House, Committee on Foreign Affairs, *U.S. Nuclear Policy*, Hearings, 103rd Congress, 2nd Session (Washington, D.C.: U.S. Government Printing Office, 1995), p. 36 (emphasis added).

20. McGeorge Bundy, William Crowe Jr., and Sidney Drell give a perfect illustration of the continuing and overwhelming confidence in "existential deterrence" in their statement: "It simply is not true that smaller plans with smaller forces will be inadequate for strategic deterrence. The possibility of even a few nuclear detonations in populated areas provides ample deterrence." See, *Reducing Nuclear Danger* (New York: Council on Foreign Relations Press, 1993), p. 95.

But whether, under the rubric of deterrence, "hawks" were promoting improved nuclear capabilities, or "doves" were advocating deep reductions, very little attention was devoted to the possibilities that:

- Washington's understanding of deterrence could be seriously flawed or limited;
- Many factors other than the lethality of mutual threats might contribute to determining whether deterrence would "work" as intended;
- Moscow might not share Washington's basic definition of what is "rational" regarding nuclear weapons, and this could matter significantly;
- Deterrence could be far less mechanistic and predictable in practice than suggested by the dominant Cold War deterrence framework; or,
- Adjusting the nuclear posture might have very little to do with the "stability" of deterrence.

SOME PAINFUL TRUTHS ABOUT DETERRENCE THEORY AND PRACTICE

Whether in the Cold War or post-Cold War period, the first step in understanding deterrence is to recognize that it is a psychological function. It is not the inevitable outcome of any particular "strategic balance;" even scrupulous efforts to establish a "stable" military balance will be irrelevant to preventing war under some plausible circumstances. Confident claims that any particular strategic nuclear balance is "stable," or that any particular adjustment to that balance will be "stabilizing" or "destabilizing" should be viewed with great skepticism because deterrence, properly understood, involves much more than comparing relative force capabilities. It involves essential questions about decision-making factors that typically are ignored in Cold War style "stability analyses." Indeed, adjusting the force balance one way or another may essentially be irrelevant to the functioning of deterrence in any particular case unless other critical conditions are present.

One such condition, for example, is that a challenger be attentive to the deterrence threats, thresholds, and commitments made by its opponent. Selective attention by rational leaders can easily undermine any basis for deterrence to function as intended.

Actual human behavior as observed in historical case studies demonstrates that desperate leaders intent on their chosen course can become inattentive to their foes' commitments and interests regardless of how clearly expressed and demonstrated. A desperate leadership's unwillingness to take inconvenient facts into account can lead it to cling to grossly unrealistic expectations about its decisions: "These case histories suggest the pessimistic hypothesis that those policy makers with the greatest need to learn from external reality appear the least likely to do so."[21]

Confidence that challengers will reliably observe the nuclear balance, recognize and believe U.S. demonstrations of will, understand the situation, calculate rationally, and then be deterred, is an inadequate basis upon which to establish American security, for even the most brilliantly presented deterrence threat may be discounted or misunderstood by a challenger. This should not be a terribly controversial point. Virtually all historical studies of deterrence have reached a similar conclusion.[22] Nevertheless,

---

21. Richard Ned Lebow, "The Deterrence Deadlock: Is There A Way Out," in Robert Jervis, Richard Ned Lebow, Janice Stein, *Psychology and Deterrence* (Baltimore, MD: Johns Hopkins University Press, 1985), pp. 182-183.

22. See, for example, Alexander George and Richard Smoke, *Deterrence in American Foreign Policy: Theory and Practice* (New York: Columbia University Press, 1974); Peter Karsten, Peter D. Howell and Artis Frances Allen, *Military Threats: A Systematic Historical Analysis of the Determinants of Success* (Westport, CT: Greenwood Press, 1984); Alex Hybel, *Power Over Rationality* (Albany, NY: State University of New York, 1993); Jervis, Lebow, and Stein, *Psychology and Deterrence*; Richard Ned Lebow, *Between Peace and War* (Baltimore, MD: Johns Hopkins University Press, 1981), p. 110; Raoul

fundamental skepticism about the reliability of deterrence is resisted strongly because it calls into question most of what has long passed for accepted wisdom: that deterrence can be "ensured" by a condition of mutual vulnerability and by manipulating the nuclear balance accordingly.

The Cold War deterrence framework has been particularly influential in the United States. Confident voices abound with claims that by adjusting the strategic balance in one fashion or another, deterrence will be "stabilized," that is, peace will be preserved. The promise that one knows how to deliver peace is a powerful attraction; it says that foes can be controlled in an area that literally involves life or death. When such promises repeatedly are offered by senior military officers, government officials, and academics from prestigious universities, people take them seriously. This is unfortunate, because such promises are hollow.

Indeed, in Washington bureaucratic institutions have been created, weapon systems vilified or justified, treaties signed, academic and governmental careers built (also in the think tank, and arms control industries), and thousands of commentaries written, on the basis of this presumed knowledge of deterrence. We came to fancy ourselves as experts at deterrence. Claiming that a factor subject to human control, the "nuclear postures," had "solved the problem" of deliberate nuclear attack was powerful stuff; it assured us of security in the context of an otherwise inescapable nuclear threat.

The Cold War deterrence framework has proven resistant to change. There is understandable reluctance to cast into doubt the

---

Naroll, Vern L. Bullogh, Frada Naroll, *Military Deterrence In History: A Pilot Cross-Historical Survey* (Albany, N.Y.: State University of New York Press, 1974), pp. 342-343; Keith B. Payne and Lawrence Fink, "Deterrence Without Defense: Gambling on Perfection," *Strategic Review* (Winter 1989), pp. 25-40; and, Keith B. Payne, *Deterrence in the Second Nuclear Age* (Lexington, KY: University Press of Kentucky, 1996).

typical official and academic treatments of deterrence that exude confidence in its functioning predictably, and in the human capability to measure it and manipulate it predictably. Promises that we can control the future to preserve our security are too attractive to be given up lightly.

COLD WAR DETERRENCE CALCULATIONS AND ASSUMPTIONS

Unfortunately, in most Cold War-style analyses of deterrence "stability," those factors that tend to render policies of deterrence unreliable simply are not taken into serious consideration:[23] Military capabilities are compared, strategic exchanges are modeled, and net war outcomes projected. If, based on the result of force exchange analysis, the net costs (in terms of targets damaged or destroyed) to a challenger are thought to be unacceptable, the challenger is expected to behave sensibly and be deterred. If an acceptable level of damage is anticipated, or even a net gain in a crisis seems likely, then an incentive to strike is presumed and the condition is considered "unstable."

Such force exchange analyses have long been employed to draw conclusions about the "stabilizing" or "destabilizing" affect of prospective changes in the U.S. strategic force posture. That is, conclusions are offered concerning how a specific change in strategic forces will affect the probability of war. The assumption in such analyses, often left unstated, is that political leaders will behave as the strategic equivalent of Adam Smith's "economic man."

---

23. Among the numerous examples see, Glenn A. Kent, Randall J. DeValk, and David E. Thaler, *A Calculus of First-Strike Stability (A Criterion for Evaluating Strategic Forces),* A RAND Note, N-2526-AF, June 1988; Paul L. Chzanowski, "Transition to Deterrence Based on Strategic Defense," *Energy and Technology Review* (January-February 1987), pp. 31-45; and Dean Wilkening, Kenneth Watman, *Strategic Defenses and First-Strike Stability*, R-3412-FF/RC (Santa Monica, CA: The RAND Corporation, November 1986).

Leaders are assumed to be ready, willing, and able, to engage in well-informed, dispassionate, rational, cost-benefit calculations, and to make their policy decisions accordingly. They recognize that value tradeoffs are involved in their decisions (i.e., they may have to choose one objective at the expense of another). They are assumed to be at least generally familiar with their opponent's threats, values, intentions, and military capabilities, able to absorb information, and able to implement value-maximizing and cost-minimizing decisions under great stress.

Early in the Cold War William Kaufman, a prominent advisor to senior U.S. defense officials, argued explicitly that such an image of U.S. opponents reflected "reality." He observed that U.S. military strategy should be based on an understanding of the Soviet Union and China as "cautious, cool, and calculating," and recommended viewing them as, "a calculating individual with a multiplicity of values, aware of cost and risk as well as advantage, and capable of drawing significant inferences from symbolic acts."[24] Kaufman subsequently concluded that under this assumption wars become "token tests of strength.... They cannot represent decisive showdowns of power."[25] That is, deterrence certainly would work because the opponents would be "cautious, cool, and calculating," and U.S. nuclear threats would be severe.

This image of the opponent as rational and pragmatic is an enormous convenience when constructing a policy of deterrence. It allows the defense planner to set aside those many factors that can limit the potential for deterrence to "work" as intended, and confidently rely instead simply on the opponent's rational

---

24. William Kaufman, "Limited War," in, William Kaufman, ed., *Military Policy and National Security* (Princeton, NJ: Princeton University Press, 1956), p. 117.

25. Ibid., p. 118.

pragmatism to preclude its decision for a "decisive showdown of power."[26]

Yet, as Fred Iklé, former U.S. Under Secretary of Defense for Policy has noted, "In the real world, nuclear forces are built and managed not by two indistinguishable 'sides,' but by very distinct governments and military organizations. These, in turn, are run by people, people who are ignorant of many facts, people who can be gripped by anger or fear, people who make mistakes—sometimes dreadful mistakes."[27]

Cold War discussions of strategic deterrence identify only two basic requirements for an effective deterrent: the capability to inflict unacceptable damage, and the manifest credibility of that threat. These well-known requirements, however, are not sufficient for deterrence to "work." An entire set of often-ignored but necessary political and psychological conditions must dominate the decision-making process on both (or all) sides if deterrence is to function as envisaged. As suggested above, these include the following, *inter alia*:

- Leaders who value avoidance of the U.S. deterrence threat more highly than whatever might be the value at stake in a contest of wills with the United States;

- Leaders capable of relatively unbiased assessments of information and, based on that information, linking decisions to preferred outcomes, while recognizing value tradeoffs in relatively dispassionate decision-making;

- Leaders who are attentive to and comprehend the intentions, interests, commitments, and values of the opponent(s);

---

26. Ibid.

27. Fred Charles Iklé, "Nuclear Strategy: Can There Be A Happy Ending?" *Foreign Affairs*, Vol. 63, No. 4 (Spring 1985), p. 10.

- Leaders who focus their cost-benefit calculations on external factors (i.e., deterrence threats) as the final determinant of their decision-making;
- Leaders who understand the military capabilities and consequences involved in their decisions, at least at a general level;
- Political systems that permit individually rational decision-makers to establish similarly rational state policies that do, in turn, control state behavior.

If one or several of these conditions is absent, there is no basis for assuming that the necessary rational, cost-benefit calculations could be conducted or would determine policy so that U.S. deterrence threats can have their intended deterrent effect. The existence and weight of these cognitive/political requirements may be very difficult to identify and measure, and attempting to do so would require an in-depth examination of each challenger to be deterred. Unfortunately, such examinations are difficult and time-consuming. It is far more convenient simply to assume the opponent will behave rationally and reasonably, and thus predictably. This convenience may help explain why the Cold War deterrence framework overwhelmingly ignored these potentially decisive factors in decision-making, and derived grand conclusions about deterrence based on the one factor that is *relatively* easily measured, i.e., the balance of nuclear forces.

When deterrence is defined only in terms of maintaining a particular level of military capability relative to an opponent, then it is not difficult to conclude that stability is relatively "easy" to calculate and predict. However, if the necessary decision-making variables identified above are taken into serious consideration, it is easy to understand that deterrence is a much more complicated process.

Regardless of the "strategic balance," when the challenger is not dispassionate, well-informed, or reasonable, as frequently has been the case in historical experience, deterrence cannot be assumed to function predictably. It cannot be "ensured" under any circumstances, and manipulating the force balance may be of trivial significance.

Chapter 3

WHY THE COLD WAR DETERRENCE FRAMEWORK IS INADEQUATE

How is it possible to reach conclusions that question much of what has for years passed for accepted wisdom regarding deterrence? The answer is relatively straightforward: historical studies consistently demonstrate that the deterrence theory assumption of well-informed leaders operating rationally, reasonably, and thus predictably, frequently does not correspond with actual crisis decision-making; and deterrence, therefore, can fail or not apply.

Take, for example, the most important assumptions in deterrence theory, the assumed prevalence of rational, well-informed calculation in decision-making. Case studies often demonstrate that decisions about peace and war are not well-informed, thought through, or made dispassionately. As Oxford professor Robert O'Neill has observed, "Many of those who initiate wars either do not understand what they are doing or fail to realize the size of the gamble they are taking."[1]

Studies of deterrence that are based on evidence drawn from centuries of actual politico-military case studies, and incorporate basic concepts of human psychology and cognitive processes have matured since the mid-1980s. These validate the proposition that a

---

1. "The Use of Military Force: Constant Factors and New Trends," *The Changing Strategic Landscape*, Part II, in Adelphi Papers, No. 236 (London: International Institute For Strategic Studies, 1989), p. 3.

wide variety of factors typically shape leadership decision-making, factors that cannot be derived from a methodology that simply assumes states and leaders to be similarly motivated, rational and reasonable.

Numerous factors can lead a challenger to decision-making that is surprisingly unreasonable, even though narrowly rational: an individual leader's personal beliefs and characteristics, a leadership's political goals, ideology, perception of threat, determination, and decision-making process, *inter alia*. Personal beliefs and modes of thought have been the dynamic behind some of the most significant and surprising foreign decision-making of this century—they matter greatly.

Several of the most common such factors are illustrated below.

PERSONAL BELIEFS, GOALS, AND VALUES

Personal beliefs and modes of thought that appear to have significantly shaped state policies in the past include leaders' spiritual beliefs, their (frequently distorted) perceptions of themselves and their opponents, concepts of personal and/or national honor, intellectual rigidity or adaptability, respect for others or the lack thereof, deceitfulness or openness, risk acceptance or tolerance, aggressiveness or caution, and maliciousness or sympathy. History abounds with examples of leaders' personal and political beliefs—ranging from the grossly criminal to the sublime—shaping decision-making in unreasonable and thus surprising ways.[2]

---

2. As Jonathan Roberts observes, "The personality of an individual determines the reaction to information and events. A leader's nationality, passion, idealism, cynicism, pragmatism, dogmatism, stupidity, intelligence, imagination, flexibility, stubbornness, and so on, along with mental disorders such as depression, anxiety, and paranoia, shape reactions and decision during a crisis." *Decision-Making during International Crises* (New York: St. Martin's Press, 1988), pp. 162-163.

In a series of seven case studies examining the outbreak of war, for example, Professor John Stoessinger concluded that in each case, a "fatal flaw or ego weakness" in a leader's personality was of decisive importance: "With regard to the problem of the outbreak of war, the case studies indicate the crucial importance of the personalities of leaders. I am less impressed by the role of abstract forces, such as nationalism, militarism, or alliance systems, which traditionally have been regarded as the causes of war. Nor does a single one of the seven cases indicate that economic factors played a vital part in precipitating war. The personalities of leaders, on the other hand, have often been decisive."[3]

Following a monumental analysis of why states go to war, Yale historian Donald Kagan reaches a similar conclusion that, in decisions for war and peace, "considerations of practical utility and material gain" actually play a "small" role, while "some aspect of honor is decisive."[4] The path to war is not only about security and material gain, but also, "demands for greater prestige, respect, deference, in short, honor."[5] In pursuit of these often amorphous and intangible goals, leaders knowingly will pursue high-risk policies and court disaster.[6]

Leaders' basic ideological beliefs and perceptions also have been significant, including, for example, perceptions of threat (whether accurate or grossly distorted), theories about the nature of international relations, the prerogatives and obligations of the leadership, the state and the citizen, notions of national honor and

---

3.   John G. Stoessinger, *Why Nations Go to War* (New York: St. Martin's Press: 1993), p. 213.

4.   Donald Kagan, *On The Origins Of War* (New York: Doubleday, 1995), p. 8.

5.   Ibid., p. 569.

6.   Donald Kagan, "Honor, Interest, and the Nation State," in, *Honor Among Nations*, Elliot Abrams, ed. (Washington D.C.: Ethics and Public Policy Center, 1996), pp. 8-9.

sovereignty, and the view a leadership has of its own place in history. Leaders' views on such matters can be the direct determinant of their decision-making, autonomous of (and even contrary to) what seems to an outside observer to be pragmatic, rational and reasonable. They have guided policies in ways that were surprising and sometimes very dangerous for contemporary observers who anticipated reasonable behavior according to familiar norms.

For example, Gen. Wafic al Samarrai, the head of Iraq's military intelligence during the Gulf War and a lifelong acquaintance of Saddam Hussein, described war as part of Hussein's character: "His theory is war. He cannot survive without war...[Hussein] said war is glory. It is a side of his character."[7] Gen. al Samarrai emphasized that Saddam Hussein's decision-making reflected personal and political values far from Western norms and expectations. This glorification of war may help to explain his surprising readiness to invade Kuwait and subsequently to defy U.S. assembled might so soon after his years of costly warfare with Iran.

Czar Nicholas's thinking at the time of the Russo-Japanese War of 1904 demonstrates how one of the factors leading to the outbreak of war was the Czar's irrational and bigoted view of the Japanese. In Czar Nicholas's mind, it was unfathomable that a non-European power would dare to attack imperial Russia. In fact, prior to the outbreak of the war, the German Kaiser cautioned the Czar that Russia would be faced with war. The Czar's response was that there could be no war because he would not permit it. According to Count Witte, a member of the Czar's Court, "What he meant, apparently, was that Russia would not declare war and that Japan

---

7. Quoted in Tim Trevan, *Saddam's Secrets* (New York: Harper Collins Publishers, 1999), p. 300.

would not dare it."[8] In this case, decision-making was driven, at least in part, by the low esteem in which the Czar held the Japanese.

Following the initial U.S. use of an atomic weapon, Japanese War Minister Gen. Korechiki Anami attempted to persuade the Japanese Supreme Council to continue the war. He "called for one last great battle on Japanese soil—as demanded by the national honor, as demanded by the honor of the living and the dead." General Anami argued, "Would it not be wondrous for this whole nation [Japan] to be destroyed like a beautiful flower."[9] General Anami and his colleagues in the military came very close to winning the internal Japanese debate about how to confront impending defeat. Yet, in Washington the notion that national honor could be valued over national survival in this fashion is viewed with dismay and disbelief, hardly worthy of consideration as a possible dynamic of behavior. The implications of this illustration for the deterrence tautology are profound: an opponent's rationality does not necessarily equate to its susceptibility to even very lethal U.S. deterrence threats.

Mao Zedong viewed himself as god-like, unaccountable, and infallible.[10] He held an instrumental view of China's citizens, with at least occasional gross disregard for their well-being beyond serving his own grandiose political goals. He sacrificed millions of Chinese in the state-sponsored famines unleashed by his ideological vision of a "great leap forward."[11] In numerous private and public statements he expressed shocking callousness regarding

---

8.   *The Memoirs of Count Witte*, translated from the original Russian manuscript and edited by Abraham Yarmolinsky (New York: Doubleday, Page, and Company, 1921), p. 121.

9.   Quoted from, David McCullough, *Truman* (New York: Simon and Schuster, 1992), p. 459.

10. See, Li Zhisui, *The Private Life of Chairman Mao* (New York: Random House, 1994), pp. 120, 296.

11. See Jasper Becker, *Hungry Ghosts* (New York: The Free Press, 1997).

the potential for hundreds of millions of Chinese deaths from nuclear war, identifying such a horror as "no great loss."[12] That Mao could subordinate the lives of so many Chinese to his particular ideological goals left considerable room for Washington to have been surprised in a deterrence contest of wills.

Occult religious/spiritual beliefs represent another example of the type of what may be categorized as personal beliefs that can drive decision-making beyond U.S. expectations. Saddam Hussein's belief in the occult apparently helped guide his surprisingly incompetent moves during the Gulf War. Wafic al Samarrai commented on Hussein's faith in "soothsayers": "The soothsayer was a boy of twelve years old from Kirkuk. This boy soothsayer accompanied Saddam in all his special tours. There was another soothsayer from South East Asia.... These two soothsayers I know them very well. They kept telling him that he would win.... It's quite exotic about the way [Saddam] thought and the way he behaved. He thought that these soothsayers are really applying astrology and this is some kind of science."[13]

This basis for decision-making may seem impossible in a technically advanced society, but it is not limited to Third World leaders. For example, Col. Gen. Vladimir Yakovlev, Commander in Chief of the Russian Strategic Rocket Forces, identifies astrology as "a quite serious science. It helps us launch spacecraft, missiles; we use it broadly to forestall suicides among the personnel. Experience shows it is unreasonable to reject it."[14] Clearly, that General Yakovlev, by his own account, takes astrology into serious consideration with regard to the forces under

---

12. Li Zhisui, *The Private Life of Chairman Mao*, p. 125.

13. See the statements by Gen. Wafic al Samarrai, in *Frontline*, "The Gulf War, Parts I and II," 9 and 10 January 1996.

14. Quoted in, "Belarus: Russia's Rocket Troops Chief Views Cooperation, Astrology," *Vo Slavu Rodiny*, in Foreign Broadcast Information Service, *Central Eurasia-Military Affairs*, February 26, 1998, p. 2.

his command is unreasonable, even irrational by Washington's standards regarding such matters, and could have unpredictable consequences.

That serious belief in the occult could affect national decision-making is not unheard of even in Washington: Nancy Reagan dismayed senior members of the White House staff and Reagan Administration by consistently consulting a psychic astrologer from California, Joan Quigley, concerning President Reagan's activities and schedule.[15] As Gen. Colin Powell has observed, "Nancy Reagan consulted an astrologist to decide where and when the President should conduct the business of the United States."[16]

Even very private feelings can shape decision-making in surprising ways. In 1983 241 U.S. soldiers and 58 French paratroopers were killed in Lebanon by suicide truck bombings, while Italian soldiers went unharmed. Syria's Defense Minister Mustafa Tlas has helped to explain this apparent good fortune on the part of the Italians. "I gathered the heads of the Lebanese resistance and told them: 'Do anything you want to American forces or to the British and others, but I do not want a single Italian soldier hurt.'"[17] The self-expressed reason for General Tlas's generosity toward the Italian forces was his great fondness for the beautiful Italian film star Gina Lollobrigida. Perhaps America's many starlets are under-appreciated for their potential contribution to national security.

---

15. See, for example, the discussion in Donald T. Regan, *For The Record* (New York: Harcourt Brace, 1988), pp. 3-5, 70-75, 367-370.

16. Colin Powell, *My American Journey* (New York: Random House, 1995), p. 361.

17. Quoted in, "Syrian official protected Italy's troops over love for Italian actress," *The Washington Times*, January 3, 1998, p. A-5.

OVERRIDING IMPERATIVES AND CONSCIOUS, HIGH-RISK BRINKMANSHIP

Historical case studies also demonstrate that two general imperatives can drive leaders to surprising and extraordinarily risky initiatives: grave foreign and/or domestic threats that leaders believe necessitate aggression.[18] In such circumstances, leaders have pursued highly risky brinkmanship despite their foe's seemingly credible and capable deterrence commitments. Leaders can consciously choose a high-risk course involving potentially great cost because the alternative of inaction appears to lead to wholly intolerable consequences. In the context of such need-driven decision-making, high-risk behavior can be accepted and rationalized because of the expected unacceptable cost of not acting.[19] There are numerous historical examples of such imperatives leading to high-risk brinkmanship.

For example, the great historian of antiquity, Josephus, describes the sequence of events when the early-first century Roman procurator of Judea, Pontius Pilate, sought to bring Caesar's effigy into Jerusalem.[20] Previous procurators of Judea had avoided the custom of establishing such Roman images in Jerusalem. It was highly offensive to the Jews, given the Mosaic law against graven images. Pilate, however, did what the prior procurators had not.

---

18. See the excellent historical work in, Richard Lebow, *Between Peace and War* (Baltimore: Johns Hopkins University Press, 1981), chapter 9; and Lebow, "The Deterrence Deadlock: Is There A Way Out," *in Psychology & Deterrence*, Robert Jervis, Richard Ned Lebow, and Janice Gross Stein, eds. (Baltimore: Johns Hopkins University Press, 1985), pp. 180-188.

19. See the discussion in, Richard Ned Lebow and Janice Gross Stein, *When Does Deterrence Succeed And How Do We Know*, Occasional Paper, No. 8 (Ottawa: Canadian Institute for International Peace and Security, February 1990).

20. See the discussion of this event in, Josephus, *The Works of Josephus*, translated by William Whiston (Peabody, MA: Hendrickson Publishers, 1987), pp. 479-480.

Josephus tells us that Pilate brought the images of Caesar into Jerusalem under cover of darkness. The Jewish "multitudes" promptly went to Pilate to protest against the images. In reply, Pilate, "gave a signal to the soldiers to encompass them round, and threatened that their punishment should be no less than immediate death, unless they would leave off disturbing him."[21]

Pilate's threat obviously was severe, well understood, highly credible, and wholly ineffective. The Jewish multitudes, "Threw themselves upon the ground, and laid their necks bare, and said they would take their death very willingly, rather than the wisdom of their laws should be transgressed." According to Josephus, Pilate "was deeply affected with their firm resolution," and withdrew Caesar's effigy from Jerusalem.

In 416 B.C. the warriors of Melos took a similarly self-conscious and absolute position in defense of their freedom against the Athenians—who had made very credible and severe threats against them in order to end Melian neutrality in the Second Peloponnesian War. The warriors' failure to yield led to their annihilation and the colonization of Melos by Athens.

Over two millennia later, Russia's Czar Nicholas knowingly chose a high-risk war with Germany and Austria-Hungary rather than conciliation; in this case the Czar concluded that the cost of backing down in the Balkans would be intolerable. Conceding to Austria-Hungary's demands against Slavic and Orthodox Serbia would have destroyed the nationalist and Pan-Slavic basis of the (Orthodox) Russian government's domestic legitimacy. The political consensus in St. Petersburg was to wage war, even if it meant high-risk war with Germany and Austria-Hungary.[22]

---

21. Ibid., p. 480.

22. As one historian of the war's outbreak notes: "A domestic political imperative spurred Nicholas and his government to fight Austria-Hungary rather than permit a wholesale realignment of the Balkan states." John Maurer, *The Outbreak of the First World War* (Westport, CT: Praeger, 1995), p. 115.

Georgetown University Professor William Wohlforth has noted with regard to the Czar's decision-making and the Council of Ministers meeting on July 24, 1914: "Despite their clear understanding of Russia's weakness after its defeat by Japan in 1904-5 and the revolution of 1905, despite their expectation that Russia's relative power would increase in the years ahead, despite their lack of tangible or strategic interest in the Balkans, Nicholas and his ministers took their empire to war. Russia's prestige, they reasoned, could not stand further concessions to the Central Powers. The decision brought Russia into a conflict that led to the destruction of everything those men who met on July 24 held dear."[23]

Prior to the Gulf War, Saddam Hussein expressed views regarding a possible confrontation with the West that reflected values, motivation, and a willingness to accept risks and costs in conflict that later surprised Washington: "If you use pressure, we will deploy pressure and force. We know that you can harm us, although we do not threaten you. But we too can harm you.... You can come to Iraq with aircraft and missiles, but do not push us to the point where we cease to care. And when we feel that you want to injure our pride and take away the Iraqis' chance of a high standard of living, then we will cease to care, and death will be the choice for us. Then we would not care if you fired 100 missiles for each missile we fired. Because without pride life would have no value."[24]

From an Iraqi perspective, according to accounts by both senior Iraqi officials and defectors, Saddam Hussein's decision to invade was neither irrational nor unreasonable. Rather, the decision was

---

23. "Honor as Interest in Russian Decisions for War, 1600-1995," in, *Honor Among Nations*, Elliot Abrams, ed. (Washington D.C.: Ethics and Public Policy Center, 1996), p. 22.

24. Quoted in, Don Oberdorfer, "Missed Signals in the Middle East," *Washington Post Magazine,* March 17, 1991, p. 39.

driven by two mistaken beliefs: that Iraq's future would be intolerable in the absence of such a move because of a U.S.-led effort ("conspiracy") to destroy Iraq's economy;[25] and that the United States, for essentially political reasons, was unlikely to respond firmly to an Iraqi *fait accompli.*[26]

These four examples illustrate that the expectation of intolerable loss from inaction can lead to conscious, rational, high-risk decision-making, including decisions that risk survival. Again, the U.S. Cold War deterrence tautology comes unraveled in the context of a desperate willingness to run extraordinary risks in order to forestall an intolerable future.

The behavior of leaders who are highly goal-oriented, and consciously willing to accept great costs in pursuit of their goals also may fall outside the boundaries assumed in the U.S. deterrence framework. Extreme determination and willingness to sacrifice, not only to avoid loss but to secure a goal, can be consistent with the ideological and/or religious zealot, the willing martyr. There are, of course, numerous historical examples of such.

Libyan leader, Muammar al-Qadhdhafi, for example, at least sounds the part: "O brothers, the American columns do not scare us, nor do the fleets of America and the allies of America. We are the children of the martyrs. Methods of intimidation and humiliation do not work with us. If they have succeeded to the west, east, north, or south of Libya, they will not succeed in Libya.... The Libyan people prefer martyrdom to the last man and last woman.... Brothers, we say to America: We welcome

---

25. As Tariq Aziz observed following the war: "We started to realize that there is a conspiracy against Iraq, a deliberate conspiracy against Iraq by Kuwait, organized, [and] devised by the United States." As a result, according to Aziz, "Iraq had no choice but to act, either to be destroyed, to be suffocated and strangled inside its territory or attack the enemy on the outside." Statements by Tariq Aziz, *Frontline*, "The Gulf War, Part I," January 9, 1996, transcript, 1–2.

26. See, Jeffrey Record, "Defeating Desert Storm (and Why Saddam Didn't)," *Comparative Strategy*, Vol. 12, No. 2 (April-June 1993), pp. 127-128.

aggression, we welcome confrontation.... The futile people say: How can Libya resist America? We have not said only that. We are all ready to perish, and we will not surrender to America."[27]

Extreme determination and commitment to an intangible goal often is attributed only to non-Western religious or ideological zealots. That is a mistake. Such a commitment is, for example, reflected in the words of the colonial American patriot and revolutionary, Josia Quincy, in his *Observations on the Boston Port Bill* (the first of the British "Intolerable Acts"): "Blandishments will not fascinate us, nor will threats of a 'halter' intimidate, for, under God, we are determined that wheresoever, whensoever, or howsoever we shall be called to make our exit, we will die free men." If the British had sought to anticipate the susceptibility of America's colonial revolutionaries to deterrence and coercion, they would have needed to understand the high-level of personal determination driving Josia Quincy and his comrades.

During the 1962 Cuban Missile Crisis Cuban leaders Fidel Castro and Che Guevara apparently urged the Soviets in Cuba and Moscow to launch a preemptive nuclear strike against the United States in the event of an attack against Cuba. During the crisis Castro urged Soviet leader Nikita Khrushchev to prepare for such a strike, "If they [Americans] actually carry out the brutal act of invading Cuba...that would be the moment to eliminate such danger forever through an act of legitimate defense, however harsh and terrible the solution would be."[28] Khrushchev himself later said of Castro, "At that time he [Castro] was a very hot-tempered

27. "Speech by Colonel Muammar al-Qadhdhafi at Al Wahat," Tripoli Libyan Television Network, October 6, 1994, translated in, Federal Broadcast Information Service, "Al-Qadhdhafi Delivers Address at Al Wahat," NES-94-197, October 12, 1994, p. 19.

28. Quoted in, Aleksandr Fursenko and Timothy Naftali, *One Hell of a Gamble* (W.W. Norton: New York, 1997), pp. 272-273; see also, pp. 283, 286, 306.

person.... He failed to think through the obvious consequences of a proposal that placed the planet on the brink of extinction."[29]

A Soviet participant in the crisis, Col. Viktor Semykin, describes how the Cubans, ready to accept any cost, urged a Soviet missile attack: "The Cubans really insisted we use our weapons. 'Why else did you come here? Use your weapons. Fire.' They were ready for war. Maybe they believed so strongly, they were ready to sacrifice themselves. They would say, 'Cuba will perish, but socialism will win.' They were ready to sacrifice themselves."[30]

Castro's political theoretician, Che Guevara, expressed his ideological fervor and willingness to sacrifice himself and Cuba for the cause of socialism. "If the rockets had remained, we would have used them all and directed them against the heart of the United States, including New York, in our fight against aggression."[31] These are the voices of an ideological commitment that is highly resistant to cost-benefit calculation and conciliation. As one biographer notes, Che looked forward to, and worked toward, such an "ultimate showdown" with the United States; in his view, it was "the final aim of Communism."[32]

In contrast, Soviet Deputy Premier Anastas Mikoyan's reply to Che reflects a different perspective, and a cost-benefit calculus more susceptible to deterrence threats. "We see your readiness to

---

29. Quoted in James Blight, et al., *Cuba on the Brink: Castro, the Missile Crisis, and the Soviet Collapse* (New York: Pantheon Books, 1993), p. 29.

30. Col. Viktor Semykin, interviewed for, "The Missiles of October: What the World Didn't Know," *ABC News*, Journal Graphics transcript no. ABC-40, October 17, 1992, p. 21. On the basis of conversations with Castro, former Secretary of Defense Robert McNamara has confirmed that Castro was committed to the use of nuclear weapons against the United States, despite being convinced that Cuba "would have been totally destroyed," as a consequence. See, *News Hour with Jim Lehrer*, PBS TV, February 22, 2001.

31. Quoted in, Enrique Krauze, "The Return of Che Guevara," *The New Republic*, Vol. 218, No. 6 (February 9, 1998), p. 34.

32. Daniel James, *Che Guevara* (New York: Stein and Day Publishers, 1969), p. 147.

die beautifully, but we believe that it isn't worth dying beautifully."[33] Mikoyan complained in a letter to Khrushchev that with the Cuban leadership, "bitter feelings often overcome reason," and that the Cubans were, "expansive, emotional, nervous, high-strung, quick to explode in anger, and unhealthily apt to concentrate on trivialities."[34]

The Cold War deterrence framework's assumption that rationality yields reasonableness and predictability may well be useful in the context of a challenger of Mikoyan's dispassionate and pragmatic character. Such an assumption, however, is likely to lead to false conclusions about deterrence in the face of a dedicated ideological zealot such as Che Guevara. In effect, the potential for ideological fervor to so dramatically shape "rational" cost-benefit calculations is discounted or ignored by the Cold War deterrence framework. Fortunately, in 1962, relatively cautious Soviet bureaucrats were in control of the missiles, not Fidel Castro or Che Guevara. In future crises, leaders ready to "die beautifully" may be in control of missiles, and their cost-benefit calculus will not permit the predictable functioning of deterrence.

These are the types of factors affecting rational decision-making that can easily prevent the reasonable, predictable cost-benefit calculations upon which the Cold War deterrence framework is predicated. They include the willingness to risk all to maintain a threatened value or in passionate pursuit of a goal.

POLITICAL IMPERATIVES AND COGNITIVE DISTORTION

In addition, when leaders believe they must act to avoid an intolerable future, a variety of well-known cognitive processes can limit their capacity to engage in the type of well-informed, rational,

---

33. Quoted in, Krauze, "The Return of Che Guevara," p. 34.

34. Aleksandr Fursenko and Timothy Naftali, *One Hell of a Gamble*, p. 306.

decision-making necessary for deterrence to function predictably. Leaders in such circumstances can deny, ignore, reject and/or distort those elements of reality that are incompatible with the course they have chosen, or the course they believe has been forced upon them: "When policy makers became convinced of the necessity to achieve specific foreign policy objectives, they became predisposed to see these objectives as attainable…when policy makers feel compelled to act, they may employ denial, selective attention, or other psychological sleights of hand to dismiss indications of an adversary's resolve. In such circumstances, the complex and ambiguous nature of the international environment does not encourage restraint but rather encourages irrational confidence."[35]

We know that in crisis situations, decisions tend to be based on fairly simplified cognitive structures, which tend to reduce the range of options perceived by the leaders involved. There is no doubt that objective rationality in decision-making can be impaired by various psychological defense mechanisms.[36] One example of the type of psychological factors that appears to have led rational leaders to such miscalculation is the denial mechanism. Denial can affect a person who is compelled to choose among a panoply of difficult options. A choice is made, and the decision-maker subsequently simply denies the possible negative consequences associated with the chosen course and ignores information suggesting negative consequences associated with that choice.

Denial is a basic human psychological reaction to danger and involves "various degrees of nonperception, nonrecognition,

---

35. Lebow, "The Deterrence Deadlock," p. 182.

36. For a basic discussion of psychological defense mechanisms such as repression and denial, see William N. December and James J. Jenkins, *General Psychology: Modeling Behavior and Experience* (Englewood Cliffs, NJ: Prentice-Hall, 1970), pp. 659-678; and Lee Roy Beach, *Psychology: Core Concepts and Special Topics* (New York: Holt, Rinehart and Winston, 1973), pp. 187-198.

nonunderstanding, or nonacceptance of certain realities."[37] Detailed historical case studies demonstrate that this psychological defense mechanism has indeed been significant in miscalculations that resulted in the outbreak of crises and wars during both the nuclear and prenuclear age.[38] For example, some statesmen have simply refused to acknowledge the strength of a foreign threat.

Another common psychological process important in this regard has been labeled bolstering.[39] This is the psychological tendency of decision-makers who are compelled to choose from several unsatisfying courses to select the least miserable, minimize its possible negative consequences and exaggerate its positive attributes. The possibility for unwarranted overconfidence on the part of desperate leaders as a result of this psychological mechanism is obvious. As Richard Lebow observes, it blinds policy makers to the possible adverse consequences of their actions.[40]

The Gulf War may provide an example of both how an unexpected level of determination can confound expectations, and how self-serving expectations can color perception. Washington's leaders simply would not believe that Saddam could be so unreasonable, so willing to risk another war; and they filtered

---

37. See, Group for the Advancement of Psychiatry, Committee on Social Issues, *Psychiatric Aspects of the Prevention of Nuclear War*, Report No. 57 (September, 1964), p. 241.

38. Peter Karsten, Peter D. Howell, and Artis Frances Allen, *Military Threats: A Systematic Historical Analysis of the Determinants of Success* (Westport, CT: Greenwood Press, 1984), p. 21; Richard Lebow, "Miscalculation in the South Atlantic: The Origins of the Falklands War," in Jervis, Lebow, and Stein, *Psychology and Deterrence*, pp. 103, 119; and, in the same text, Lebow, "The Deterrence Deadlock: Is There A Way Out," p. 182-183.

39. See the discussion in, Lebow, *Between Peace and War*, p. 110.

40. Lebow, "Miscalculation in the South Atlantic: The Origins of the Falklands War," p. 104.

contrary information through that prism of confident disbelief.[41] April Glaspie, former U.S. Ambassador to Iraq, has observed that prior to Iraq's August 2 invasion of Kuwait the U.S. warned Saddam Hussein against military aggression.[42] If there was such a warning, it failed to deter. More to the point, even following the buildup of U.S. and Coalition forces against Iraq during the winter of 1991, Saddam Hussein refused to bow to U.S. threats and withdraw from Kuwait, leading President Bush to question the Iraqi leader's rationality.

An appreciation of Saddam Hussein's perspective, however, may help to explain this behavior that otherwise seemed inexplicable: he appears to have been both highly determined, and to have viewed the U.S. with self-serving disdain. The U.S. Air Force's meticulous study of the Gulf War, the *Gulf War Air Power Survey*, concludes: "Finally, Iraqi arrogance—which afflicted both Saddam and his generals—and which manifested itself in a predisposition to inflate Iraqi capabilities and underestimate those of their enemies, had a significant impact on his assessment of the balance of forces. These important, yet difficult to quantify, factors influenced nearly every decision made prior to the war and precluded Saddam or his advisors from accurately identifying coalition strengths and weaknesses, and recognizing Iraq's own significant shortcomings."[43]

Clearly, Saddam Hussein misjudged the United States as badly as the U.S. leadership misjudged him, basing his view of

---

41. See, Alex Hybel, *Power Over Rationality* (Albany, NY: State University of New York Press, 1993), p. 55.

42. Quoted in Don Oberdorfer, "Glaspie Says Saddam Is Guilty of Deception," *The Washington Post*, March 21, 1991, p. A-23.

43. U.S. Air Force, *Gulf War Air Power Survey*, Volume I, *Planning and Command and Control* (Washington, D.C.: U.S. Government Printing Office, 1993), p. 81.

Washington on the U.S. withdrawals from Vietnam and Lebanon.[44] Each operated from self-serving presumptions about the other that, at least in principle could have been corrected, but instead channeled events toward war.

In 1982 Britain faced a similar situation wherein the credibility of its commitment was miscalculated by a challenger, leading that challenger toward an ill-fated path of aggression that surprised the British. Decisions leading to the 1982 Falklands War with Argentina appear to have been affected by a series of self-serving miscalculations. There is little doubt that the desperate political weakness of the junta ruling Argentina led it to view the dispute with Britain over the Falklands as a vehicle for demonstrating its competence—exploiting nationalistic sentiment on the issue and elevating its domestic political authority. As one assessment of the war notes: "Within Argentina, recovery of the 'Malvinas' would not stifle internal dissent, but at least it would unite the nation for a time. It would serve as a vindication of military rule and cleanse the reputation of the armed forces."[45] At the time, General Leopoldo Galtieri, head of the junta, said to then- U.S. Secretary of State Alexander Haig, "we cannot sacrifice our honor...you will understand that the Argentinian government has to look good, too."[46]

The prospect for Argentina's aggression was heightened by the junta's self-serving view that the British commitment to the Falklands was very soft. There appears to have been a dangerous combination of the junta's strongly felt need to act and its

---

44. See, Donald Kagan, "Honor, Interest, and Nation-State," in, *Honor Among Nations*, ed., Elliot Abrams (Washington, D.C.: Ethics and Public Policy Center, 1998), p. 19.

45. See, Max Hasting and Simon Jenkins, *The Battle for the Falklands* (New York: Norton, 1983), 48. This "domestic politics" thesis also is presented in Watman and Wilkening, *U.S. Regional Deterrence Strategies*, pp. 38-40.

46. Quoted in, Alexander M. Haig, *Caveat* (New York: MacMillan, 1984), p. 277.

convenient underestimate of the risk. Prior to the war U.S. officials warned General Galtieri that the British would fight. Galtieri replied, "Why are you telling me this? The British won't fight."[47]

Following the war, General Galtieri was asked, "Didn't Argentina see the likelihood of the British responding to the invasion as they did?" Galtieri responded that he had assumed some possibility of a strong British reaction, but he had judged the probability of such to be very low: "Though an English reaction was considered a possibility, we did not see it as a probability. Personally, I judged it scarcely possible and totally improbable. In any case, I never expected such a disproportionate answer. Why should a country situated in the heart of Europe care so much for some islands located far away in the Atlantic Ocean; in addition, islands which do not serve any national interest? It seems so senseless to me."[48]

General Galtieri preferred to believe that Prime Minister Margaret Thatcher, the "Iron Lady," would not respond, even as she was facing an election cycle. Galtieri could join many other leaders, including Chamberlain in 1939, Acheson in 1941, and senior Bush Administration officials in 1990, in decrying the surprising senselessness of the opponent's behavior. In each case the confident assumption of a reasonable opponent was a convenient and self-serving belief that overshadowed considerable evidence to the contrary.

COGNITIVE DISTORTION: DRUG USAGE

In addition to surprising personal characteristics, a willingness to risk self-sacrifice to preserve a threatened value or achieve a cherished goal, and cognitive distortions, other factors may limit

47. Ibid., p. 280.

48. Oriana Fallaci, "Galtieri: No Regrets, No Going Back," *Times* (London), June 12, 1982, p. 4.

the informed, rational and reasonable decision-making necessary for deterrence to operate predictably. One little-noted such factor is drug usage. This may, at first, seem not to be a serious concern with regard to national decision-makers. Yet it must be recognized that leaders under the influence of a variety of drugs have governed great powers with dictatorial authority. Adolf Hitler, for example, took large, daily dosages of both stimulants and sedatives, as prescribed by his personal physician, Theodor Morell. And in 1944 Hitler began receiving frequent cocaine treatments, using an inhalator twice a day. The combination of these drugs and other unusual medical treatments may have contributed to Hitler's temper tantrums, hallucinations, and paranoia.[49]

Dr. Jerrold Post has observed regarding Hitler's drug usage: "The precise effects of this pharmaceutical cocktail of cocaine, amphetamines, and other stimulants on Hitler's mental state are difficult to gauge. Suffice it so say, in the jargon of the street, that Hitler was simultaneously taking coke and speed. Methamphetamine alone would have had major deleterious effects on Hitler's decision-making. Many of the effects of amphetamines would have been augmented by cocaine."[50] Hitler was not the only National Socialist leader so influenced. Reichsmarschall Hermann Goering was a morphine addict, possibly blinded to reality by morphine's euphoric effect.[51] Albert Speer, under interrogation immediately following the war observed that "in the last months

---

49. See the discussion in, Robert Waite, *The Psychopathic God: Adolf Hitler* (New York: Da Capo Press, 1977), pp. 351-356. See also, Jonathan Roberts, *Decision-Making during International Crises* (New York: St. Martin's Press, 1988), p. 203; and, Bert Park, M.D., *Ailing, Aging, Addicted* (Lexington, KY: University Press of Kentucky, 1993), p. 55.

50. See Jerrold Post, M.D., and Robert Robins, *When Illness Strikes The Leader* (New Haven: Yale University Press, 1993), pp. 70-72.

51. Waite, *The Psychopathic God*, pp. 54-55. See also, Christian Zentner and Freidemann Bedurftig, *The Encyclopedia of the Third Reich* (New York: De Capo Press, 1997), pp. 354-355.

one had always to deal with drunken men." An American participant in the interrogation noted that Speer "went on to guess that when the history of the Third Reich was written, it would be said that it drowned in a sea of alcohol."[52]

According to recently declassified U.S. State Department documents, senior U.S. officials considered former South Korean President Park Chung Hee to be dangerously unstable, largely because of his heavy use of alcohol. They were particularly concerned in 1965, following an unsuccessful North Korean terrorist attack against President Park himself, that he was "almost irrationally obsessed" with the desire to retaliate militarily against North Korea. Park's drinking was so heavy at the time that President Johnson's special envoy, Cyrus Vance, described him as "a danger and rather unsafe." Vance went on to observe that, "President Park will issue all sorts of orders when he begins drinking.... His generals will delay any action on them until the next morning. If he says nothing about those orders the following morning, then they just forget what he told them the night before."[53] In this case, sensible South Korean generals apparently provided a barrier to the implementation of presidential decision-making obviously skewed by alcohol consumption. In other past cases, as is discussed below, subordinates have had less leeway to ignore suspect orders.

China's Chairman Mao Zedong suffered from severe insomnia. As a result, according to his personal physician, Dr. Li Zhisui, Mao became addicted to barbiturates. At one point he was taking ten times the normal dosage of sleeping pills, enough to kill a person. According to Dr. Li, Mao initially used chloral hydrate to relieve

---

52. John Kenneth Galbraith, *A Life In Our Times* (Boston: Houghton Mifflin Company, 1981), p. 193.

53. U.S. Department of State, *Foreign Relations of the United States, 1964-1968*, Volume XXIX, *Korea*, at <www.state.gov/www/about_state/history/vol_xxix/index.html>, accessed January 29, 2001.

his insomnia, but became addicted, often mixing it with sodium seconal. Ultimately, Mao used drugs "when receiving guests and attending meetings. He also took them for his dance parties."[54] How Mao's drug addiction may have shaped his decision-making is unclear, but that it could have done so is certain.

One possibly significant case occurred in 1971. Just before falling asleep, and in a drowsy, slurred directive to his private nurse, Wu Xujun, Mao countermanded an earlier decision agreed to with Zhou Enlai. In doing so, Mao may have changed the course of history. In that earlier decision Mao and Zhou had agreed to *deny* the request from the U.S. table tennis team, then in Japan, for a sporting engagement in China. Through the fog of barbiturates, Mao rescinded that decision and approved the American team's request. The Chinese invitation thus extended led to the famous "ping-pong diplomacy" of the 1970s and facilitated an historic opening to Washington.[55]

Whether or not barbiturates shaped Mao's decision to rescind the position he had earlier agreed to with Zhou obviously cannot be known with certainty. That Mao made a decision of some political magnitude under the influence of barbiturates is certain.

Washington, of course, is not immune to the possibility of drug usage affecting policy. President John Kennedy, for example, reportedly used steroids (cortisone and desoxy certicosterone acetate) to treat his Addison's disease, and apparently took them in excess.[56] More to the point, however, is that in 1961 it appears that Kennedy also began receiving by injection large doses of combined amphetamines and steroids from a now-discredited

---

54. Dr. Li Zhisui, *The Private Life Of Chairman Mao* (New York: Random House, 1994), pp. 109, 112-113, 440.

55. Ibid., p. 558.

56. Park, *Ailing, Aging, Addicted*, pp. 168-171. See also, Roberts, *Decision-Making during International Crisis*, pp. 185, 203-204.

physician.[57] The potential side effects of steroids taken in excess are similar to those of amphetamines taken in excess: "delusions, agitation, anxiety, insomnia, and irritability, not to mention their addictive effects when taken in combination."[58] It is not possible here to identify the extent to which President Kennedy's decision-making may have been influenced by the excessive use of steroids and amphetamines. One such effort, however, suggests strongly that these drugs contributed to Kennedy's poor performance at the fateful 1961 Vienna Summit with Nikita Khrushchev, and to his reclusiveness following the summit.[59]

ADOLF HITLER: A STUDY IN UNEXPECTED DECISION-MAKING

Adolf Hitler's personal character and brutal ideological beliefs provide multiple illustrations of both rational and irrational factors shaping policy in unreasonable and unexpected ways, sometimes decisively. A very brief synopsis demonstrates conclusively the point that leadership decision-making that lies far outside Washington's expectations of what is reasonable may occur in even the most advanced, "modern" societies. Adolf Hitler was the legally appointed leader of the country that at that time had the highest educational standards in the world. Germany was technically advanced and culturally sophisticated. Hitler repeatedly and publicly declared his brutality, extreme hatreds and ideological goals. Nevertheless, through most of his years of leadership he and much of his political program were wildly popular.

There is a tremendous amount of documentary evidence concerning Hitler's character, thought, and political beliefs. And in many cases Hitler himself made the direct connection between these and the policies he intended to implement when in authority.

---

57. Park, pp. 170-183.
58. Ibid., p. 171.
59. Ibid., pp. 181-183.

As German historian Eberhard Jäckel observes, "Perhaps never in history did a ruler write down before he came to power what he was to do afterward as precisely as did Adolf Hitler."[60]

For all Hitler's manipulative and oratory skills, he was at heart an ideological zealot. The ideology of National Socialism, which strongly reflected Hitler's personal imprint and was a fusion of extreme political and quasi-religious beliefs, had an internal logic and consistency.[61] Indeed, few leaders were more consistent in implementing policies that reflected their personal character and expressed ideological beliefs. As Robert Waite observes, "Hitler believed his ideas. More important, they formed the foundation upon which he reordered society. Indeed, never in human history has a political theory been so ruthlessly carried out in practice."[62]

Hitler considered the history of international relations to reflect nature's struggle for survival, governed only by the "laws of the jungle." In accord with then-fashionable ideas of Social Darwinism, he claimed that human progress was the product of this struggle.[63] Perhaps most importantly, Hitler placed race, as opposed to class, or individuals, at the center of nature's competition. Hitler stated that his elevation of the concept that race is the dominant force in history was his greatest triumph: "If I try

---

60. Eberhard Jäckel, *Hitler in History* (Hanover: Brandeis University Press and University Press of New England, 1984), p. 24. For a popular assessment of selected Nazi propaganda intended to demonstrate that Hitler's views expressed in the early 1930's were ample warning of his subsequent behavior see, John Laffin, *Hitler Warned Us* (New York: Barnes & Noble Books, 1998).

61. For an elaboration of National Socialism's attempted fusion of political and religious belief see, Michael Burleigh, *The Third Reich: A New History* (New York: Hill and Wang, 2000). See also, Jay Gonen, *The Roots of Nazi Psychology* (Lexington, KY: University Press of Kentucky, 2000), pp. 1-15.

62. Robert Waite, "Afterward," in, Walter Langer, *The Mind of Adolf Hitler* (New York: Basic Books, 1972), p. 259.

63. Adolf Hitler, *Mein Kampf* (Boston: Houghton Mifflin, 1943), pp. 131-132, 134-135, 151, 153; see also, Adolf Hitler, *Hitler's Secret Book*, Introduction by Telford Taylor (New York: Bramhall House, 1986), pp. 5-7.

to gauge my work, I must consider, first of all, that I've contributed, in a world that had forgotten the notion, to the triumph of the idea of the primacy of race."[64] He identified brutality and supposedly superior Aryan "race value" as the keys to success in nature's racial survival of the fittest. Consequently, Hitler's fundamental ideological convictions included the need for "ruthless brutality" and Aryan "racial purity."

Correspondingly, Hitler despised and ridiculed "bourgeois" Judeo-Christian virtues as contrary to the struggle of nature and as foreign shackles meant to hobble the "superior" Aryan race. The hardness and ruthlessness necessary to succeed in this race-centered Darwinian struggle required freedom from "conscience and morality."[65] Said Hitler: "In the end, only the urge for self-preservation can conquer. Beneath it so-called humanity, the expression of a mixture of stupidity, cowardice, and know-it-all conceit, will melt like snow in the March sun."[66]

Hitler reveled in the role of "barbarian," and celebrated his liberation from most traditional moral standards in favor of a state of nature in which the strongest, the ruthless, and the most brutal would dominate.[67] He cultivated "ruthless brutality," particularly in combating those he considered to be the "race poisoners" of Aryans, notably Jews, Gypsies, Poles, and Russians.

---

64. *Hitler's Secret Conversations, 1941-1944*, Normai Cameron and R.H Stevens, translators (New York: Farrar, Straus, and Young, 1953), October 21-22, 1941, p. 67.

65. Walter Langer, *The Mind of Adolf Hitler: The Secret Wartime Report* (New York: Basic Books, 1972), p. 190; and, Waite, *The Psychopathic God*, p. 16.

66. *Mein Kampf*, p. 135.

67. Hitler boasted with regard to himself and his party: "We have no scruples. I have no bourgeois hesitations.... Yes, we are barbarians! We want to be barbarians! It is an honorable title." Quoted in, Hermann Rauschning, *Hitler Speaks* (London: Thornton Butterworth, 1939), pp. 86-87.

Hitler wrote in the first volume of *Mein Kampf* (1924) that the proper role of the "Folkish" state was to strengthen Germany in its struggle for survival and dominance. For Hitler, strengthening Germany called for two primary tasks. The first was to promote Germany's "race value" with an "iron fist": "The Folkish state...must set race as the center of all life. It must take care to keep it pure," and, "A state which in this age of racial poisoning dedicates itself to the care of its best racial elements must some day become Lord of the earth."[68] Non-Aryan peoples were thought to threaten Germany's "race value" by "poisoning" Aryan blood with their own "lower race value." Germans suffering from physical or mental disabilities were thought to pose a similar threat. Hitler ordered the suppression and mass murder of these peoples based on this supposed threat to Aryan race value, a threat purportedly inherent in their blood. An individual's innocence and due process in the American legal sense meant nothing.

In Hitler's ideology his second state task was to solve Germany's supposed overpopulation problem by securing territory in Russia in a war of conquest and annihilation.[69] Hitler believed that this would provide the necessary space for German farmers to feed the growing German population; it would also provide a critical security buffer zone. German citizens, in Hitler's view, possessed no inalienable individual rights per se; rather, they were to be unquestioning instruments in this Darwinian struggle for survival, as directed by their Führer.

Hitler's public speeches and private discussions, his two volumes in *Mein Kampf*, and his 1928 book, *Hitlers Zweites Buch* [published in English as *Hitler's Secret Book*] demonstrate

---

68. *Mein Kampf*, p. 403, 686. See also, *Hitler's Secret Book*, p. 210.

69. *Mein Kampf*, p. 140 and *Hitler's Secret Book*, pp. 46-48, 74, 124, 139. See also Jürgen Förster, "Hitler's Decision In Favor of War Against the Soviet Union," in, Militärgeschichtliches Forschungsamt, *Germany and the Second World War*, Vol. IV (New York: Oxford University Press, 1998), pp. 25-38.

comprehensively that Hitler held these ideological beliefs from very early in his political career. Once in power, he clearly acted upon them.[70] Telford Taylor wrote of Hitler in the introduction to *Hitler's Secret Book*, "Perhaps more than any other man of this century he was able to transmute his own thoughts into events, and a corresponding concern and fascination thus attaches to this record of his thoughts."[71]

In October 1939, for example, Hitler ordered the initial implementation of a euthanasia program he had planned in 1935, to eliminate those Germans "unworthy of life" ["*Vernichtung Lebensunwertes Leben*"], including the mentally ill, the incurable, those crippled by accident, and babies with birth defects. Hitler lauded as wise and humane the "destruction" of "sick, weak, deformed children" because it would strengthen the race. He criticized contrary policies as "mendaciously sentimental, bourgeois-patriotic nonsense."[72] A national euthanasia program, including adult victims, ultimately involved the sterilization of 350,000 Germans and the murder of up to another 200,000.[73]

This program was an extension of Hitler's particular fusion of ideology and metaphysics, his embrace of Social Darwinism; it was his murderous effort to promote nature's process of natural selection.[74] Hitler's purpose for the program, which established

---

70. See, for example, the discussion in Eberhard Jäckel, *Hitler's Weltanschauung: A Blueprint for Power* (Middletown, CT: Wesleyan University Press, 1973), pp. 47–66.

71. *Hitler's Secret Book*, p. XXV.

72. *Hitler's Secret Book,* pp. 17-18.

73. See, for example, the discussions in, Gerhard Weinberg, *Germany, Hitler & World War II* (New York: Cambridge University Press, 1996), p. 6; Sebastian Haffner, *The Meaning of Hitler* (Cambridge, Mass: Harvard University Press, 1979), pp. 132-133; Waite, *The Psychopathic God*, pp. 388, 414; Sherwin Nuland, "The Final Pollution," *The New Republic* (June 14, 1999), pp. 37-38; and, Jäckel, *Hitler in History*, pp. 32, 49-50.

74. See the discussion in, Gonen, *The Roots of Nazi Psychology*, pp. 20-21, 38.

techniques and personnel for the coming extermination campaigns against Jews, Gypsies, Poles, and Russians, was to raise Germany's blood "purity" and "race value," and thereby strengthen Germany's position for racial struggle. He similarly considered the initial deportation and subsequent genocide of European Jewry as a means of ridding the Aryan race of an international enemy and thereby strengthening the German nation in its expanding empire. This "purification" clearly reflected Hitler's pathological antisemitism, and his ideological beliefs about the purpose of the state and how to strengthen Germany for the war of conquest to be waged against the East.

Hitler was explicit in his genocidal intentions. In a speech to the Reichstag on January 30, 1939, for example, Hitler, referring to "a certain foreign people" said "We will banish this people." Only slightly later in the speech he threatened European Jewry with "a crisis of yet inconceivable proportions;" and minutes later, taking the role of "prophet," said that another world war would lead to "the annihilation [*Vernichtung*] of the Jewish race in Europe." [75]

Germany's 22 June 1941 invasion of the Soviet Union, *Operation Barbarossa*, was undertaken, at least in part, to secure Hitler's long-sought-after *Lebensraum*, the territorial basis for creation of a *Grossgermanisches Reich* [Great Germanic Empire]. Hitler's decision for *Barbarossa* was the culmination of his basic view of international relations as a brutal, state-of-nature, racial struggle, his belief that Germany needed territory, to be had only in the East, and his belief in the inherent inequality of peoples, in this case the inferiority of "Slavdom."

Hitler saw the Soviet Union as ripe for, and deserving of, conquest because the "inferior," "subhuman" Slavic barbarians

---

75. See, Max Domarus, *Hitler: Speeches and Proclamations 1932-1945, The Chronicle Of A Dictatorship*, Vol. III, 1939-1940 (Wauconda, IL: Bolchazy-Carducci Publishers, 1997), pp. 1448-1449.

ultimately would be incapable of mustering an effective defense.[76] Hitler had observed regarding the coming destruction of the Soviet Union, "We have been chosen by fate to be the witnesses of a catastrophe which will be the most powerful substantiation of the correctness of the folkish theory of race."[77] Slavs were, in Hitler's mind, fit only to serve as slaves following their conquest: "The Slavs are a mass of born slaves, who feel the need of a master."[78] Hitler's contempt for Slavs had its immediate policy effect. In his view, the Soviet Union would collapse quickly. Because of his confidence in Aryan superiority, his troops were not provided with winter uniforms, nor were preparations made for the Russian winter.[79] As a result, by early-December 1941, "General Winter" had contributed much to halting the German offensive outside of Moscow.

Hitler's timetable for and conduct of the war also was shaped significantly by his view of himself as a person and a leader. Hitler believed that in 1918 "Providence" had called him in a supernatural "heavenly vision" to set him on his political path to save Germany. He was the irreplaceable, "infallible" German Messiah; only he had the calling and strength to pursue the "hard" programs he believed were necessary to create a bright future for the Aryan race. In addition, by 1938 Hitler believed that his health was failing and that natural causes would soon end his life. Consequently, Hitler made little serious provision for successors and demanded the rapid preparation for war, lest he die before

---

76. *Hitler's Secret Book*, pp. XXII, XIV. See also, Jäckel, *Hitler's Weltanschauung: A Blueprint for Power*, pp. 38-39.

77. Jäckel, *Hitler's Weltanschauung: A Blueprint for Power*, p. 38.

78. *Hitler's Secret Conversations,* September 17, 1941, p. 28.

79. John Stoessinger, *Why Nations Go To War*, pp. 214-215.

victory.[80] It was his "irrevocable decision to solve the problem of German 'living-space' before 1945 at the latest."[81]

Hitler also was a high-risk and even self-destructive gambler, a personal characteristic borne out in many of his foreign policy initiatives. As Edward Mead Earle notes, "Hitler so firmly believed in his destiny that in both the military and political spheres he took risks from which most generals would shrink."[82]

Against all military advice and in the face of overwhelming French military superiority, Hitler knowingly risked political suicide when he ordered the militarization of the Rhineland in March 1936. Hitler later said, "a retreat on our part would have spelled collapse.... The forty-eight hours after the march into the Rhineland were the most nerve-wracking in my life. If the French had then marched into the Rhineland we would have had to withdraw with our tails between our legs, for the military resources at our disposal would have been wholly inadequate for even a moderate resistance."[83] Despite a last minute bout of nerves, Hitler knowingly took this risk based on his "intuition" that France would not respond forcefully.

Hitler clearly scorned cautious risk-calculation in foreign policy: "As the political leader, however, who wants to make history, I must decide upon one way, even if sober consideration a thousand times tells me that it entails certain dangers and that it also will not lead to a completely satisfying end."[84] If success was

---

80. See, H.R. Trevor-Roper, "The Mind of Adolf Hitler," in *Hitler's Secret Conversations,* p. xxi. See also, Haffner, *The Meaning of Hitler,* pp. 18, 108; and, Waite, *The Psychopathic God,* p. 389.

81. Quoted in, H.R. Trevor-Roper, "The Mind of Adolf Hitler," p. xxi.

82. Edward Mead Earle, "Hitler: The Nazi Concept of War," in, *Makers of Modern Strategy: Military Thought from Machiavelli to Hitler,* Edited by Edward Mead Earle (Princeton, NJ: Princeton University Press, 1961), p. 505.

83. Donald Kagan, *On the Origins of War* (New York: Doubleday, 1995), p. 360.

84. *Hitler's Secret Book,* p. 40.

in doubt, Hitler believed that will, energy, and "brutal ruthlessness" would overcome.[85] Convinced he was guided and protected by "Providence," Hitler appears to have had unique confidence, even against long odds, in the inner "voice" guiding him:

> Neither threats nor warnings will prevent me from going my way. I follow the path assigned to me by Providence with the instinctive sureness of a sleepwalker.[86]

> Trust your instincts, your feelings, or whatever you like to call them. Never trust your knowledge.[87]

> I will not act; I will wait, no matter what happens. But if the voice speaks, then I know the time has come to act.[88]

> The spirit of decision consists simply in not hesitating when an inner conviction commands you to act.[89]

Because Hitler believed himself to be the infallible German Messiah, guided by "Providence," he felt accountable to no person or institution. Under the "Führerprinzip" (absolute power in his hands alone) he frequently ruled by decree, without consultation or written orders. Soon after becoming German Chancellor he did away with even the pretense of cabinet meetings. His monumental decision to declare war on the United States on December 11, 1941, was done without consultation. German policy came to be

---

85. Ibid., p. 41.

86. Adolf Hitler, Speech, Munich Exhibition Halls, March 14, 1936. Quoted in, Max Domarus, *Hitler: Speeches and Proclamations 1932-1945, The Chronicle of a Dictatorship*, Vol. II, 1935-1938 (Wauconda, IL: Bolchazy-Carducci Publishers, 1992), p. 790.

87. Rauschning, *Hitler Speaks*, p. 184.

88. Ibid., p. 181

89. *Hitler's Secret Conversations, 1941-1944*, September 17, 1941, p. 26.

determined by his will and whim. As an example of the latter, in 1943 Hitler unexpectedly cancelled the V-2 Rocket program on the basis of an unpleasant dream he had about the missile. Restoration of the program required the personal intervention of Reich Minister Albert Speer and the program's leading technical expert, Wernher Von Braun. In effect, the program suffered at least a two-month delay as a result of Hitler's dream.[90]

The conscious role of hate in Hitler's programs also was an element of his basic character, political views, and ultimately his policies. With years in Spandau prison to reflect, Albert Speer concluded that the core of Hitler's personality was "pathological hatred."[91] Allen Bullock, in his classic account of Hitler, states simply that "hatred intoxicated Hitler."[92] Hitler clearly hated strongly and considered the emotion of hate to be the strongest mechanism for action and motivating political support: "There is only defiance and hate, hate and again hate." And Goebbels quotes Hitler as stating (in private), "God has graced our struggle abundantly. God's most beautiful gift bestowed on us is the hate of our enemies, whom we in turn hate from the bottom of our hearts."[93]

---

90. See, Wesley Frank Craven and James Lea Cate, eds., *The Army Air Forces in World War II, Volume III, Europe: Argument To V-E Day* (Washington, D.C.: Office of Air Force History, 1983), pp. 87-88.

91. Quoted in Waite, *The Psychopathic God*, p. 330.

92. Alan Bullock, *Hitler, A Study in Tyranny* (New York: Harper and Row, 1962), p. 383.

93. Quoted in John Lukacs, *The Hitler Of History* (New York: Knopf, 1997), pp. 71-72. Although Hitler frequently referred to "God" and "Providence," he clearly was violently anti-Semitic and anti-Christian with disdain for the Judeo-Christian conception of God. Hitler appears to have worshiped his brutal conception of nature and natural selection, and his own ego. Indeed, Hitler consciously sought in National Socialism to fuse virulent forms of religious devotion and political zealotry into an overarching political-religious movement. See the brilliant discussion of this theme in, Michael Burleigh, *The Third Reich: A New History*, pp. 9-14, 252-267. There is some evidence that members of the National Socialist leadership were interested in the

Hitler's embrace of hatred, indeed its elevation to an organizing principle, became a powerful dynamic of the Nazi regime and found expression in the exceptionally brutal and aggressive policies authored by Hitler, as described above and as practiced within the Nazi Party itself. This hatred eventually was extended to all of Germany.

The failure of the Cold War deterrence framework, the deterrence tautology, to take into account the vicissitudes of actual leadership decision-making is dramatically illustrated by Hitler's so-called Nero orders of March 18 and 19, 1945, the goal of which can only have been national self-destruction.[94] The Führer Order of March 18 called for the removal of all civilians from western Germany, by foot and without supplies—a death march. The order of March 19 essentially sought to destroy all the material assets within the Reich necessary for civilian survival. Hitler's desire for national self-destruction is wholly outside the scope of possible behavior as recognized by the Cold War deterrence framework; it was nevertheless wholly consistent with Hitler's character, ideology, and rejection of "bourgeois" moral standards.

Albert Speer apparently protested these Nero orders. Hitler's reply, "If the war is lost, then the nation will be lost also. There is no need to show any consideration for the foundations which the German nation needs for its most primitive survival. On the contrary, it is better to destroy those things ourselves. Because this nation has shown itself the weaker, and the future belongs exclusively to the stronger nation from the East. In any event, what remains after this struggle are only the inferior, for the good have

---

occult. See, for example, Nicholas Goodrick-Clarke, *The Occult Roots of Nazism* (New York: NYU Press, 1992), and, Dusty Sklar, *Gods and Beasts: The Nazis and the Occult* (New York: Thomas Crowell, 1977).

94. See the discussions in, Haffner, *The Meaning of Hitler*, pp. 158-160. See also, Whitney Harris, *Tyranny on Trial* (Dallas: Southern Methodist University Press, 1999), pp. 472-473.

died in battle."[95] Speer later said of Hitler, "He betrayed [Germans] with intent. He tried to throw them definitely into the abyss."[96]

If he and Germany were to lose the war, Hitler's ego and belief in natural selection required that the final act be a Wagnerian *Götterdämmerung*, and that the German people themselves perish for failing him. Hitler's ultimate values had nothing to do with the protection and promotion of Germany. In the end, he sought the destruction of Germany in the service of his own brutality and ego: "I have to attain immortality even if the whole German nation perishes in the process."[97] Hitler's desire to ensure the destruction of Germany also fit his conception of history as nature's brutal and racial struggle for survival: in the test of combat that Hitler so glorified, "Slavdom" had proven itself to be the stronger race. Thus, Germany, in Hitler's view, should perish. On this point, Hitler said, he was "cold as ice."[98] Such decision-making lies far outside the boundaries of the U.S. Cold War deterrence framework, which is, "founded on the theory that an adversarial state or coalition group will act according to the logic of national or group self-interest."[99]

Not all policy, even in National Socialist Germany, has its origins in a leadership's particular, and possibly peculiar, psyche and belief system. Obviously, all leaderships, including Hitler's, operate within a broader context that facilitates or impedes their

---

95. Quoted in, Haffner, *The Meaning of Hitler*, p. 159.

96. Harris, *Tyranny on Trial*, p. 472.

97. As quoted by Hitler's physician, Dr. Theo Morell. Military Intelligence Service Center, U.S. Army, O.I. Special Report 36 (April 1947), *Adolf Hitler: A Composite Picture*, National Archives, cited in Waite, p. 409.

98. Jäckel, *Hitler in History*, p. 89.

99. As stated by Adm. Hank Chiles in testimony supporting his nomination to be Commander in Chief of U.S. Strategic Command. See, U.S. Senate, *Nominations Before the Senate Armed Services Committee,* Hearings, 103rd Congress, 2nd Session (Washington, D.C.: U.S. Government Printing Office, 1994), p. 227.

capability to translate ideas into policy. Nevertheless, as the above historical illustrations demonstrate, these factors clearly can shape decision-making in significant ways that are likely to be missed by the expectation of an opponent's rational, reasonable pragmatism—a fact borne out by the West's disastrous misjudgment of Hitler. Even when presented with accounts of the Holocaust during the war, American leaders tended to respond with disbelief. Supreme Court Justice Felix Frankfurter, for example, reportedly responded to a wartime eyewitness account of the Holocaust by saying, "I am unable to believe you."[100]

COLD WAR DETERRENCE ASSUMPTIONS CONTRADICT REALITY

The assumption of the Cold War deterrence framework, that deterrence will "work" in the context of secure and severe mutual threats because decision-making will be well-informed, dispassionate, and rational cum reasonable, ignores or discounts the variety of factors illustrated above. A comparison of the Cold War deterrence framework with the incredibly broad spectrum of human motivations, goals, thought and values highlights the point that this framework cannot capture the reality of human decision-making. As a result, it is inadequate at best, and potentially grossly misleading.

This problem, largely ignored by a generation of defense officials and academic commentators,[101] was noted relatively early

---

100. Quoted in, Deroy Murdock, "A Hero Who Taught the World," *Washington Times*, August 27, 2000, p. B-5.

101. The most notable exceptions to this criticism are, Fred Charles Iklé, memo, *Possible Consequences of a Future Spread of Nuclear Weapons*, January 2, 1965, Committee File, *Committee on Nuclear Proliferation*, NSF, Boxes 6-7 LBJ Library; Iklé, "Can Nuclear Deterrence Last Out the Century?" *Foreign Affairs*, Vol. 51, No. 2 (January 1973); Iklé, "Nuclear Strategy: Can There Be a Happy Ending?" *Foreign Affairs*, Vol. 3, No. 4 (Spring 1985); and Alexander George and Richard Smoke, *Deterrence in American Foreign Policy: Theory and Practice* (New York: Columbia University Press, 1974).

in the Cold War by those comparing human cognitive processes with deterrence theory. In 1964 the American Group for the Advancement of Psychiatry issued a pessimistic assessment of the long-term prospects for deterrence because, "it rests on certain dubious psychological assumptions."[102] Two pioneering scholars in the subject of deterrence, Alexander George and Richard Smoke, similarly emphasized the "hazard" of establishing specific policy prescriptions based on deterrence theory: "Substantively, deterrence theory is seriously incomplete, to say the least, for a normative-prescriptive application."[103]

The marriage of historical studies, psychology, and political science has produced studies on deterrence that confirm this problem. As Professor Robert Jervis observes, "Deterrence posits a psychological relationship, so it is strange that most analyses of it have ignored decision makers' emotions, perception, and calculations and have instead relied on deductive logic based on the premise that people are highly rational...once one looks in detail at cases of international conflict, it becomes apparent that the participants almost never have a good understanding of each other's perspectives, goals or specific actions. Signals that seem clear to the sender are missed or misinterpreted by the receiver; actions meant to convey one impression often leave quite a different one; attempts to deter often enrage, and attempts to show calm strength may appear as weakness."[104] From such considerations, professor Ned Lebow concludes, "These empirical findings raise serious questions about the utility of deterrence."[105]

---

102. *Psychiatric Aspects of the Prevention of Nuclear War*, Report No. 57 (September 1964), p. 268.

103. George and Smoke, *Deterrence in American Foreign Policy*, p. 83.

104. "Introduction: Approach And Assumptions," in Jervis, Lebow, and Stein, *Psychology and Deterrence*, op. cit., p. 1.

105. Lebow, "The Deterrence Deadlock: Is There a Way Out," in Ibid., p. 183.

The introduction of nuclear weapons to the mix of factors operating does not "fix" this problem. The tremendous lethality of nuclear weapons may usefully focus leadership attention on occasion. Even very lethal threats, however, cannot bring to an end the enormous capacity of leaders to have poor judgment, impaired rationality, to pursue "unreasonable" goals and embrace unreasonable values, to be ignorant, passionate, foolish, arrogant, or selectively attentive to risks and costs, and to base their actions on severely distorted perceptions of reality. As much as we might wish it not to be so, these factors play to some degree in virtually all crisis decision-making, and in some crises, they—not the particular character of the nuclear balance—will dominate decision-making. This conclusion ultimately calls into question confidence in the Cold War deterrence framework.

Even the most hard-headed practitioners of *realpolitik*—assuming their opponent to be driven by rational, pragmatic, predictable calculation—will be vulnerable to gross surprise if they do not recognize that rational decision-making may be shaped by surprising goals and values, and by such imponderables as belief in astrology, dreams, or an inner "voice."

The review above illustrates the extent to which decision-making that is rational in a narrow instrumental sense may appear irrational to outside observers because it is shaped by unfamiliar and unexpected goals and values. The Cold War deterrence framework, with its mirror-imaging and convenient assumption of pragmatic, rational and reasonable challengers cannot accommodate leaders who are willful and motivated by unfamiliar, extreme goals and values. It is not a challenger's irrationality that is likely to surprise and frustrate Washington's expectations for deterrence in these cases, although such will be the charge. What will appear as irrationality and frustrate deterrence policy is likely to be a challenger's unexpected behavior that is driven by political goals and values misunderstood or dismissed in Washington.

The notion that significant decision-making can be shaped by factors such as an individual leader's character and belief system contradicts the expectation of rational and pragmatic decision-making in response to the overriding great structural forces of history. The U.S. foreign policy community seems particularly susceptible to dismissing the notion that a challenger's unfamiliar or unreasonable personal characteristics or political beliefs could drive its response to U.S. deterrence policy in shocking directions, perhaps because the idea seems old-fashioned and moralistic. It does not fit our experience in a vibrant democracy where policy is less likely to reflect the particular psyche and will of the executive than is the case in an oligarchy or dictatorship (one of the great benefits of democracy). Consequently, Washington typically expects the repugnant, unusual, unwanted, or eccentric beliefs and qualities of a foreign leader to be washed out as the political process forces conformance to more acceptable norms—as frequently happens in American politics. As the variety of illustrations offered above demonstrates, however, this leavening process does *not* take place in many political contexts.

Washington simply finds it difficult to accept that seemingly odd and distasteful foreign political beliefs, not Washington's own conception of rational pragmatism, can drive foreign decision-making. Perhaps the relatively high level of pragmatism that defines American politics leads to expectations of the same abroad. Political theories and goals that do not conform to Washington's norms and expectations typically are dismissed as temporary trappings, expedient political slogans that will be discarded pragmatically, not a serious basis for anticipating policy.

The Clinton Administration's response to India's nuclear tests again illustrates the point. The campaign commitment to nuclear testing by the then-newly-elected government in India was dismissed as retrograde "old think" in Washington. Once in power, the new government was expected to become reasonable and move away from nuclear weapons. When the new government instead abided by its commitment, the response in Washington was to question the rationality of Indian decision-making. Instead of seeking to understand why India's new political leaders placed a high value on nuclear tests, a condescending "how could they be so foolish?" attitude permeated most Clinton Administration pronouncements and unofficial commentary.

Again, history demonstrates convincingly that in many societies extreme political and personal belief systems can drive decision-making in ways that are "unthinkable" to those who do not share or are unfamiliar with those beliefs. This is not a new thesis. In the 1950s, for example, Nathan Leites, a brilliant scholar at the RAND Corporation, pioneered the study of elite belief systems and their significance. Leites demonstrated how particular beliefs about history and politics shape leadership perceptions, expectations, norms, and courses of action.[106] Professor Adda Bozeman long warned against basing expectations of foreign behavior on the assumption that leaders and countries are "structurally alike in essence" and driven predictably by common themes.[107] Unfortunately, Leites's thesis and Bozeman's admonition never penetrated much of Washington, leaving it more vulnerable to surprise and susceptible to the Cold War deterrence tautology.

---

106. See, Nathan Leites, T*he Operational Code of the Politburo* (New York: McGraw-Hill, 1951); and, *A Study of Bolshevism* (Glencoe, IL: Free Press, 1953). See also, Alexander George, *The "Operational Code": A Neglected Approach To the Study of Political Leaders and Decision-Making*, RM-5427-PR (Santa Monica, CA: RAND, September 1967).

107. See, Adda Bozeman, "War and the Clash of Ideas," *Orbis*, Vol. 20, No. 1 (Spring 1976), p. 102.

Chapter 4

COLD WAR DETERRENCE THOUGHT IN THE POST-COLD WAR WORLD

Despite the end of the Cold War and the attendant dramatic changes in the international environment, much of the official and expert discussion of nuclear deterrence throughout the 1990s continued to reflect the past practice of assuming that challengers would be rational and reasonable, and thus predictably deterrable in familiar ways. Deterrence continued to be viewed as a function of lethal threats, and a goal that could be achieved with assurance.

Numerous statements by prominent civilian and military officials and commentators reflect this view. For example, as the commander in chief of the U.S. Strategic Command in 1997, Gen. Eugene Habiger expressed this basic formulation: "Ultimately, deterrence is a package of capabilities, encompassing not just numbers or weapons, but an assured retaliatory capability provided by a diversified, dispersed, and survivable force with positive command and control and effective intelligence and warning systems."[1] Of course, only by assuming all future challengers to be rational cum reasonable can deterrence be reduced to a "package of capabilities." In reality, deterrence is far more complex. Viewing it only as the effect of even very lethal capabilities will lead to false expectations about its effectiveness, at least on occasion.

---

1. U.S. Senate, Committee on Armed Services, *Statement of General Eugene E. Habiger*, March 13, 1997, p. 4 (mimeo).

An October 1998 public report by the Department of Defense's Defense Science Board entitled *Nuclear Deterrence* attempts to "define concepts of deterrence relevant to the changing world."[2] In doing so it describes the deterrence requirement for "the *assurance* that no rational adversary could believe they could gain by employing nuclear weapons (or other weapons of mass destruction) against the US or an ally under the US nuclear umbrella." (Emphasis added). The report subsequently focuses almost entirely on U.S. capabilities for nuclear threat to provide that "assurance."

For the reasons described above, regardless of how lethal U.S. threats may be, there can be no "assurance" that any particular challenger, including a rational challenger, will conduct the type of cost-benefit calculations necessary for deterrence to work. Nevertheless, confidence in the old Cold War deterrence framework continues to dominate, including confidence that mutual vulnerability will assuredly produce deterrence "stability."

For example, in recent U.S.-Russian discussions in Moscow, the State Department's Senior Advisor for Arms Control and International Security, John Holum, went to great lengths to reassure Russia that its deterrent would not be compromised by any U.S. plans for a National Missile Defense (NMD) system. Instead, Holum promised that U.S. NMD would conform to the "classic" deterrence stability framework: U.S. NMD would be so limited that it could not interfere with Moscow's capability to "carry out an annihilating counterattack" against the United States.[3]

---

2.   Department of Defense, Office of the Under Secretary of Defense For Acquisition & Technology, Report of the Defense Science Board Task Force, *Nuclear Deterrence*, October 1998 (emphasis added.)

3.   John Holum is quoted in, Steven Lee Myers and Jane Perlez, "Documents Detail U.S. Plan to Alter '72 Missile Treaty," *New York Times*, 28 April, 2000, p. A-1. For the reported text of Holum's "Talking Points," with the Russians see, "Documentation: ABM Treaty 'Talking Points,'" *Comparative Strategy*, Vol. 19, No. 4 (October-December 2000), p. 365.

Senior members of the Clinton Administration, including Vice President Albert Gore and Secretary of Defense Cohen, similarly attempted to assure China that U.S. defenses would not be designed to "destabilize" deterrence, that is, to undermine Chinese capabilities to threaten American soil with long-range missiles and nuclear weapons. Why not? Because, according to Gore, deterrence based on the Cold War framework remains a "durable strategy."[4]

Similarly, John Holum stated that the U.S. had no intention of pursuing a capability to defend itself against Chinese nuclear-armed missiles. Why not? Because, "We believe deterrence works in the context of the U.S.-China relationship, as with Russia;"[5] and, "We are satisfied with the stable deterrent relationship with China."[6]

The Director of Central Intelligence, George Tenet, also stated that with regard to Russian and Chinese missile threats to the United States, "We are familiar with Russian and Chinese capabilities to strike at military and civilian targets throughout the United States. To a large degree, we expect our mutual deterrent and diplomacy to help protect us from this, as they have for much of the last century."[7]

The occasion of senior U.S. officials reassuring potential challengers that Washington has no intention of intruding on their capability to launch "annihilating strikes" against America can

---

4. "Excerpts From Gore's Remarks on Bush, the Presidential Race and the Issues," *New York Times*, June 14, 2000, p. A-20.

5. *The President's NMD Decision and U.S. Foreign Policy*, Conference on International Reactions to U.S. National and Theater Missile Defense Deployments, Stanford University, March 3, 2000 (mimeo).

6. Quoted in, John Pomfret, "Taiwan May Get Antimissile Technology," *Washington Post*, July 9, 2000, p. A-19.

7. *The Worldwide Threat in 2000: Global Realities of Our National Security ('as prepared for delivery')*, Statement by Director of Central Intelligence, George J. Tenet, Before the Senate Foreign Relations Committee, March 21, 2000, p. 2 (mimeo).

only be understood in the context of the Cold War deterrence framework for "stability." Such assurances are wholly the product of a framework for deterrence in which the opponents' reasonableness is assumed and thus mutual vulnerability is considered a very high-confidence basis for deterrence "stability."

U.S. civilian leaders and commentators throughout the 1990s also expressed confidence in the Cold War deterrence framework with regard to regional powers such as North Korea, Iraq, and Iran. The general rationale for doing so is the assertion that because deterrence "worked" against the massive Soviet nuclear threat, it should easily work against the more limited threats from regional challengers. Deterring North Korea, Iran, or another rogue state from severe provocation essentially is viewed as a goal automatically covered by the nuclear deterrence policies and capabilities that are thought to have deterred the greater threat from Moscow throughout the Cold War.

For example, in July 1995 Jan Lodal, then Principal Deputy Assistant Secretary of Defense, confidently observed with regard to rogue threats, "Nuclear deterrence worked throughout the Cold War, it continues to work now, it will work into the future.... The exact same kinds of nuclear deterrence calculations that have always worked will continue to work."[8] In 1996 Defense Secretary William Perry observed that "no rogue nation today has ICBMs; only the established nuclear powers have ICBMs. And if these powers should ever pose a threat, our ability to retaliate with an overwhelming nuclear response will serve as a deterrent. Deterrence has protected us from the established nuclear arsenals for decades, and it will continue to protect us."[9]

---

8. Quoted in, Jan Lodal and Ashton Carter, with selected reporters, July 31, 1995, Washington D.C., News Conference Transcript, pp. 9-11 (mimeo).

9. Quoted in, Bill Gertz, "Perry: Missile Defense Unnecessary," *Washington Times*, April 26, 1996, p. A-6.

More recently, Representative Cynthia McKinney, a member of the House Armed Services Committee, similarly claimed, "Clearly, if our nuclear arsenal and conventional military superiority deterred the Soviet Empire, it can do the same to Korea or Iraq."[10] Or, as prominent commentator John Pike of the Federation of American Scientists stated explicitly, "I am assuming that deterrence will work with these [regional] countries as it worked with Josef Stalin and Chairman Mao: 'We'll turn you into a sea of radioactive glass 20 minutes later.'"[11]

Even when senior U.S. defense officials acknowledged the need to consider the particular views of a challenger in this regard, they hastily returned to great confidence in Washington's continuing capability to deter because, as senior Defense Department official Walter Slocombe asserts, "few dictators are, in fact, indifferent to the preservation of key instruments of their state control or to the survival of their own regimes or indeed their own persons and associates."[12] The presumption, of course, is that the United States can threaten these values, the challenger in turn will understand and respond reasonably, and therefore U.S. deterrence threats will continue to "work."

In fact, historically few leaders have shown themselves to be "indifferent" to their own survival and that of their regimes. They also have nevertheless demonstrated a great variance in the priority they attach to such values. Other values such as liberty, religious or

---

10. "Should the U.S. Have a Missile Defense System?" *American Legion Magazine*, Vol. 148, No. 1 (January 2000), p. 42.

11. Quoted in, Rowan Scarborough, "It's Not 'Star Wars' II, Republicans Say In Fighting Missile Defense," *Washington Times*, January 23, 1995, p. A-1, A-9.

12. See the testimony of Walter B. Slocombe, Under Secretary of Defense for Policy, in, U.S. Senate, Committee on Governmental Affairs, Subcommittee on International Security, *The Future of Nuclear Deterrence*, Hearings, 105th Congress, 1st session (Washington, D.C.: U.S. Government Printing Office, 1997), pp. 6–7.

ideological devotion, revenge, national honor, and personal glory have, on frequent occasion, been accorded higher priority by leaders than the survival of their regimes or themselves, and they have consciously, willingly risked, and sometimes sacrificed, themselves and their own countries in service of these higher values.

Nevertheless, senior U.S. military officials share this confidence in deterrence vis-à-vis rogue states. For example, the U.S. Commander in Chief of the Pacific Command has stated that "the North Korean leaders also know that if a major conflict starts, they know that not only will they lose the conflict, but it will be the end of their regime. So there is a very strong deterrent capability which I think will be successful."[13] The fundamental assumption behind this continuing confidence in deterrence, reflecting the clear heritage of the Cold War framework, is that challengers will view the world and make decisions predictably, and thus deterrence will work reliably: what the North Korean leadership knows, how it estimates risk, how it prioritizes values, how its decision-making will operate, what its cost-benefit calculus will be, and how it ascribes credibility to U.S. threats; all these factors and more will come together reliably and predictably, and U.S. deterrence threats will thus be "successful."

It is not an overstatement to note that confidence with regard to the deterrence of North Korea is questionable. We in Washington cannot be confident even in fully identifying the leadership of North Korea, the so-called Hermit Kingdom, much less how it will make decisions in time of crisis. As U.S. Ambassador Stephen Bosworth has noted, "Politically, I think we know very little about the country, how decisions are made, or who is in the ascendancy

---

13. U.S. Department of State, International Information Programs, Washington File, On The Record Press Briefing, *Transcript: Adm. Blair Briefing on Korea, India-Pakistan, China-Taiwan*, April 5, 2000, <http://usinfo.state.gov>.

and who is not."[14] The former senior American commander of U.S. forces in South Korea, Army Gen. John Tilelli, similarly observed, we don't understand "what is going on between the ears" in North Korea.[15]

In 1998 General Eugene Habiger indicated great confidence in deterrence with the sweeping statement that no states are "undeterrable" because, "in my view, every nation has its price when it comes to being deterred."[16] The implication, of course, is that so long as Washington is able to threaten the necessary "price," the challenger will respond reasonably, and thus deterrence will "work." Unfortunately, in the absence of a serious investigation of the specific challenger in question, and in some cases even following such an investigation, it may not be possible to know whether there is in fact such a "price," or how that price might be threatened effectively for deterrence purposes.

Many academic commentators and political activists similarly express continuing confidence in the Cold War deterrence formula. For example, Harvard professor Stephen Walt claims, "If we could deter the 'evil empire' for four decades, we can almost certainly deter today's rogue states." [17] Spurgeon Keeny, executive director of the Arms Control Association, goes so far as to claim repeatedly and against all logic that even "irrational" challengers will be deterred reliably because U.S. threats are so lethal: "Even

---

14. "Dealing with North Korea: Ambassador Stephen W. Bosworth," *The Nuclear Roundtable, Meeting Summary*, Henry L. Stimson Center, May 31, 1996, p. 1.

15. Quoted in, "The Far East, Know Thine Enemy," *Air Force Times*, December 20, 1999, p. 6.

16. U.S. Senate, Committee on Armed Services, *Department of Defense Authorization For Appropriation For Fiscal Year 1999 And The Future Years Defense Program, Part 7*, Hearings, 105th Congress, 2nd Session (Washington D.C.: U.S. Government Printing Office, 1998), p. 494.

17. Steven Walt, "Rush to Failure," *Harvard Magazine* (May-June, 2000), p. 35.

fanatical, paranoid regimes are deterred by the prospect of catastrophic consequences,"[18] and, "Even the most 'irrational' rogue state would be deterred from threatening, much less undertaking, such an attack [against the United States] by the prospect of overwhelming U.S. retaliation."[19]

MIT's George Lewis repeats the mistake of equating an opponent's rationality and the U.S. capacity to issue severe threats with the certainty of deterrence: "Underlying the concern over nuclear blackmail is the notion that emerging missile states such as North Korea or Iraq may be 'undeterrable'—that is, their leadership may not be sufficiently rational to be deterred by the prospect of U.S. nuclear retaliation. There is little, if any, evidence in support of such an argument. However isolated and repressive these regimes may be, the one thing their leaders value highly and have been sufficiently rational to maintain—their hold on power— is precisely what would be lost in a U.S. retaliatory attack."[20]

---

18. "Inventing an Enemy," *New York Times*, June 18, 1994. And, in a report by the Progressive Policy Institute, nuclear physicist Peter Zimmerman expresses a level of confidence in deterrence that exceeds the logical boundaries of deterrence theory: "Deterrence at the nuclear, chemical, and biological weapons level is likely to function against even fairly irrational regimes." See Peter Zimmerman, *Missile Defense And American Security*, Progressive Policy Institute Defense Working Paper, No. 2, May 1996, p. 12.

19. Spurgeon Keeny, "The New Missile 'Threat' Gap,*" Arms Control Today* (June/July 1998), p. 2. It should be sufficient to note here the most basic and well-understood premise of deterrence theory: "…it should be emphasized that no qualification of the notion of rationality can be fitted into deterrence doctrine and leave that doctrine standing whole as an explanation of the successful avoidance of nuclear war—as more, that is, than a frantically hopeful hunch. If it is diluted with any really non-rational propositions, its logical structure, at least, must begin to collapse," Phillip Green, *Deadly Logic: The Theory of Nuclear Deterrence* (Columbus, OH: Ohio State University Press, 1966), p. 164.

20. George Lewis, Lisbeth Gronlund, and David Wright, "National Missile Defense: An Indefensible System," *Foreign Policy* (Winter 1999-2000), pp. 128-129. Stephen Walt makes essentially the same argument in "'Rush to Failure,'" p. 35.

Lewis's assertion reflects continuing confidence in the old Cold War deterrence tautology. It is, however, an obvious non sequitur to leap from the accurate observation that leaders care about threats to their lives and power, to the conclusion that their rationality combined with severe U.S. threats ensures successful deterrence.

Such confidence in deterrence is based on the demonstrably false underlying assumption that "rogue" leaders will consistently be reasonable as defined in Washington, and thus predictable and controllable: Washington will be capable of threatening rogue leaders' power and lives, and those leaders will understand and respond reasonably to such grievous U.S. threats. They will therefore be deterred. This argument leaves no room for the fact that leaders can hold to distorted, self-serving interpretations of reality, rely on dubious sources of information, be motivated by extreme emotions and goals, and esteem some values more highly than their own lives and positions.

Attempts to justify continued confidence in deterrence typically go no further than the assertions rogue leaders will be "rational," just as the Soviets were during the Cold War. And, just as assuredly, rogue leaders will prove conveniently reasonable and thus deterrable. All rational challengers will: truly value most highly that which Washington can threaten; comprehend and believe U.S. threats to those values; calculate that conciliation to Washington is preferable to risking U.S. wrath; and thus be deterred reliably and predictably. Hitler's ultimate desire for the destruction of Germany, Japanese War Minister Anami's belief that Japan's destruction would have been "wondrous," and Castro's embrace of Cuban national martyrdom should haunt those who continue to assert such confident claims about deterrence.

If the reliable functioning of deterrence truly were simply a matter of possessing a lethal nuclear threat and choosing rational opponents, the prospects for deterrence working predictably would be brighter. The U.S. possesses a sizable nuclear arsenal, and there appear to be few functionally irrational opponents. Unfortunately, however, deterrence is not so predictable because manifestly rational opponents can be driven in their decision-making by dynamics that appear wholly unreasonable and are therefore unexpected. As a result, their behavior can surprise and deterrence can fail unexpectedly.

The Cold War deterrence framework has inspired most past national security managers and academic commentators to have overwhelming confidence in their capability to "know" and "ensure" deterrence. During the Cold War, the requirement was simply to manipulate U.S. and Soviet nuclear arsenals to maintain mutual nuclear threats. Because likely Soviet behavior was assumed to be rational, reasonable, and predictable, America's Cold War debate about deterrence requirements focused near-exclusively on the number and types of weapons available, that is, the magnitude of mutual threats.

Until the mid-1970s, for example, consideration of "what would deter" the Soviet Union generally was devoid of any decision-making factors potentially unique to the Soviet Union other than the state of its strategic force capabilities. Other potentially important factors could have included Soviet domestic threat perceptions, the regime's political strength or vulnerability, cultural norms, and/or the specific values, health, determination, political goals, and cost and risk tolerances of Soviet leaders.

Instead, as noted above, U.S. thinking about deterrence generally was based on the convenient "mirror imaging" assumption that Soviet decision-making would be guided by the same general factors that guided American decision-making. "Mirror imaging" lent itself to quantitative stability analyses that involved positing two generic states of similar character, and then modeling strategic force exchanges. This type of analysis largely ignored input from the relevant behavioral sciences such as psychology; it also lacked serious input from political science, history, and anthropology. Because Soviet reactions to deterrence threats were expected to stay within familiar and predictable bounds, deterrence analysis shifted to the single variable of the force balance.

Focusing on the force balance and essentially assuming all other factors to be equal is inadequate because deterrence is a psychological process, and nonmilitary factors can be decisive to the outcome of deterrence threats. Because a specific leadership's perception of cost and benefit may be unique to its particular culture, worldview, political ideology and circumstances, values and goals, or even the personal health of an individual leader, i.e., to what and how it thinks, a methodology that limits expectations of a challenger's decision-making to rational pragmatism, at least on occasion, will lead to surprises.

Very recently some official statements on the subject of deterrence have begun to reflect an appreciation of the inadequacy of deterrence policy based on the Cold War framework. This recognition is reflected in the expressed concern that regional challengers may be "undeterrable," or at least not subject to the same types of deterrence calculations that presumably "worked" in the past. The U.S. Commission on National Security, for example, in commenting on the future of deterrence made the point explicitly: "Deterrence will not work as it once did; in many cases it may not work at all."[21]

The new features of the post-Cold War period magnify the inadequacies of the Cold War deterrence framework. The post-Cold War international environment holds out a much wider variety of potential opponents and contexts in which U.S. deterrence policies must operate. And, far less is known about several potential challengers, including North Korea, for example. Consequently, the scope is much greater for potential challengers' unfamiliar or idiosyncratic factors to significantly shape their responses to U.S. deterrence policies.

---

21. U.S. Commission on National Security, *New World Coming: American Security in the 21st Century*, September 15, 1999, p. 8.

This is *not* to suggest that assessing deterrence will be more difficult in the post-Cold War period because so-called rogue states will be "irrational," whereas Soviet leaders were rational. It should not be assumed that the leadership of Iran or North Korea, for example, will be any more or less rational than were Soviet leaders.

There is, however, ample evidence that Washington is less familiar with the variety of factors that could be significant in rogue leadership decision-making than it was vis-à-vis Soviet decision-making. This lack of familiarity will greatly challenge Washington's capacity to anticipate a rogue challenger's cost-benefit calculus, and thereby to establish reliable deterrence policies. As Gordon Craig and Alexander George observe, "Not all actors in international politics calculate utility in making decisions in the same way. Differences in values, culture, attitudes toward risk-taking, and so on vary greatly. There is no substitute for knowledge of the adversary's mind-set and behavioral style."[22]

Decades of close U.S.-Soviet interaction, beginning with the World War II alliance, and the enormous subsequent level of attention paid to Moscow following World War II, provided Washington with a relatively high level of familiarity with Soviet leaders and their decision-making. Yet, even in this optimal case, Washington was seriously surprised or unprepared on a number of occasions with regard to the functioning of deterrence threats vis-à-vis the Soviet Union. [23] For example, during the 1962 Cuban Missile Crisis, in a contest of wills directly involving nuclear deterrent threats, the superpowers came, "within a hair breath of nuclear war."[24] Just how close the world came to nuclear war was

---

22. George Craig and Alexander George, *Force and Statecraft*, Third Edition (New York: Oxford University Press, 1995), p. 188.

23. See, for example, Peter Pry, *War Scare* (Westport, CT: Praeger, 1999).

24. Robert McNamara, "For The Record," *Washington Post*, June 18, 1998, p. A-24.

not appreciated until well after the crisis; based on the post-Cold War availability of information, Robert McNamara, Secretary of Defense during the crisis, concluded "We lucked out."[25]

Even so, the advantage of familiarity can no longer be assumed in Washington's efforts to deter the variety of prospective rogue challengers. It is a mistake to assume that the effect of U.S. deterrence policies will be predictable because such opponents will behave according to familiar, "reasonable" norms. Washington's serious misunderstanding of Japan in 1941, China in 1950, and most recently Saddam Hussein, is illustrative of the problem.[26] Alexander George has observed in this regard that U.S. efforts to deter and engage Saddam Hussein prior to the Gulf War were undermined by Washington's lack of familiarity with the dynamics of his decision-making: "Limited knowledge of Muslim culture, psychology, and ways of thought and expression added to the difficulty of inferring Saddam Hussein's real beliefs, calculations, and intentions from his unusual rhetorical style and added uncertainty to efforts to influence him. Dealing with leaders from a culture so different from our own added to the familiar problem of ensuring that what one says is being understood and is taken seriously."[27] After decades of relative familiarity with the Soviet Union, the challenge to deterrence posed by the lack of familiarity has reemerged with a vengeance in the post-Cold War era.

In addition, rogue leaders themselves, including Saddam Hussein, are known to be relatively unfamiliar with the variety of factors that shape Washington's decision-making. Consequently, the lack of familiarity that can seriously undermine the predictable

---

25. Ibid.

26. See, for example, Alex Hybel, *Power over Rationality* (Albany: State University of New York Press, 1993), pp. 51-56.

27. Alexander George, *Bridging the Gap: Theory & Practice in Foreign Policy* (Washington, D.C.: United States Institute of Peace Press, 1993), p. 42.

functioning of deterrence is likely to be mutual in at least some potential post-Cold War cases.

Exacerbating this problem is a possibility frequently alluded to but rarely stated explicitly: leaders of rogue states may be more likely to hold worldviews well outside norms understood in Washington because "the often bloody trail of leadership selection" in such countries "encourages the recruitment of paranoid personalities because those who lead 'fighting organizations' may find paranoid qualities functional in their leadership roles."[28] In short, the types of political leaders who come to the fore through bloody revolutionary movements are least likely to fit nicely into Washington's conceptual box of rational, reasonable, predictable decision-makers.

The Cold War deterrence framework does not take these potentially decisive post-Cold War factors into account: under conditions of relative ignorance, assuming rational, reasonable, and predictable challengers may establish grossly misleading expectations about their behavior; confidently predicting the outcome of deterrence in this manner is therefore extremely risky. During the post-Cold War period, past practices of mirror-imaging, or simply assuming an opponent to be reasonable according to familiar standards, will not provide a reliable basis for anticipating the outcome of deterrence. In short, a new deterrence framework is particularly important given the variety of factors that can dominate crisis decision-making, and the relative lack of mutual familiarity that will hamper U.S. post-Cold War relations with many potential challengers, most notably the rogue states.

An additional factor is likely to further limit the applicability of the Cold War deterrence framework to the post-Cold War period.

---

28. Barry Wolf, *When the Weak Attack the Strong: Failures of Deterrence*, A RAND Note, N-3261-A (Santa Monica, CA: RAND, 1991), p. 16. See also Robert Tucker, "The Dictator and Totalitarianism," in *A Source Book for the Study of Personality and Politics*, Fred Greenstein and Michael Lerner, eds. (Chicago: Markham Publishing, 1971), pp. 469-470.

Washington has added a new and demanding mission for its deterrence policy, i.e., preventing a regional power from escalating to the use of weapons of mass destruction (WMD), even while U.S. conventional forces are defeating the challenger on or near its own territory. In the future, Washington will want the option of intervening militarily against regional powers which, on some occasions, will possess the capability for WMD escalation, including WMD use against the United States itself. In such cases, Washington will want its deterrence policy to accomplish that which it said was impossible for the Soviet nuclear deterrent vis-à-vis NATO during the Cold War, i.e., provide Moscow with confidence that it could prevent NATO's WMD escalation even while defeating NATO on Western territory, "deterring NATO's deterrent."

U.S. Cold War deterrence theory posited that, although the Soviet Union possessed significant conventional force advantages in Europe, Soviet fear of NATO's threat of nuclear escalation (nuclear "first use") would deter it from any sizable Soviet conventional or nuclear attack. It was believed that NATO's nuclear escalation threat presented an unavoidable risk of costs to the Soviet leadership that would far outweigh the benefits of any purposeful offensive aimed at Europe. The Soviet leadership would be deterred because it could never be confident that it could exploit its conventional force superiority without triggering NATO nuclear retaliation.

When a regional power has the capability to target the United States with WMD, why should Washington have any greater confidence that it could exploit U.S. conventional superiority without triggering WMD escalation by the regional foe than it credited the Soviet Union with having during the Cold War? What profound new advantage would Washington have that Moscow did not? By what new calculation will Washington be able to confront a challenger's WMD escalation threat to America and project force against it nonetheless?

There is a problem here for U.S. deterrence policy beyond the unpredictability of opponents. It is a problem that appears not to be understood whatsoever by those who confidently assert that the deterrence of future regional aggressors involves simply the extension of the U.S. deterrence policies that "worked" against the Soviet leadership during the Cold War: U.S. deterrence goals vis-à-vis the Soviet Union were different than are U.S. post-Cold War deterrence goals vis-à-vis regional aggressors.

In the Cold War, the West held out the threat of nuclear escalation if the Soviet Union projected force into NATO Europe; in the post-Cold War period it will be regional aggressors threatening Washington with nuclear escalation in the event the United States needs to project force into their regional neighborhoods. In such a contest of wills, the U.S. may be at a great disadvantage in terms of the costs, benefits, and the stakes involved in most prospective regional crises. U.S. leaders are very unlikely to be more cost/risk tolerant in terms of prospective military and/or civilian losses; the reverse probably is true. The stakes involved in a regional conflict are unlikely to be greater for the U.S.; the reverse probably is true. In short, Washington will want effective deterrence in regional crises where the challenger is able to threaten WMD escalation and it is more willing to accept risk and cost.

Concern about this new U.S. deterrence mission is not fanciful or an instance of "worst-case analysis." Some regional powers desire WMD and long-range delivery means for the self-expressed purpose of deterring U.S. power projection by threatening Washington with WMD escalation, especially including nuclear threats. They seek to trump U.S. conventional superiority by threatening WMD escalation just as NATO sought to deter the Warsaw Pact during the Cold War. Deterring Washington in this fashion clearly is the intention of China and some regional rogues.[29] In the midst of NATO's bombing campaign against Serbia then-Yugoslav President Slobodan Milosevic expressed his appreciation of, and desire for, such a coercive strategy and capability against the United States: "You are not willing to sacrifice lives to achieve our surrender. But we are willing to die to defend our rights as an independent Sovereign nation.... Missiles and other sophisticated weapons will not always be the monopoly of high-tech societies.... America can be reached from this part of the world."[30]

The question this rogue strategy introduces is, who will deter whom? During the post-Cold War period, regional powers may frequently have a coercive advantage against the United States—an advantage that Washington exploited against the Soviet Union with great confidence in the past. During the Cold War, NATO believed that its threat of nuclear escalation would keep Moscow's conventional superiority in check. Ironically, regional powers now aspire to, and express confidence in, the same deterrence strategy to prevent U.S. force projection into their regions. This is a very new deterrence ballgame for the United States and there is no basis for assertions that the old rules will apply.

---

29. See, for example, the discussion of North Korean nuclear threats to the United States by Kim Myong Chol, a North Korean writer reportedly with close ties to the government in Pyongyang, in, *N. Korea Makes Public Threat to Blow Up US Mainland*, accessed at, www.kimsoft.com/1997 on March 3, 2000; and, "North Korea prepared to fight to the end as Kim Jong-il has his own version of *The Art of War*," *Asia Times*, April 10, 1996, p. 9.

30. Slobodan Milosevic, text of interview in, "We Are Willing to Die to Defend our Rights," *Washington Times*, May 1, 1999, p. A-8.

Chapter 5

THE DILEMMA OF POPULAR USAGE AND A NEW DIRECTION

A general finding from this review is that the outcome of deterrence and coercive threats can be affected significantly by the participant's modes of thought and the context. Various factors that may be unique to the context and challenger, including idiosyncratic leadership beliefs, can be decisive in determining whether deterrence threats "work." Confidence should not be placed in generic formulas for deterrence directed toward a wide spectrum of challengers because of the large number of leadership and context variables that can be decisive.

Confident generalizations about the effectiveness of deterrence should wane with greater recognition that diverse leadership thought and beliefs can push rational decision-makers in surprising directions, and deterrence can fail unexpectedly as a result. The fundamental flaw in the Cold War deterrence framework is the underlying assumption that a rational opponent will be a reasonable, predictable, and deterrable opponent, an assumption most obviously revealed in the convenient practice of mirror-imaging. This assumption and practice have facilitated Washington's extreme overconfidence in deterrence and in the U.S. capacity to create deterrence "stability" mechanistically simply by managing the nuclear balance.

Unfortunately, popular usage of the word "deterrence," at this point, is anchored firmly to its Cold War mooring. Every interested member of Congress, college professor, journalist, concerned physicist, lawyer and physician confidently knows what will "ensure" deterrence—what is "stabilizing" and "destabilizing"—courtesy of the elegance of the Cold War framework. Less well-known is that this confidence and elegance are misplaced and misleading, respectively.

A dilemma suggested by this study is whether to banish the term deterrence for being hopelessly tied to its Cold War usage, or to work toward a healthier understanding of the term. The latter course probably is preferable, if only because the former is impractical.

If we are to continue using the term "deterrence," an important initial remedial step is to recognize the danger of intellectual hubris. Despite near-constant past claims by U.S. civilian officials, military leaders, and prominent academics, no particular nuclear balance, no weapon system, no declaratory policy, no technological advance, no presidential statement, no intelligence breakthrough, and no organizational gimmick can predictably "ensure" deterrence. Doing so would require omniscience and omnipotence, qualities even Washington lacks.

We ultimately cannot prevent leaders from making decisions based on ignorance, folly, the self-serving or self-induced distortion of reality, or a conscious willingness to court disaster. At some point in America's future deterrence assuredly will again unexpectedly fail as a result of one or a combination of these factors. Indeed, the prospects for failure probably have increased with the post-Cold War diversity of challengers. And, with WMD proliferation the consequences of deterrence failure are increasingly severe.

American leaders and involved academics need to come to grips with the fact that Washington can establish deterrence policies, but it cannot control the results of those policies with the predictability assumed in the Cold War past. The post-Cold War environment leads us back to Carl von Clausewitz's classic insight about war and politics throughout the ages; uncertainties predominate and no "fix" can remove the "fog" that denies high confidence in the predictability of an opponent's behavior.

If discussions of deterrence are to have a chance of being more insightful than misleading, the Cold War assumption of a rational cum reasonable and predictable opponent must be discarded in favor of as much information as possible concerning the specific opponent and the specific context. In this manner, the opponent's cost-benefit calculus may be more accurately modeled and the likely effectiveness of U.S. deterrence threats in practice may be more accurately anticipated. As part of the policy-formulation process, a challenger's particular thought, beliefs, and values must be examined to reduce the prospect for wholly surprising responses to U.S. deterrence threats.

The need to investigate seriously such factors has grown as U.S. leaders increasingly are likely to confront relatively unfamiliar opponents such as Iran, North Korea, Libya, and Iraq. Unfortunately, U.S. confrontations with willful and unfamiliar regional challengers, including so-called rogue states armed with weapons of mass destruction, appear to be on the rise. U.S. leaders will need the best possible basis for anticipating an opponent's behavior, and the convenient course of assuming an opponent to be rational and reasonable (and hence predictably deterrable), entails increasing risk.

There is no adequate alternative to the hard task of attempting to ascertain the particular opponent's modes of thought and core beliefs, assessing how they are likely to affect its behavior, and formulating U.S. deterrence policy in light of those findings. In the absence of this, expectations about the behavior of that particular leadership will reflect a dangerous ignorance. Such ignorance clearly cannot be eliminated by even very serious efforts to "know the enemy." But it may be reduced. Continued reliance on the convenient assumption of a rational and reasonable opponent now risks the type of foreign policy debacles that have followed such an assumption in the past—with the unprecedented additional threats posed by mass destruction weapons.[1]

Moving toward a more empirically-based approach to deterrence policy will not come easily. Assuming opponents to be rational and reasonable, as defined in Washington, is attractive for several reasons. Spinning out untutored certitudes about how a foreign leadership sees the world and should behave is relatively easy, and extreme confidence in deterrence is comforting; the close examination of particular leadership characteristics and beliefs involves considerable work and intellectual humility. In addition, the latter approach will be opposed actively by some in government because it has the potential to lead to the politically unpopular conclusion that U.S. deterrence policies may be inadequate or irrelevant in very serious circumstances.[2]

In addition, a more empirical approach to deterrence could easily require senior civilian officials and military personnel to rely more on the findings of regional and country specialists concerning how an opponent is likely to behave than on their own impressions and images of the opponent. That is, it could challenge the egos and power of senior policy makers by making them more reliant on lower-level country specialists, intelligence analysts, and independent academics.

It may, of course, be difficult to decipher a challenger's thought and political beliefs, and anticipate how those factors are likely to drive decision-making. Indeed, the considerable difficulty involved in seeking to understand a challenger helps explain the widespread preference simply to assume an opponent to be reasonable, and then extrapolate its likely behavior. Nevertheless, taking the time

---

1. Yale Professor Martin Shubik provides a very useful discussion of the unprecedented increase in the potential lethality posed by weapons of mass destruction in, "Terrorism, Technology, and the Socioeconomic of Death," *Comparative Strategy*, Vol. 16, No. 4 (October-December 1997), pp. 399-414.

2. Several briefings of the thesis presented here to senior and mid-level Department of Defense officials in 1999 and 2000 have underscored this point.

and effort to establish a more informed basis for deriving expectations of foreign behavior becomes more important as the international environment becomes increasingly less forgiving of U.S. mistakes.

Accumulating pertinent information about a challenger will never be complete, and the relevant information is likely to change over time. Consider, for example, the very different dynamics underlying Hitler's decision-making at three critical junctures over the course of only nine years: the militarization of the Rhineland in 1936; his declaration of war on the United States in December 1941; and his "Nero" orders for the destruction of Germany and subsequent suicide in 1945.

Attempting to become familiar with the decision-making dynamics of foreign leaders, for the purpose of establishing an informed basis for deterring and coercing them, is not a trivial undertaking. And, it must be acknowledged that even extensive efforts at acquiring information concerning the factors underlying a challenger's decision-making will not preclude surprising, unpredictable behavior based on unfamiliar or wholly obscure motives, goals, and values. Even well-informed policies of deterrence will not be predictably effective.

Reducing the level of ignorance concerning the opponent in pertinent areas, however, may be possible in every case. And doing so should serve to increase the likelihood of effectiveness for U.S. deterrence policies by making those policies relatively more informed by the opponents' various motivations and cost-benefit calculations.

Attempting to derive deterrence policies from such a specific examination of challenger and context represents a dramatic break from the Cold War deterrence framework. It represents a more empirical approach to deterrence, in contrast to the Cold War's convenient method of mirror-imaging and deductive logic. A more empirical approach to deterrence would not, however, be a break from the practice of military and political leaders for millennia prior to the Cold War. For example, in the Fourth Century B.C.

Sun-tzu identified effective policies of deterrence and coercion as the highest form of strategy, and far preferable to success on the battlefield. To be so successful according to Sun-tzu, however, requires that one "know the enemy."[3]

The methodology developed below is designed to provide a simple tool for tailoring deterrence policies to specific antagonists and contexts. The primary areas of interest in this framework are characteristics of: the pertinent leaderships/countries, their motivations, goals, and determination, the nature of decision-making, the object of the friction (the "stakes" involved), the regional political/security context, and the sources of power available to the participants.

The optimal U.S. deterrence policy ideally would be informed by these factors. That is, the U.S. force structure, threat, and declaratory policy, for deterrence purposes, are the dependent variables; they are not the starting points of consideration. To a large extent they should be derived from findings about the challenger and the context. This seemingly logical sequence, unfortunately, is not the norm.

In the late 1990s, for example, two frequently heard assertions from prominent government officials and academic commentators were that conventional forces could largely substitute for nuclear forces for deterrence purposes, and/or that deterrence would be "stable" at START III force levels (possibly 2,000-2,500 warheads) and below. The 1997 report of the National Defense Panel offers the following reassuring conclusion: "Effective deterrence of potential nuclear adversaries can be maintained at the reduced levels envisioned by START III and beyond."[4] Without investigating the particular character of any potential opponent,

---

3. Sun-tzu, *The Art of War*, translation by Ralph D. Sawyer (New York: Barnes and Noble, 1994), pp. 167-168, 177-179.

4. National Defense Panel, *Transforming Defense: National Security in the 21st Century* (December 1997), p. ii.

this report confidently predicts the continuing effectiveness of U.S. deterrence against an open set of challengers ("potential nuclear adversaries"), in the context of an unknown U.S. nuclear threat potential ("START III and beyond"), over unknown stakes. It is not overstatement to observe that such statements must be hollow. They reflect heroically unrealistic confidence in the authors' capacity to anticipate the future behavior of unknown challengers over unknown stakes.

Whether a particular type of threat will be suitable for deterrence "working" will depend on factors specific to the leaderships and countries involved and the context, some of which may be highly tolerant of cost and risk, obsessively-driven, inattentive, ignorant, and/or under enormous domestic political stress. In some cases, START III force levels of 2,000-2,500 nuclear weapons might be excessive for deterrence, in other plausible cases deterrence may require more, or be impracticable altogether regardless of the number of nuclear weapons. The challenge is to reduce our ignorance regarding such matters prior to a crisis, and structure policy accordingly. Conveniently assuming opponents to be informed and reasonable will not provide the basis for such discernment.

Consequently, the framework proposed here is designed specifically to "get inside" the decision-making process of the challenger, and to ascertain as far as possible the basis for its decision-making with regard to a specific context and flashpoint. In principle, this should facilitate formulation of a more effective deterrence policy because it will provide a better basis for anticipating a challenger's behavior.

Correspondingly, this framework establishes a tool for identifying and characterizing the various factors (some likely unique, others subject to generalization) that may be critical to the functioning of deterrence and coercive threats in a specific case, and subsequently tailoring U.S. deterrence policies to that specific challenger and context.

The following six-step process is an initial effort to define a methodology supportive of a new, more empirical approach to deterrence:

1. The first step would be to identify the countries and leaderships likely to be involved in a challenge to the United States. For example, a possible challenger could be identified and the variety of potential flashpoint issues in its relations with the United States described. The juxtaposition of plausible U.S. and challenger goals with regard to a particular flashpoint would be summarized, including what might be U.S. deterrence objectives in particular crisis scenarios.

2. The second step would be to identify those country/context characteristics that could be significant to the functioning of U.S. deterrence/coercive threats vis-à-vis a specific challenger and flashpoint.

   These characteristics would include, for example, questions addressing the challenger's general susceptibility to deterrence on this particular issue:
   Rationality/predictability: Does the challenger's past history of decision-making on this issue suggest predictable, reasonable decision-making will dominate? Has Washington previously been surprised by the challenger's apparently "irrational" behavior? Are there severe domestic political imperatives or unyielding ideological goals that may dominate decision-making and even distort perceptions of reality? In cases where a single leader rules supreme, is that leader known to suffer from significant physical or mental health problems, drug addictions, or other factors that could easily limit rational behavior?

Leadership: Who are the leaders likely to control decision-making on the flashpoint in question? What is known about their will and determination on the issue? What are the likely motivations and constraints on their behavior? To what extent are their pertinent personal characteristics, such as willingness to conciliate, known?

Familiarity and focus: Is the challenger's leadership sufficiently familiar with Washington's goals and "style" to comprehend the nature of U.S. demands and threats? Is that leadership paying attention? To what level of detail is the leadership likely to be attentive to U.S. declaratory policy?

Communication: What is the optimal method for communicating with the challenger's leadership regarding the flashpoint in question?

Value and cost/risk structure: Where does the issue in question fit in the value structure of the challenger's leadership? What is likely to be the challenger's tolerance to risks and costs with regard to the specific stakes in question? Does the leadership hold core values involving the issue in question (e.g., regime survival, regional power relations, cultural, ideological or—in other cases—religious commitments, etc.) that might be decisive in decision-making?

Options: What are the options open to the challenger in the context? Is conciliation to U.S. demands (to avoid the U.S. deterrent threat) likely to be an acceptable option or intolerable? Is conflict with the United States likely to appear acceptable, and if so, under what conditions? Are all options, possibly including conciliation to U.S. demands, likely to appear intolerable? If so, is there any indication that one alternative or another is "less intolerable?"

Precedent/credibility: Does the United States have a demonstrated commitment to the interest in question that is likely to facilitate the credibility of its deterrence policy?

Opportunities for learning: What are the potential opportunities for learning about the country/leadership/context prior to and even during the decision-making period? This could involve "learning by doing." The U.S. could take actions, outside of a crisis context, specifically designed to test a challenger's reactions and optimal modes of communication in an effort to gain information and reduce uncertainties about deterrence policies.

Priorities and Value Trade-off (political, economic, etc.): What value would be paramount in the challenger's decision-making and take priority in any need to trade-off values? For example, how might conciliation or conflict with the United States over the specific issue of contention affect the challenger's other foreign policy or economic development goals? When the challenger must trade-off one goal for another in its decision-making, what effect might that trade-off have on decision-making regarding the crisis flashpoint? If, for example, establishing or maintaining economic relations with the United States is an important goal of the challenger, what effect would that goal have on the challenger's decision-making with regard to provocation of the United States in pursuit of a foreign policy goal?

U.S. Regrets/Retaliatory options: What is the challenger likely to believe about the potential regrets for Washington if the challenger is not conciliatory and the U.S. executes its deterrent threat? These regrets for Washington could be the result of the challenger's own retaliatory capabilities, domestic U.S. considerations, allied reactions, and/or the likely reaction from other potential U.S. foes. What freedom of action might the challenger believe it has if it perceives U.S. regrets to be high?

3. The third step would be to use the findings in the above areas to construct a strategic profile of the challenger likely to pertain to the specific flashpoint in question. The profile would emphasize those national and leadership characteristics of the challenger likely to shape its cost-benefit calculus and decision-making with regard to deterrence in the specific context. Such a profile of the challenger would include informed judgments, when possible, concerning the degree to which the challenger might be: expected to engage in rational decision-making and predictable behavior; susceptible to deterrent threats; conciliatory on the issue of contention; highly determined or not, and tolerant or intolerant of cost/risk; cognizant of U.S. demands and threats; confident in its own military and deterrence policies; driven by considerations beyond the specific flashpoint; and willing to attribute credibility to U.S. threats, inter alia.

4. The fourth step would be to use the national profile thus created to help determine whether the challenger is likely to be amenable to any plausible U.S. deterrent threat in this particular context: is the challenger, in this case, likely to be deterrable in principle? If not, then alternatives to deterrence policies obviously would take on greater priority.

If the challenger appears to be deterrable, in principle, then the question of specific U.S. deterrence and declaratory policy options must be assessed in light of the above profile. Each characteristic or set of characteristics of the country/leadership/context profile is likely to be significant to U.S. considerations of its deterrence and/or declaratory policy options. Viewed comprehensively, the profile would facilitate a more informed U.S. decision concerning the basic question of its approach to deterrence, including what should be the character of its threats to be most effective.

Subsections of the profile would assist in addressing some of the more detailed U.S. questions concerning the most advantageous deterrence policy. For example, the challenger's will, the value it places on the issue of contention, and its cost/risk tolerance in a confrontation with Washington over the issue, all could affect the effectiveness of various U.S. threat options, including declaratory policy, the instrument and targeting options. Similarly, the challenger's likely estimation of U.S. regrets involved in executing various threat options would affect the challenger's view of its own freedom of maneuver and the credibility of the U.S. threat, and thus its value for deterrence.

Cultural factors influencing the challenger's leadership, and possibly idiosyncratic characteristics of individual leaders would affect the optimal channel of communication, style of communication, and even the person(s) selected to convey the U.S. deterrent threat. (In some political cultures, for example, a close relative of the president would be accorded more credibility than even a very senior U.S. official.)

In short, the country/leadership/context profile would be used to inform U.S. threat and declaratory policy options, with some U.S. options likely to appear more appropriate to the particular challenger and context than others.

The completion of profiles for a variety of challengers and contexts could permit the categorization of challengers and the formulation of generalizations about the deterrence of challengers within those categories. For example, regional cultural norms may provide the basis for some generalizations, as may regime type.

5. The fifth step would be to identify those deterrence/ declaratory policy options suggested by the country/ leadership/context profile, and compare those options with the type of deterrence policy options available to Washington given U.S. political and military capabilities and constraints in this specific context.

   For example, if the challenger's will, cost/risk tolerance, and perception of its own freedom in this case suggests that only the most severe U.S. threats would be likely to sustain deterrence, or that deterrence is likely to be irrelevant, then the question of competing U.S. priorities (such as the avoidance of serious civilian and military casualties, or alliance relations) could come to dominate consideration of the optimal possible U.S. deterrence/declaratory policy.

   Here a feedback loop would be used to create a comparison between the deterrence/declaratory policy requirements suggested by the specific challenger and context, and the deterrence/declaratory policy options realistically available to Washington given its military tools and broad foreign policy goals.

6. The sixth step would be to identify the potential value of various prospective U.S. capabilities as suggested by the contrast between deterrence need, as identified by country/leadership/context profiles, and pertinent U.S.

capabilities and constraints. For example, what military capabilities or declaratory policies might help fill a gap in the U.S. capacity to support the various requirements for deterrence suggested by the profile of the specific challenger and context?

As numerous deterrence profiles are completed on a variety of potential challengers and flashpoints, and numerous prospective deterrence policies are assessed, it may be possible to point to those U.S. capabilities most valuable for deterrence purposes over a large number of cases. It may also be possible to identify those capabilities most suited for deterrence in selected cases that are judged to be critical because of their likelihood or lethality.

Clearly, the framework described above is not a magic formula for eliminating the uncertainties surrounding deterrence. It suggests a more empirical method for prioritizing U.S. capabilities for deterrence purposes, but it does not establish a basis for ensuring deterrence. There is no such basis. In some cases there will be relatively high confidence in the information needed to complete the deterrence framework. In other cases, the information will be questionable and uncertain. Indeed, in some important cases, North Korea for example, there may be very little information of high confidence. On these occasions it will be particularly important to recognize that which is unknown, the fragility of deterrence, and the potential value, therefore, of preparing for deterrence either to fail or not apply. Even when a profile is incomplete and of modest confidence, however, it could help to avoid some of the gross mistakes and errors in the conduct of deterrence and coercion that have afflicted the policies of the United States and many others in the past. To recognize that which is not known and that this ignorance will contribute to the unpredictability of deterrence, is no mean accomplishment.

The goal of this proposed approach to deterrence is to identify those specific categories of information about a challenger that could be critical to its decision-making, gather information in those areas, and use it to better anticipate a challenger's likely cost-benefit calculus, and thus its potential decision-making and behavior. This approach could help highlight factors that could lead a challenger toward cognitive distortion and/or highly unusual decision-making.

This proposed framework almost certainly will require modification upon specific application. It is intended to be an initial suggestion as to a methodology for identifying and gathering information with regard to a specific challenger and context. Put into practice, it should facilitate U.S. deterrence policies that are less vulnerable to surprise failure because those policies would be better informed concerning the opponent's likely cost-benefit calculus, and how best to influence its behavior based on that calculus. But, as emphasized above, nothing can eliminate the potential for challengers to behave unpredictably.

Based on findings culled from historical research on deterrence, the following areas of inquiry may be particularly pertinent in any attempt to "know the enemy," that is, to gain a useful understanding of an opponent's beliefs, will, values, and likely cost-benefit calculations under specific conditions. These areas are organized according to the six-step process described above:

A DETERRENCE FRAMEWORK

Step 1. Identify antagonists, issue, objectives, and actions.
   1.1   Antagonists
   1.2   Issue
   1.3   Adversary's objectives
   1.4   Actions to be deterred
   1.5   U.S. objectives

Step 2.   Identify and describe those factors likely to affect the adversary's decision-making in the context of this specific flashpoint and U.S. deterrent threats.
- 2.1   Degree of rationality and predictability as indicated by past behavior
- 2.2   Leadership characteristics
  - 2.2.1   Individuals with responsibilities for the issue at hand
  - 2.2.2   Leadership motivations
  - 2.2.3   Leadership determination
  - 2.2.4   Operational code (worldview and strategic style)
  - 2.2.5   Political-psychological profiles of key decision-makers
  - 2.2.6   Adversary's understanding of and attention to the U.S.
    - 2.2.6.1   Previous interactions with the U.S.
    - 2.2.6.2   Attention to U.S. declaratory policy
    - 2.2.6.3   Likelihood the adversary will (mis)comprehend U.S. demands and threats
- 2.3   Value and cost/risk structure
  - 2.3.1   Location of the issue in the value hierarchy of the adversary's leadership
  - 2.3.2   Other relevant values of the adversary's leadership
  - 2.3.3   Cost/risk tolerance of the adversary's leadership with regard to this issue
- 2.4   Options
  - 2.4.1   Military options available to the adversary
  - 2.4.2   Adversary's freedom to conciliate or provoke
- 2.5   Adversary's belief about the costs the U.S. will incur if its deterrent threat is executed
  - 2.5.1   Costs from the adversary's retaliation
  - 2.5.2   Political costs at home and abroad
- 2.6   Communications

      2.6.1 Optimal method for communicating with the adversary

      2.6.2 Possibilities for misperception

  2.7 Credibility of U.S. threats

      2.7.1 Past pledges or actions demonstrating U.S. commitments

      2.7.2 Other special circumstances

Step 3. Construct a strategic profile of the adversary with regard to the crisis in question.

  3.1 Predictability of the adversary's behavior

  3.2 Cost/risk tolerance

  3.3 Influence of considerations beyond immediate issue

  3.4 Will, determination, and freedom to conciliate or provoke

  3.5 Cognizance of U.S. demands and threats

  3.6 Credibility of U.S. deterrent threats

  3.7 Susceptibility to U.S. deterrent threats

Step 4. Assess whether the challenger is likely to be susceptible to deterrence policies in this particular case; and, if so, the nature of those policies.

Step 5. Identify available U.S. deterrence policy options.

  5.1 U.S. policy

  5.2 Punitive or denial threats

  5.3 Military actions

  5.4 Related diplomatic steps

  5.5 Means for communicating threats

  5.6 Likely adversary reactions and implications for options

  5.7 Indicators for determining option effectiveness

  5.8 Opportunities for learning

  5.9 Possible real-time modifications to improve option effectiveness

  5.10 Domestic and allied constraints on U.S. actions

  5.11 Expected results

Step 6.   Identify the gap between the likely requirements for deterrence and available U.S. deterrence policy options. Describe different, new, or additional military capabilities and policies that may be needed.

    6.1   Key military capabilities for supporting the deterrent options most suited to the challenger in this case

    6.2   Related declaratory policy and diplomatic measures

In no case could the collection of the desired information outlined above be fully accomplished. All attempts to become so well-informed in each of these potentially key areas will be frustrated to a greater or lesser degree by a lack of data, ambiguous data, conflicting data, and the possible intentional disinformation campaigns of some adversaries. The point here is to reduce the margin of ignorance, and to be more aware of what is not known, so that U.S. deterrence policies can be established on a more informed basis, and thus be more likely to work in practice.

Chapter 6

TESTING THE DETERRENCE FRAMEWORK

A U.S.-China Crisis over the Status of Taiwan

The following is a case study intended to explore the possible value of the new deterrence framework described in the previous chapter.[1] The intention here is not to "fill in" or even address each of the points in the outline; some elements of the outline are impractical for the chosen case and others are well beyond the scope of this effort. Nor is the goal here to predict a future crisis, or to influence U.S. policy with regard to current events. It is to provide an initial check of the methodology, and to test the proposition that a more empirical deterrence framework will lead to markedly different expectations regarding deterrence than would be the case under the Cold War framework.

---

1.   I am indebted to my colleagues Kurt Guthe, John Kohout, Willis Stanley, and Bernard Victory of the National Institute for Public Policy, and to Prof. Thomas Christensen of MIT, for their contributions to this case study. In a series of extensive roundtable discussions in 1999 my colleagues and I applied the methodological framework described above to this case study. Kurt Guthe performed much of the research for the case study and provided a detailed, annotated outline that addressed each point of the methodology, "Deterring PRC Aggression against Taiwan: An Application of a Deterrence Framework." The case study presented here draws on and highlights this extensive work.

In this case study, a crisis scenario is postulated and the potential for deterrence examined based on an investigation of the specific participants and the factors likely to motivate their behavior in the crisis. The results of this examination are then compared to the general deterrence expectations that would be derived from the Cold War deterrence framework. Such a case study should help shed light on whether the framework proposed here holds promise for improving the basis for future U.S. deterrence policies.

This case study involves most prominently the United States, China, and Taiwan. The development triggering the crisis in this scenario is a formal declaration of independence by Taiwan. This declaration is assumed to be more definitive, and significantly more threatening to Beijing, than Taiwanese President Lee Teng-hui's July 1999 call for a "special state-to-state relationship" between the People's Republic of China (PRC) and Taiwan.[2]

COMPETING OBJECTIVES

The immediate U.S. objective in this hypothetical confrontation over Taiwan's independence would likely be to prevent China

---

2.   In a July 9, 1999 interview with Deutsche Welle radio, President Lee said, "The 1991 [Taiwanese] constitutional amendments have placed cross-straits relations as a state-to-state relationship or at least a special state-to-state relationship rather than an internal relationship between a legitimate government and a renegade group, or between a central government and a local government. Thus, the Beijing authorities' characterization of Taiwan as a 'renegade province' is historically and legally untrue." "Interview with Lee Teng-hui, President of the Republic of China (Taiwan)," transcript of Deutsche Welle radio interview, July 9, 1999, <http://www.dwelle.de/english/interview.html>. Lee reaffirmed this policy in a National Day speech on October 10, 1999. See Foreman, "Taiwan Backs China Reforms," Associated Press, October 9, 1999, <http://www.taiwansecurity.org/AP/AP-991009-Taiwan-Backs-China-Reforms.htm>. The Taipei government has not, however, renounced the possibility of eventual reunification with the mainland, which a declaration of independence would do.

from resolving the crisis by force. The broader goals would likely include to:

- Protect the United States from attack;
- Protect U.S. overseas territory, installations, and forces;
- Preserve U.S. freedom of action abroad;
- Help defend U.S. allies against aggression;
- Maintain the U.S. strategic position in the Asia-Pacific region (preserve the reputation of the U.S. as a reliable ally of Japan, South Korea and other security partners in East Asia);
- Support peaceful settlement of the PRC-Taiwan dispute;
- Deter the use of force in the PRC-Taiwan dispute, including: missile and air attack against Taiwan; Chinese seizure of offshore islands; a naval blockade of Taiwan; nuclear use against Taiwan; invasion of Taiwan; conventional attack on U.S. forces; nuclear attack on U.S. forces; nuclear strikes on the United States;
- In particular, minimize U.S. military and civilian casualties in any intervention.

The PRC's immediate objective following Taiwan's declaration would be to deny or "roll back" Taiwanese independence. The deeper purposes for doing so would include to:[3]

---

3. DoD, *Future Military Capabilities and Strategy of the People's Republic of China*, Report to Congress Pursuant to Section 1226 of the FY 98 National Defense Authorization Act (Washington, D.C.: Department of Defense, July 9. 1998), pp. 1-2; and David Finkelstein, "China's National Military Strategy," in *Liberation Army in the Information Age*, CF-145-CAPP/AF, edited by James C. Mulvenon and Richard Yang (Santa Monica, CA: RAND, 1999), pp. 108-113.

- Ensure the survival of the current leadership and Communist regime;

- Sustain the legitimacy of the Chinese Communist Party (CCP), now dependent largely on Chinese nationalism rather than Communist ideology;[4]

- Protect the lives, reputations, and legacies of Chinese leaders;

---

4. "China's transition from Marxism-Leninism-Mao Zedong Thought to nationalism as the basis of political legitimacy also made the Taiwan problem more sensitive. Throughout the 1980s Marxism declined worldwide as a credible ideology. China's 'opening to the outside world' made its citizens more aware of the high levels of prosperity and freedom commonplace elsewhere. Within China experimentation with market economics demonstrated the creative powers of capitalism. The CCP's [Chinese Communist Party's] response to ideological questioning was to wage repeated campaigns against 'spiritual pollution,' 'bourgeois liberalism,' and other such maladies, but each successive campaign became less effective. The upheaval of 1989, when wide sections of the Beijing populace called for political reform only to be met by brutal repression, further reduced the appeal of Marxism-Leninism. Shortly afterward Communist rule collapsed in Eastern Europe. Then the USSR itself disappeared. By the early 1990s there was a vast gulf between the formal ideology used to justify continued CCP rule of China and belief in that ideology by the urban and educated populace.

One major response of the CCP to that 'crisis of faith' was to use nationalism to fill the void. The new justification of CCP rule was not construction of socialism and communism, but development of power and wealth for China. Education and propaganda organs began to stress 'patriotic' indoctrination. Patriotism (*aiguo zhuyi*) became China's new political orthodoxy, its new standard of political correctness. The central aim of this doctrine was to wipe out a century of 'humiliation' and establish China as a front-ranking country in the world. In that context, movement toward the incorporation of Taiwan into China, into the PRC, would be a major gain for the leader achieving it. Allowing Taiwan to 'drift away' would dam a leader's political aspirations." John W. Garver, *Face Off: China, the United States, and Taiwan's Democratization* (Seattle, WA: University of Washington Press, 1997), pp. 49-50.

- Enhance the role of the People's Liberation Army (PLA) as the defender of Chinese sovereignty and territorial integrity (PLA's institutional aim);

- Safeguard the sovereignty and territorial integrity of China;

- Maintain or improve the PRC's status in Asia;

- Oppose U.S. predominance in Asia;

- Minimize the costs associated with actions to regain Taiwan, including physical destruction, economic disruption, and international isolation.

To achieve some or all of these goals in this scenario it will be critical for China to avoid, deter, or defeat potential U.S. military intervention in any PRC-Taiwan conflict triggered by the Taiwanese declaration and a Chinese military response. Based on past precedent and/or recent Chinese discussions of this scenario it is possible to identify some Chinese actions that would likely be threatened or, in some cases, carried out against the United States if it intervened against the Chinese use of force against Taiwan: cyberattack, terrorism, and other asymmetric responses against the U.S.;[5] attacks on Asian allies of the U.S.; conventional or nuclear

---

5. Michael Pillsbury, "Chinese Views of Future Warfare: Implications for the Intelligence Community," prepared for a hearing of the Senate Select Committee on Intelligence, September 18, 1998 (photocopy), pp. 3, 7-8, 9-10.

Unrestricted Warfare, a 1999 book that two PLA colonels wrote after the U.S. intervention in the 1996 Taiwan Strait crisis, describes a variety of asymmetric attacks the PRC could employ against the U.S. According to a Chinese newspaper article that discussed the book, "No-limit warfare transcends all models of warfare, breaking all limits, and using all means, particularly nonmilitary means, for an alternative alignment that is unique to us, striking at the enemy from all angles, at all levels, and in all areas, to meet our war aims." Sha Lin, "Two Senior Colonels and 'No-Limit Warfare.'" *Zhongguao Qingnian Bao*, June 28, 1999, p. 5, Foreign Broadcast Information Service translation, FTS19990728000697.

combat with U.S. forces;[6] and nuclear threats against the U.S. homeland.

CHINESE DECISION-MAKING: THE STAKES

There are numerous factors that could contribute to Chinese decision-making in the event of a Taiwanese declaration of independence. The initial point to note is that China's leadership appears fully capable of rational decision-making. Past behavior indicates a significant degree of rationality and predictability. For example, although Chinese goals may reflect values that are obscure or strange to U.S. observers, renowned China specialists Steve Chan and Allen Whiting have found Chinese conflict behavior to be highly calculated and consistent over the course of decades.[7]

For more on *Unrestricted Warfare*, see Qiao Liang and Wang Xiangsui, *Unrestricted Warfare: Assumptions on War and Tactics in the Age of Globalization*(Beijing: PLA Literature and Arts Publishing House, February 1, 1999), in Foreign Broadcast Information Service translation, FTS19991221001362; John Pomfret, "China Ponders New Rules of 'Unrestricted Warfare,'" *Washington Post*, August 8, 1999, p. A-1; and David Harrison and Damien McElroy, "China's Military Plots 'Dirty War' Against the West," *London Sunday Telegraph*, October 17, 1999.

6.   PRC preparations for nonnuclear war with the U.S.: "...Open source writings and R&D efforts indicate that PLA planners do consider the possibility of U.S. intervention [in a PRC-Taiwan conflict]. Mark A. Stokes, *China's Strategic Modernization: Implications for the United States* (Carlisle, PA: Strategic Studies Institute, Army War College, September 1999), pp. 141-143; see also, Harlan Jencks, "China's 'Punitive' War on Vietnam: A Military Assessment," *Asian Survey*, Vol. 19 (August 1979), pp. 156-159, 160; and Garver, pp. 128-129.

7.   Chan examined five military conflicts: "(1) Korean War, 1950; (2) the Sino-American confrontation over Quemoy, 1958; (3) the Sino-Indian border conflict, 1962; (4) the escalation of the Vietnam War, 1964-1965; and (5) the Sino-Soviet border clashes, 1969. Steve Chan, "Chinese Conflict and Behavior: Assessment from a Perspective of Conflict Management," *World Politics*, Vol. 30 (April 1978), pp. 394-400. See also, Alan Whiting, *The Chinese Calculus of*

Understanding the dynamic or motivation behind Chinese behavior is extremely important to any effort to anticipate the Chinese cost-benefit calculus in this scenario. It is beyond the scope of this effort to identify the myriad personal idiosyncratic traits, attitudes, and drives that could influence the actions of individual Chinese leaders. There is, however, evidence pointing to the more general political motivations that would animate the PRC leadership in this case. These motivations are likely to be critical to Chinese decision-making, and thus the outcome of any U.S. deterrence threats.

For example, "The most sensitive strategic issues for China are sovereignty, territorial integrity, and what one might call the 'buffer areas' of the 'near-abroad.'"[8] China's leaders view the question of Taiwan as involving the most fundamental considerations of sovereignty and territorial integrity. Denying Taiwanese independence, and ultimately gaining control of Taiwan appears to be perceived by the PRC leadership as a survival interest, both in terms of the personal political fortunes of the leadership and the Communist regime in general.[9] Taiwan's status

---

Deterrence: India and Indochina (Ann Arbor, MI: University of Michigan Press, 1975), pp. 202-203. In line with the findings of Chan and Whiting, China specialist Bates Gill has remarked, "The Chinese have historically shown themselves to be highly calculating when it comes to moving up the escalation ladder." But, he also cautioned, "That doesn't leave out the possibility of mistakes and miscalculation." Quoted in Jonathan S. Landay, "Risks in a Chinese Invasion of Taiwan," *The Christian Science Monitor*, September 3, 1999, p. 3.

8. Prepared Testimony of Larry Wortzel, U.S. House of Representatives, Armed Services Committee, June 21, 2000, p. 3 (mimeo).

9. "The erosion of the national ideology based on Marxism, Leninism, and Maoism has left Beijing with only an inchoate nationalism on which to base its legitimacy. Instead of being guided by the ideals, values, and principles of a vibrant nationalism—which would be appropriate for the leaders of a nation that is the heir to a great civilization—China's politicians determine their foreign and domestic policies according to a peculiar form of hard-nosed pragmatism.

is not a second-order issue, it is an issue of the highest priority. Gaining control of Taiwan would provide enormous political benefit for the Chinese leadership, while a successful Taiwanese bid for independence would be seen as carrying an intolerable political price. As Bates Gill, a noted Chinese area specialist at the Brookings Institution, has emphasized, "Losing Taiwan would bring down the government in Beijing."[10] It is the apparent belief in this point by the Chinese leadership that raises the stakes for China in a crisis over Taiwanese independence.

Gaining control of Taiwan, or at least denying it independence, would likely contribute greatly to the legitimacy of the CCP regime. The status of Taiwan has particular significance because the CCP regime has lost its previous ideological basis for legitimacy and now has resorted largely to nationalism. Reunification with Taiwan is a course of action well-suited to rally Chinese nationalism, now the key prop of the regime.[11] It would

---

...Chinese pragmatism provides a very practical set of rules for clinging successfully to power, and clinging to power is the principal concern of China's current leaders." Lucian W. Pye, "Understanding Chinese Negotiating Behavior: The Roles of Nationalism and Pragmatism," in Kim R. Holmes and James J. Przystup, eds., *Between Diplomacy and Deterrence: Strategies for U.S. Relations with China* (Washington, D.C.: Heritage Foundation, 1997), pp. 220, 236.

"China today has a political system with weak institutions and atrophied mechanisms of control within the context of hegemonic rule. The ruling elite are undergoing wholesale generational turnover and a political succession. The new elite is a conglomerate of apparatchik-technocrats who, thus far, pursue incrementalist policies intended above all to preserve their power and maintain social order." David Shambaugh, "Containment or Engagement in China? Calculating Beijing's Response," *International Security*, Vol. 21 (Fall 1996), pp. 194-195.

10. Presentation at the National Defense University, Center for Counterproliferation Research, Workshop, *China 2010: Deterrence in Transition*, June 9, 2000.

11. "Preventing Taiwan's independence would be important to any Chinese regime, but it is a critical nationalist issue for the Chinese Communist

contribute to the important nationalist concept of what might be called "Chinese Manifest Destiny." Bringing Taiwan back into the fold would end the "century of shame and humiliation" (the legacy of Chinese weakness in the face of depredations by Western and Japanese imperialists, including Japanese rule of Taiwan from 1895 to 1945) and consolidate the "Middle Kingdom."[12] In addition, gaining control of Taiwan would eliminate a self-

---

Party government. The party has, by way of market reforms, all but obliterated the second of the two adjectives in its name. Almost no influential figure in Chinese government or society believes in communism any more, and that has created a vacuum that nationalism, always a strong element in the party's legitimacy, is filling. As many analysts have noted, nationalism is the sole ideological glue that holds the People's Republic together and keeps the CCP government in power. Since the Chinese Communist Party is no longer communist, it must be even more Chinese." Thomas J. Christensen, "Chinese Realpolitik," *Foreign Affairs*, Vol. 75 (September-October 1996), p. 46.

12. "[Chinese] contemporary sensitivities are especially acute when they involve the territorial integrity of China and help explain some of the problems surrounding the issue of mainland-Taiwan relations. See, Bates Gill, *The Deterrence Series: Chemical and Biological Weapons and Deterrence Case Study 6—People's Republic of China* (Alexandria, VA: Chemical and Biological Arms Control Institute, 1998), p. 8.

"For mainland China...bringing Taiwan back into the fold of the motherland is perhaps the most deeply felt commitment of the Communist Party leadership in Beijing and the officer corps of the 2 million-strong PLA, who regard themselves as the guardians of the Chinese revolution and the defenders of Chinese sovereignty. Indeed, recovering Taiwan is as strong an imperative in the Chinese national consciousness as Manifest Destiny was in the American consciousness a century ago, when nationalism and commercialism combined in a burgeoning vision of an America stretching from ocean to ocean." Patrick E. Tyler, *A Great Wall: Six Presidents and China: An Investigative History* (New York: Public Affairs, 1999), p. 10.

"China is acquiring the political, economic, and military power to reassert its self-defined traditional Middle Kingdom role in Asia. Under these circumstances perceived threats to territorial integrity and sovereignty strike at the foundations of national identity." Allen S. Whiting, "The PLA and China's Threat Perceptions," *The China Quarterly*, No. 146 (June 1996), p. 615.

governing political, economic, and social system that stands as an attractive alternative to Beijing's authoritarian rule.[13]

In short, Chinese leaders consider a Taiwanese bid for independence to be intolerable because, if achieved, it could severely challenge the basis of the CCP's claim to legitimacy. China's leaders fear that Taiwanese independence could lead to the fall of other "dominoes," notably the non-Han regions of Tibet, Xinjiang, and Inner Mongolia.[14] This fear that the "loss" of Taiwan could have catastrophic domestic political implications, and could in fact lead to the collapse of the regime, is consistent with the traditional Chinese linkage of "danger from without" (foreign threats) to "trouble from within" (internal disorder).[15] Deng Xiaoping and other senior Chinese leaders have long discussed Taiwanese independence as intolerable both in terms of the Communist regime's interests and the personal position of Chinese

---

13. "Taiwan threatens the legitimacy of Communist rule, because it represents a successful political and economic alternative." Douglas Porch, "The Taiwan Strait Crisis of 1996: Strategic Implications for the United States Navy," *Naval War College Review*, Vol. 52 (Summer 1999), p. 26.

14. "Chinese leaders will go to extraordinary lengths to prevent Taiwan's independence in part because they fear a national breakup. Chinese analysts believe that national integrity would be threatened by an uncontested declaration of Taiwanese independence, especially because of decades of propaganda about Taiwan's unbreakable links to the motherland. They subscribe to a domestic domino theory in which the loss of one piece of sovereign territory will encourage separatists elsewhere and hurt morale among Chinese forces who must defend national unity. The most notable concerns are with traditionally non-Han regions such as Tibet, Xingjiang, and Inner Mongolia." Christensen, p. 46. See also Porch, p. 25; and John Lewis and Xue Litai, "China's Search for a Modern Air Force," *International Security*, Vol. 24 (Summer 1999), p. 93.

15. "There is thus a tendency for the Chinese leadership to look for 'hostile foreign forces' behind domestic unrest and even deviance within the Communist party, and a suspicion that other nations have ulterior motives in dealing with China. " Shambaugh, "Containment or Engagement in China?," p. 194. See also Whiting, *The Chinese Calculus of Deterrence*, p. 203.

leaders. For Deng, "Whoever lost Taiwan must step down and stand condemned through the ages."[16]

Such statements, particularly those involving Taiwan, may be dismissed by some as self-serving bluster. Chinese nationalism and the related attachment to Taiwan, however, appear to run very deep and wide. As Paul Heer of the Council on Foreign Relations has observed:

> On foreign policy, the common denominator is a genuine commitment to Chinese nationalism, the inevitable result of China's bleak history of vulnerability to foreign powers. Public and private statements by [Chinese President] Jiang and [Chinese Premier] Zhu show that even they are hard-liners in this respect—staunch nationalists unwilling to compromise on core sovereignty issues, especially Taiwan. ...it is misguided to presume that the occasional, harshly nationalistic rhetoric of Jiang and Zhu and other supposed moderates is the product of political pressure and not genuine. There simply is no compelling evidence to show that Jiang and Zhu do not believe what they say, both publicly and privately, on core foreign policy and sovereignty issues.[17]

Thus, a crucial point in anticipating the Chinese deterrence cost-benefit calculus with regard to Taiwan is to understand the significance of Chinese nationalism for CCP rule and its implications for Taiwan. Ideology no longer is viewed as a secure basis for the legitimacy of China's leadership. As a result, Chinese

---

16. Quoted in Hua Di, *China's Security Dilemma to the Year 2010* (Stanford, CA: Center for International Security and Arms Control, October 1997), p. 5.

17. Paul Heer, "A House United," *Foreign Affairs*, Vol. 79, No. 4 (July-August 2000), p. 20.

leaders appear to view their hold on power as somewhat fragile,[18] and increasingly dependent on the exploitation of Han Chinese nationalism. The importance of nationalism is evident in virtually every move of the CCP regime, and seems to reflect a basic underlying value of the Chinese people. As one journalist has reported, "You always do hit the wall with the Chinese when the National Question comes up. It makes no difference if you are talking with Communists or Nationalists, old or young, government flacks or dissidents. ...The attachment of the Chinese to every inch of the territory of the old Manchu empire is rooted so deep it cannot be touched by reason or argument."[19]

The connection between the domestic political condition in China to the status of Taiwan is clear: Chinese leaders link the issue of Taiwanese independence with the maintenance of China's territorial integrity and Communist regime survival; a successful Taiwanese bid for independence would call into question the emerging basis for CCP legitimacy–nationalism.

The Chinese leadership itself is responsible for raising the stakes to the point that denying Taiwan independence is a political imperative. It has consciously moved to exploit nationalism as the basis for its legitimacy, and in its domestic propaganda has constantly placed Taiwan's status within that context. Recently, the

---

18. "[One] element affecting the *weltanschauung* of China's current elite is the experience of the 1989 mass demonstrations, massacre, international isolation, and collapse of Communist Party rule elsewhere. The events left an indelible mark on the psyche of these elites, and the siege mentality that resulted has by no means fully abated despite the new confidence deriving from China's international rehabilitation and growing economic power." Shambaugh, "Containment or Engagement in China?," pp. 203-204. Interestingly, President Jiang Zemin recently asked for a series of briefings by Chinese scholars on the subject of collapsing governments and specifically the fate of their leaders. Reported in, "Jiang Asks What Brings Collapse," *Far Eastern Economic Review*, June 8, 2000, p. 12.

19. John Derbyshire, "Hitting the Great Wall of China," *Weekly Standard*, June 5, 2000, p. 15.

Chinese leadership has even lowered the threshold for this political imperative with regard to Taiwan. For years China declared that a Taiwanese declaration of independence would trigger "resolute measures," including the use of force, to resolve the Taiwan question. In February 2000, China's State Council issued a white paper on Taiwan. It lowered the threshold for the use of force by adding a new condition: if Taiwan postponed indefinitely reunification negotiations with China.[20] Far from backing away from its declared commitment with regard to Taiwan and the use of force, the Chinese leadership appears to have expanded that commitment. It has contributed to creating the conditions that make denying Taiwan independence a domestic political imperative.

This point is critical to the scenario under consideration. By placing Taiwan at the center of its exploitation of nationalism, China's leadership has elevated the stakes involved in a Taiwanese declaration of independence to include regime (and possibly personal leadership) survival. This is likely to render U.S. deterrence goals in this case much more challenging because, for Chinese leaders, the stakes hardly could be higher. The same cannot be said for the leadership in Washington. This asymmetry in stakes will likely color several very important considerations with regard to deterrence, including leadership will and determination, and each side's likely cost and risk tolerance.

LEADERSHIP DETERMINATION

As noted above, a leadership's level of determination with regard to a particular objective can significantly influence its perception of cost and benefit, and thus its readiness to conciliate or resist deterrence threats. In the case of a crisis over the issue of

---

20. See the discussion in John Pomfret, "Chinese Military Backs Beijing's Latest Warning to Taiwan," *Washington Post*, February 24, 2000, p. A-17.

Taiwanese independence, as noted above, the stakes are seen by the Chinese leadership as very high indeed.   Consequently, it is important to recognize that the PRC leaders (and populace) are united and strongly determined to prevent an independent Taiwan. Debate within the leadership on the subject would turn on other questions (e.g., when to use force, what type of force to use, how to deal with the danger of U.S. intervention), not whether Taiwan should be, or deserves to be, independent.

Repeated expressions by senior officials of the high cost China would be willing to absorb to prevent Taiwan's independence appear to reflect this consensus. For example, PLA Lt. Gen. Xiong Guangkai, Deputy Chief for Intelligence and Foreign Affairs, and member of the Taiwan Affairs Leading Small Group, has claimed (to former U.S. official Charles Freeman, 1995)[21] that China would be willing to lose "millions of men" and "entire cities" to prevent Taiwan's independence.

Numerous repeated expressions obviously may only be bluster intended to intimidate foreign leaders. They also, however, are

---

21. "In recent months, [former Assistant Secretary of Defense for International Security Affairs Charles Freeman] said he has relayed a number of warnings [issued by PRC officials] to United States Government officials. 'I have quoted senior Chinese who told me' that China 'would sacrifice 'millions of men' and 'entire cities' to assure the unity of China [i.e., prevent Taiwan's independence].'" Patrick E. Tyler, "As China Threatens Taiwan, It Makes Sure U.S. Listens," *The New York Times,* January 24, 1996, p. A3.

"During one visit to Beijing in October 1995, Charles W. Freeman Jr. was told by one PLA leader that China was prepared to sacrifice millions of people, even entire cities, in a nuclear exchange to defend its interests in preventing Taiwan's independence.

Although Freeman did not disclose who made this threat, others identified the Chinese official as Xiong Guangkai, the deputy chief of general staff of the PLA and its chief of military intelligence." James Mann, *About Face: A History of America's Curious Relationship with China, from Nixon to Clinton* (New York: Alfred A. Knopf, 1999), p. 334. See also Bill Gertz, *Betrayal: How the Clinton Administration Undermined American Security* (Washington, D.C.: Regnery Publishing, Inc. 1999), pp. 90-91.

consistent with: a high level of leadership determination and commitment based on the high stakes involved; the view that the Chinese people are tough and able to absorb great costs; [22] and a leadership view of the citizenry common in authoritarian regimes, i.e., the role of the population is to serve the state and suffer as necessary (the "masses" tend to be viewed, in Stalin's terms, as "nuts and bolts" to be expended as necessary for state purposes). [23]

This latter view certainly appears to be an element of the "operational code" of the Chinese leadership. [24] It is significant for consideration of deterrence because it suggests strongly that the Chinese leadership would calculate costs differently than would a liberal democracy such as the U.S., which is known widely to be highly sensitive to casualties, military and civilian. Other elements of the Chinese leadership's operational code also could be significant, including a strategic style that emphasizes: seizing opportunities, [25] seeing the potential benefits of action while

---

22. Thomas J. Christensen, Associate Professor of Political Science at MIT, discussion at the National Institute for Public Policy, September 24, 1999.

23. "The Chinese...differentiate much less than the Americans between human and material costs. Traditional Chinese ideology of warfare clearly encourages the Chinese people to fight and die for a holy and moral cause." Shu Guang Zhang, *Deterrence and Strategic Culture: Chinese-American Confrontations, 1949-1958* (Ithaca, NY: Cornell University Press, 1992), p. 282.

24. The operational code is a construct that was developed to understand the worldview of elite groups, beginning with the Soviet leadership. See Alexander L. George, "The 'Operational Code': A Neglected Approach to the Study of Political Leaders and Decision-Making," *International Studies Quarterly*, Vol. 13 (June 1969): pp. 190-222; and Nathan Leites, *The Operational Code of the Politburo* (New York: McGraw-Hill, 1951).

25. "Take opportunistic action...Beijing must focus narrowly on the short run and take instant advantage of whatever the latest circumstances may offer.

The world of Chinese communist factional politics today closely resembles the unstructured near-anarchy of post-Cold War international politics. Moreover, because China's political leaders operate in fluid domestic and international political environments in which sudden success and terrible disaster seem equally possible, they frequently adopt strategies and tactical ploys designed to outmaneuver one another and outwit the foreigners. Their

discounting risks,[26] treating crises as situations of opportunity as well as danger,[27] and, seeking brilliant stratagems to achieve maximum gains at minimal cost.[28]

---

behavior will seem to the outsider more like the tricks of street-smart people than the prudent calculations of national leaders.

The leaders in Beijing believe they must be quick to exploit favorable openings because they assume that everyone else will try to do the same, and they prefer to take the initiative. In this regard, the Chinese approach to problems will be the opposite of the U.S. approach. U.S. leaders idealize to an inordinate degree the importance of long-range thinking, and quite often are criticized if they try to deal with too many short-run considerations." Pye, pp. 222-223.

26. "The Chinese believe in keeping an eye on the potential benefits of an encounter and in discounting the risks. This Chinese tendency in cost-benefit calculations—accentuating the possible payoffs of success and playing down the risks—is the exact opposite of the American tendency. The compulsive need to take advantage of any opportunity encourages China's leaders to take risks....

This, of course, is the calculus of aspiring parties that are striving for advancement, whether political or economic. It is the opposite of the approach taken by status quo leaders who worry more about potential losses and setbacks. U.S. decision makers are more likely to be sensitive to the costs and dangers, and to assume that the Chinese will feel the same. The Chinese tend to assume that Americans, being hypercautious, will accept an unfavorable compromise or back down in any confrontation. Thus, both Chinese and American calculations are likely to miss the mark." Ibid., pp. 233-234.

27. "The American concept of 'crisis' differs from the Chinese. ...U.S. strategists...viewed crisis as a dangerous situation and conceived of it in a strictly negative sense. ...American crisis-management methods...primarily responded to and aimed at resolving—rather than initiating and escalating—crisis situations.

...The Chinese approach to crisis is different. ...the Chinese tend to view crisis dialectically. The term 'crisis' in Chinese stands for a situation [*shi*] embodying both danger [*wei*] and opportunity [*ji*]. Mao Zedong stressed that all crisis situations were dialectical in terms of their strong and weak points, their advantages and disadvantages, their danger and opportunity. He believed that these elements could be transformed into their opposites under certain circumstances. Thus, Mao and other leaders considered any crisis to be both negative and positive, believing that a dangerous situation could be turned to advantage." Shu Guang Zhang, p. 279.

ATTITUDES TOWARD THE USE OF FORCE

Chinese leaders frequently express their attitude about the use of force with regard to a Taiwanese declaration of independence: they have repeatedly threatened to use force to prevent an independent

---

28. "Operational plans as we know them must be sound and promise success, even at a certain cost; but the Chinese 'stratagem' is intended to be more like a masterstroke, not just solid but brilliant. This doctrine of strategic cleverness has fascinating names, such as 'kill with a borrowed knife,' or 'let the plum tree wither in place of the peach,' or 'the empty city;' and the point of this ingenuity is to add psychological acumen to operational skill, and thus to secure victory at a far lower cost than might be expected, even at no cost at all.

...The Chinese recognize that prolonged fighting can be disastrous, but unlike Clausewitz, who expected things to be difficult or to go wrong as a consequence of 'friction,' the Chinese tend to calculate—as the Germans and Japanese once did—that their own brilliant stratagems, executed by their own well-trained forces, can somehow work—unlike anybody else's—in practice as on paper. And *that* is the key to the danger today. Those who extol the subtlety of Chinese uses of force in international politics are certainly right about one thing: the Chinese do put great stock in their ability to get more with less, and they do aspire to play the diplomatic and military game with a skill that will assure maximum winnings at minimal cost. The problem is that China's reach regularly exceeds its grasp. The brilliant stratagem turns out in practice to *qiongbing duwu*, or 'exhaust forces in protracted fighting,' as the classical Chinese phrase puts it." Waldron, "The Art of Shi," *The New Republic*, Vol. 216 (June 23, 1997), pp. 39-40 (emphasis in original).

"Whether the PLA can actually succeed in an invasion of Taiwan may be immaterial. ...In a future Strait crisis, revolutionary nationalism, combined with 'niche' weapons like tactical ballistic missiles, may seem to Beijing to compensate for its overall military weaknesses. Suffice it to say that the 1996 Strait incident illustrated that military options can be attractive given an impoverishment of political thinking or a perceived absence of peaceful alternatives. This is a special danger in China, where the strategic culture assumes that great risks can bring great rewards. Sun-tzu argued that bluff, audacity, and deception can compensate for lack of raw power. Chinese officers assert that technological superiority is immaterial if one adopts 'correct strategic principles, proper strategies, flexible tactics and high operational efficiency.' It is this line of reasoning, as Waldron points out, that causes China's reach regularly to exceed its grasp." Porch, p. 30.

Taiwan.[29] For example, Chinese Foreign Ministry Spokesman, Sun Yuxi, is reported in a PRC-owned newspaper, *Wen Wei Po*, as indicating that "any one, the Taiwan authorities included, who engages in 'Taiwan independence' will lead Taiwan to the disaster of a war. The mainland side has explicitly stated that 'Taiwan independence' means war."[30] And, of course, China did use force in the 1954, 1958, and 1996 Taiwan Strait crises.[31] In general, Chinese leaders view the use of force as a "normal and legitimate" means of settling international disputes.[32]

---

29. "On 12 July [1999], the CPC Central Committee held an enlarged political bureau meeting on the topic of 'deterioration of the political situation in Taiwan.' Persons in charge of the three armed services, four general departments, all military regions, and group armies attended the meeting.

...At this enlarged meeting of the political bureau, Jiang Zemin pointed out: ...If Li Teng-hui and the Taiwan authorities, as well as the Taiwan independence forces, do not rein in at the brink of the precipice immediately and stop letting Taiwan independence, two Chinas, and one China and one Taiwan materialize into action, policy, and program, we shall immediately announce moves to liberate Taiwan by military means and complete the great cause of national reunification." Lo Ping, "Political Bureau Studies New Strategy Against Taiwan," *Cheng Ming*, No. 262 (August 1, 1999), pp. 9-11, Foreign Broadcast Information Service translation, FTS19990807000271.

30. As reported in, Liu Ying, "FM Spokesman: The Ball Is in Taiwan's Court," *Wen Wei Po*, July 5, 2000, (Internet Version), translated in Foreign Broadcast Information Service, Document ID: CPP20000705000011.

31. For capsule summaries of the 1954 and 1958 crises, see Michael Brecher and Jonathan Wilkenfield, *A Study of Crisis* (Ann Arbor, Mich.: University of Michigan Press, 1997), pp. 383-385. For an account of the 1996 crisis, see Barton Gellman, "Reappraisal Led to New China Policy," *The Washington Post*, June 22, 1998, pp. A1, A16. On the 1954 and 1958 crises, see Gordon H. Chang, *Friends and Enemies: The United States, China, and the Soviet Union, 1948-1972* (Stanford, CA: Stanford University Press, 1990), pp. 116-142, 183-197. On the 1996 crisis, see Garver, *Face Off: China, the United States, and Taiwan's Democratization*, pp. 49-50.

32. "To some world leaders, warfare is now obsolete and unlikely. This is not China's view...Chinese authors expect many 'local wars' in the next two decades, perhaps some as large as the Korean War in 1950 or the Gulf War in 1991. There is a sense that it is normal and legitimate to use force to resolve

In particular, Beijing repeatedly has warned Washington that U.S. defense of Taiwan in such a case could lead to war.[33] Elements of China's military modernization program appear aimed at countering intervention by U.S. aircraft carriers and other forces in a PRC-Taiwan conflict (e.g., new antiship missiles, improved submarine and antisubmarine warfare capabilities, advanced long-range strike aircraft).[34] Chinese nuclear-armed ICBMs appear intended to deter U.S. actions to defend Taiwan. (The PRC currently has approximately 20 DF-5 ICBMs, most of which are

---

international disputes." Michael Pillsbury, *Dangerous Chinese Misperceptions: The Implications for DOD* (Washington, D.C.: DOD Office of Net Assessment, 1998), p. 7.

33. PRC ambassador to the U.S. Li Zhaoxing, news conference, Aug. 19, 1999: "We cannot rule out the force option. We want to prepare ourselves to stop any Taiwan independence or foreign intervention." Tom Raum, "Envoy Threatens Force to Resolve Row with Taiwan," *The Washington Times*, Aug. 20, 1999, p. A13. See also, Lo Ping, pp. 9-11; and Bill Gertz, "China's Talk of Forces Buildup Over Taiwan Raises New Fears," *Washington Times*, August 10, 1999, p. A-3.

34. "China is...developing and acquiring air and naval systems intended to deter the United States from involvement in a Taiwan Strait crisis and to extend China's fighting capability beyond its coastline." George J. Tenet, Director of Central Intelligence, prepared statement before the Senate Armed Services Committee, February 2, 1999 <http://www.odci.gov/cia/public_affairs/speeches/ps020299.html>.

"China's military modernization program—focused on naval, air, and strategic forces—continues, despite slowing economic growth. China has apparently placed a priority on increasing the size and survivability of its nuclear capability, as well as investment in warfighting capabilities designed to improve their ability to deter the U.S. from involvement in any Taiwan Strait crisis." Vice Adm. Conrad C. Lautenbacher, Jr., Deputy Chief of Naval Operations for Resources, and Paul M. Lowell, Deputy Director, Naval Intelligence, in Senate Armed Services Committee, *Department of Defense Authorization for Appropriations for Fiscal Year 2000 and the Future Years Defense Program, Part 2*, Hearings, 106th Cong., 1st sess. (Washington, D.C.: U.S. Government Printing Office, 1999), p. 24. See also, Michael Swaine, *The Role of the Chinese Military in National Security Policymaking*, revised edition, MR-782-1-050 (Santa Monica, CA: RAND, 1998), p. 40.

targeted against the U.S.)[35] As Professor Arthur Waldron has observed, "Planning to conquer Taiwan militarily proceeds apace in China, along two lines. One is to perfect a lightning war stratagem, using missile barrages, special forces, or whatever, to somehow topple the Taipei government in a matter of hours. This is a dangerous fantasy, but people take it seriously. Second, is how to keep the United States out. Here nuclear threats are key, but not the sole resource. Capability [is] being developed to attack US carrier task forces."[36]

Clearly, China is willing to threaten and possibly willing to use nuclear weapons to achieve its aim of denying Taiwanese independence.[37] It may be important in this regard to recall that one reason Mao Zedong initiated China's nuclear weapons program in the late 1950s was the perceived need to prevent future U.S. "bullying" over Taiwan.[38] PLA military doctrine contemplates nuclear use in the theater, and at least one Chinese official has threatened a nuclear attack on the United States to deter U.S. intervention: "In the 1950s, you three times threatened nuclear

---

35. "China has about 20 CSS-4 [DF-5] ICBMs, in addition to shorter-range missiles. Most of these are targeted against the United States, and modernization efforts will likely increase the number of Chinese warheads aimed at the United States." Robert D. Walpole, speech at the Carnegie Endowment for International Peace, September 17, 1998, <http://www.odci.gov/cia/public_affairs/speeches/archives/1998/walpole_speech_091798.html>.

36. Prepared Testimony, Arthur Waldron, House of Representatives, Armed Services Committee, June 21, 2000, p. 5 (mimeo).

37. See, Alistair Iain Johnston, "China's New 'Old Thinking': The Concept of Limited Deterrence," *International Security*, Vol. 20 (Winter 1995/96), pp. 5-6, 8, 16, 28-29, 35, 41.

38. "The Chinese originally developed their nuclear plans and force structure in response to what they saw as nuclear blackmail by the United States during the Korean War and Taiwan crises of the 1950s." Thomas Woodrow, Defense Intelligence Agency, in Hans Binnendijk and Ronald N. Montaperto, eds., *Strategic Trends in China* (Washington, D.C.: National Defense University Press, 1998), pp. 86-87. See also, John Wilson Lewis and Xue Litai, *China Builds the Bomb* (Stanford, CA: Stanford University Press, 1988), p. 231.

strikes on China [during the Korean War and the 1954 and 1958 Taiwan Strait crises], and you could do that because we couldn't hit back. Now we can. So you are not going to threaten us again because, in the end, you care a lot more about Los Angeles than Taipei" (Xiong Guangkai to Charles Freeman).[39]

A willingness to wage war against the United States in the event of a Taiwanese declaration of independence is compatible with the political significance of the issue for the PRC leadership. It also is compatible with the traditional Chinese willingness to fight over issues of territorial integrity. The PRC, for example, previously fought the U.S. (in the Korean War) to forestall a perceived threat to its territorial integrity.[40] Alastair Iain Johnston's statistical analysis of historical cases in which the PRC threatened or used force indicates that China is more dispute-prone than most major powers, more likely to resort to higher levels of force in armed confrontations, and more likely to employ higher levels of violence in territorial disputes.[41]

Of particular importance in this regard is another possible element of the CCP's operational code: a belief that provocation and belligerence can serve a useful deterrent effect.[42] What may

---

39. Barton Gellman, "U.S. and China Nearly Came to Blows in 1996," *Washington Post*, June 21, 1996, pp. A-1, A-20. Politburo Standing Committee member Qiao Shi raised the issue of a U.S.-PRC nuclear exchange during a discussion with a visiting American professor in January 1996." Garver, *Face Off: China, the United States, and Taiwan's Democratization*, p. 129.

40. See, Shu Guang Zhang, pp. 89, 96, 115.

41. Alistair Iain Johnston, "China's Militarized Interstate Dispute Behavior, 1949-1992: A First Cut at the Data," *The China Quarterly*, No. 153 (March 1998), pp. 5, 9, 11-17, 29.

42. For the Chinese, "the best deterrence is belligerence." Whiting, *The Chinese Calculus of Deterrence: India and Indochina*, p. 202. "...The Chinese regard the use—not merely the demonstration—of force as an important means for crisis management. Sun Tse taught: 'To win one hundred victories in one hundred battles is not the acme of skill. To subdue the enemy without fighting is the supreme excellence.' But his principle of field operations stresses taking preemptive action to obtain strategic advantage. Its essence is to take short-term

appear to U.S. observers as recklessness and a decision to use force could, in fact, be the prelude to a Chinese attempt to deter rather than to rely on force directly.

POLITICAL-PSYCHOLOGICAL PROFILES OF
KEY DECISION-MAKERS

Various psychological, professional, political, and idiosyncratic characteristics of individual leaders can be significant in determining their cost-benefit calculus, and their likely behavior in crisis. Whether an individual leader's profile is key to anticipating decision-making in any particular crisis will depend on numerous factors including, obviously, the significance of the individual in

---

military action [*fabin*] to prevent the enemy from launching general war [*famou*]. Mao and other CCP [Chinese Communist Party] leaders perfectly understood this principle. Their decision to intervene in Korea, their diplomacy of tension regarding the Taiwan Strait, and Mao's 'rope around the neck' concept all reflected this Chinese calculation that short-term belligerency would serve as a means of general deterrence." Shu Guang Zhang, p. 280.

"[Mao] believed that the key to winning wars was to make your enemy believe that you have no fear of war. ...He once told a visitor that the warmonger image he had acquired suited his purposes, laced as it was with Mao's sober calculation—even conservatism—in military strategy. Mao understood the art of war, and, over the years, his warmonger image instilled greater caution in the Soviet Union and other adversaries who contemplated attacking China." Patrick E. Tyler, *A Great Wall: Six Presidents and China: An Investigative History*, p. 11.

"The history of the years 1969-1971 suggests that Mao decided on a strategy of provocation to force the Soviets to face up to the reality of a Sino-Soviet war, to signal his unwillingness to be intimidated, and to highlight to other states similarly threatened by the Soviets their common cause in dealing with the aggressive leadership in the Kremlin. His vehicle for provoking the Soviets was a controlled application of force on a desolate and frozen border island where Chinese and Russian forces patrolled contested territory." Richard H. Solomon, *Chinese Negotiating Behavior: Pursuing Interests Through 'Old Friends'* (Washington, D.C.: United States Institute for Peace Press, 1992), pp. 90-91.

question to decision-making outcomes. In states with highly centralized and/or personalized power structures, an individual leader's particular personality, political goals, beliefs, psychological makeup and/or value structure, for example, could be decisive to state behavior. In states with decentralized decision-making, the effect of any particular individual's mode of thought will presumably be lessened.

A serious assessment of this type vis-à-vis Chinese leaders is well beyond the scope of this study. And, in general, it may be the dynamic least accessible to investigation. Political leaders and the party structures within which they operate frequently guard such information.

In some cases, however, there are large bodies of personally-authored, spoken and written material, produced over a long period of time, from which to derive a useful leadership profile. The United States has experience in the psychopolitical profiling of foreign leaders, beginning with the insightful profile of Adolf Hitler by Walter Langer for the wartime Office of Strategic Services.[43] Some of that work apparently has been considered quite helpful by the senior political leadership.[44]

In the case of China, the information publicly available may simply be insufficient to construct useful profiles. The roster of known key decision-makers (leaders and their advisers) in China probably is incomplete, and the biographic information available on those individuals known to be significant on particular issues probably is inadequate.[45] In 1996 then-Director of the Central

---

43. Walter C. Langer, *The Mind of Adolf Hitler* (New York: Basic Books, 1972).

44. See, Thomas Omestad, "Psychology and the CIA: Leaders on the Couch," *Foreign Policy*, No. 95 (Summer 1994), pp. 105-122.

45. See, for example, DIA's biographic sketches of Gen. Chi Haotian, the PRC's Defense Minister, and Lt. Gen. Xiong Guangkai, the Deputy Chief of the General Staff. Defense Intelligence Agency (DIA), "General Chi Haotian," biographic sketch, October 1995 (sanitized and declassified), in National

Intelligence Agency, John Deutch, acknowledged that the intelligence community knows, "very little about Beijing's future leadership and intentions."[46] It should nevertheless be noted that an available Department of Defense (DoD) assessment characterized senior PLA officers as physically and intellectually isolated, "suspicious of the outside world." They reportedly are influenced by a "strongly nationalistic outlook" that could "color negatively the leadership's approach to international developments seen impacting China's sovereignty or security" (e.g., conflict over Taiwan).[47]

While such an assessment may be too general to provide useful guidance for establishing U.S. deterrence policy toward China in this scenario, it does strongly suggest the inadequacy of a deterrence policy based on mirror-imaging, a methodology typically unable to see threat in one's own behavior. Chinese decision-making that reflects an isolated, suspicious, and nationalistic outlook could easily fall outside the unschooled assumption that Chinese leaders ultimately will understand Washington's positions with analytical detachment, and will react reasonably, according to norms familiar in Washington.

Security Archive, *China and the United States: From Hostility to Engagement, 1960-1998*, Electronic Briefing Book, Document 13, <http://www.gwu.edu/~nsarchiv/NSAEBB/NSAEBB19/13-01.htm> and Defense Intelligence Agency (DIA), "Lieutenant General Xiong Guangkai," biographic sketch, October 1996 (sanitized and declassified), in National Security Archive, *China and the United States: From Hostility to Engagement, 1960-1998*, Electronic Briefing Book, Document 15 <http://www.gwu.edu/~nsarchiv/ NSAEBB/NSAEBB19/15-01.htm>.

46. Tim Weiner, "CIA Chief Defends Secrecy, in Spending and Spying, to Senate," *New York Times*, February 23, 1996, p. A-5.

47. Department of Defense (DOD), *The Security Situation in the Taiwan Strait*, Report to Congress Pursuant to the FY 99 Appropriations Bill (Washington, D.C.: Department of Defense, February 1, 1999), p. 17.

ADVERSARY'S ATTENTION TO AND PERCEPTION OF THE U.S.

How a challenger perceives the United States clearly is critical to its reaction to U.S. deterrent threats, or even if U.S. deterrent threats can be recognized as such. As John Stoessinger concludes in his study of the relationship between perception and international conflict, the simplified perceptions that leaders hold of other countries, leaders, and peoples frequently are decisive in their decision-making. Unfortunately such perceptions can be partially or completely divorced from reality for long periods of time.[48]

It is clear, for example, that the Japanese leadership's distorted view of the U.S. political condition was a critical element in its ill-fated decision to attack Pearl Harbor in 1941. Fifty years later, Saddam Hussein's refusal to withdraw from Kuwait, despite U.S. demands and military buildup in the region, reflected a similarly mistaken view of the U.S. There are numerous additional examples of foreign leaders holding distorted views of the U.S., and as a result misunderstanding U.S. signals and likely behavior.[49]

Such distortion can undermine the intended functioning of deterrence policies, with foreign leaders misunderstanding the character and intention of U.S. policies and thus responding in surprising ways. Consequently, a question of interest is whether the opponent is likely to devote attention to U.S. threats and signals, and adequately understand them as intended.

In the case under discussion, it appears that Chinese leaders devote considerable attention to the United States, and particularly its policy pronouncements regarding Taiwan. Indeed, in this regard PRC officials are sticklers about the details and nuances of the

---

48. See, John Stoessinger, *Nations in Darkness* (New York: Random House, 1971), pp. 184-185.

49. See, for example, the series of mutual misjudgements leading to and during the Spanish-American War. Lewis Gould, *The Spanish-American War and President McKinley* (Lawrence, KS: University Press of Kansas, 1982).

diplomatic record and will hold their U.S. counterparts responsible for past words and commitments.[50] Lucian Pye observes that they appear to "take their cues about U.S. policy from public postures," rather than utterances in private closed-door meetings.[51] U.S. adjustments to its public positions, which may be intended to signal flexibility or decisiveness, may instead be interpreted by Chinese leaders as evidence that the U.S. is uncertain, ill-prepared, or devious.[52]

A general perception that U.S. strategic aims vis-à-vis China are malevolent, that the U.S. is plotting to subvert the CCP regime and dismember China,[53] or that Washington has a strategy to

---

50. Solomon, *Chinese Negotiating Behavior: Pursuing Interests Through 'Old Friends,'* p. 127.

51. "The Chinese distrust anything that is said in private closed-door meetings, for they assume that hypocrisy prevails in face-to-face situations in which everyone must strive for harmony and courtesy should reign. People in private will say whatever they think the other party wants to hear, and everyone can pretend to be 'old friends.' Therefore, to know where the other stands on serious matters, the Chinese look to public writings and utterances.

...U.S. politicians...believe they can learn the real views of another only in face-to-face private conversations, because whatever the other may say in public is probably said only to get elected or to satisfy some constituency. Thus, it is the autocratic Chinese political culture—not the democratic American one—that respects public rhetoric.... This disconnect is at the root of much of the conflict in Sino-U.S. relations." Pye, p. 232.

52. "Shifts in position, sometimes seen by the U.S. side as a legitimate way to find a solution that will accommodate the concerns of both parties, are seen by the Chinese as uncertainty, lack of preparation, or even deviousness." Ibid., p. 238.

53. "Chinese authors seem obsessed with the notion that the United States is actively trying to subvert their government and dismember their nation.

...Chinese threat perceptions in the near-term focus on several possibilities [including] U.S. subversive efforts 'to give financial assistance to hostile forces inside and outside Chinese territories and wait for the opportune moment to stir up turbulence'" Pillsbury, *Dangerous Chinese Misperceptions: The Implications for DOD*, pp. 6, 13.

restrain, contain, and encircle, rather than "engage" China,[54] could easily contribute to a distorted interpretation of U.S. initiatives, signals, and positions.[55]

Chinese leaders have given due attention to U.S. posturing and declarations in the past, but frequently misunderstood U.S. signals and goals by interpreting U.S. behavior as much more threatening than deserved.[56] For example, fundamental to Chinese intervention in the Korean War was Mao's belief that the U.S. would use Korea as a staging area for an invasion of China. In the 1954 Taiwan Strait crisis Chinese authorities viewed increased U.S. military activity in the Taiwan Strait as preparation for an invasion of the mainland. Similarly, U.S. escalation of the war in Vietnam led Chinese leaders to fear that the U.S. was preparing to attack

---

54. "[In 1995], a senior Chinese official, Wang Jisi, told an American visitor that he had just returned from a retreat for Chinese specialists on America. These specialists served as a collective advisory group to the Communist Party leadership, including Li Peng and Jiang Zemin.

'I want to tell you the consequences of this retreat,' he told the visitor. 'The first point is that America is in decline and, therefore, it will try to thwart China's emergence as a global power. In the opinion of the participants, the United States is the only country that poses a threat to China's security.'

...'You know,' Wang told his visitor, 'for historical reasons Japan has always been the most unpopular country for the Chinese, but I can tell you that among China's senior leaders, the United States is the most unpopular country.'" Tyler, *A Great Wall: Six Presidents and China: An Investigative History*, pp. 36-37.

55. "There is a rich literature analyzing the powerful human tendency to filter information through preestablished belief systems and to structure perceived data in ways that accord with deeply held values. If Chinese nationalist values dictated that Taiwan's early unification with the mainland was a good thing, people embracing those values would make observed facts harmonious with them." Garver, pp. 114-115.

"...as Admiral [Eric] McVadon [former Naval and Defense Attaché in Beijing, 1990-1992] notes, once its arduous process of reaching a decision is complete, the PRC quashes or dismisses attempts to modify that decision, whether by internal doubters or outside forces." Porch, p. 41.

56. Stoessinger, *Nations in Darkness*, pp. 9-91.

China.[57] And, most recently, PRC officials mistakenly viewed the U.S. B-2 bombing of the Chinese embassy in Belgrade as deliberate.

VALUE AND COST/RISK STRUCTURE

Understanding the status of denying Taiwan independence in the Chinese leadership's hierarchy of values is critical to anticipating the likely Chinese cost-benefit calculus to the extent possible in this case. As noted above, the value of rolling back a Taiwanese declaration of independence appears to be very high. Indeed, this study suggests strongly that Chinese leaders consider "losing Taiwan" as having the gravest potential consequences for them personally and for CCP regime: preventing Taiwanese independence essentially is a survival interest near the top of the Chinese leadership's value hierarchy. The political significance of Taiwan, and the apparent willingness of Chinese leaders to use force, possibly including nuclear force to prevent Taiwan's independence, are indicators of the high cost/risk tolerance Chinese leaders are likely to have regarding Taiwan.

Correspondingly, Beijing's position on the matter is long-standing, unambiguous, and unyielding: Taiwan is part of "one China." For the foreseeable future, the status of Taiwan appears to be the one issue China would choose to fight over: "Beijing assesses that, barring a declaration of independence by Taiwan, the chance of a large-scale unavoidable conflict is almost negligible over the next decade and a half."[58] The Chinese leadership's repeated threats to use force may have led to a "commitment trap"

---

57. Whiting, *The Chinese Calculus of Deterrence: India and Indochina,* pp. 189-194.

58. Department of Defense (DOD), *Future Military Capabilities and Strategy of the People's Republic of China,* Report to Congress Pursuant to Section 1226 of the FY 98 National Defense Authorization Act (Washington, D.C.: Department of Defense, July 9, 1998), p. 2.

wherein a failure to respond would be viewed as fatally undermining the leadership's credibility in general. In contrast, the standing of the regime would be enhanced if Taiwan's "separatists" were forced to accept Beijing's terms for reunification.

Other Relevant Values

Economic growth and modernization are priority Chinese values. China's economic development clearly could be disrupted in various ways by armed conflict with Taiwan and the U.S. (e.g., decline in trade, war damage and the costs of reconstruction, an increased postwar defense burden necessitated by a more hostile outside world). It appears that under most circumstances, concerns about the adverse economic consequences of military action against Taiwan would help discourage PRC leaders from resorting to force. Economic trouble, and associated social problems, could undermine support for the regime.

Because Taiwan's independence also would threaten the regime, however, Chinese leaders are likely to incur high economic costs willingly for the sake of regaining Taiwan.[59] Beijing undoubtedly was aware of some of the likely costs of coercive military action against Taiwan, but nonetheless conducted its missile "tests" against Taiwan in 1995 and 1996.[60] Subsequently,

---

59. "China's leaders place priority on economic growth. However, they might deliberately risk or even sacrifice economic development if: they felt Chinese sovereignty to be at stake; Taiwan were to declare independence; they had to choose between internal stability and continued economic development." Montaperto, p. 45.

"'Some people think that China won't start a war now because it has made economic development its centre,' says the mainland's *China Business Times*, 'This kind of notion is completely mistaken.'" "Taiwan's High-Stakes Game," *The Economist*, Vol. 352 (August 21, 1999), pp. 31-32.

60. Prior to the 1995-1996 Taiwan Strait crisis, "[m]any U.S. leaders and analysts had believed that Beijing would not risk 'upsetting the apple cart' of

during the 1999 Taiwan crisis, PRC Defense Minister Chi Haotian reportedly told a gathering of senior military officers that in the event of war Beijing would suspend "economic construction," protect the mainland, reunify China, and then resume economic development.[61] If, as suggested above, the status of Taiwan is a survival issue for the CCP, this value hierarchy is fully understandable.

War to prevent Taiwanese independence appears to be one case in which the Beijing authorities would be willing to incur the economic losses of military action. The political benefit to the regime from ensuring "one China" could be decisive in decision-making, not the costs to economic development. Of course, sustaining political and economic goals simultaneously is the preferred alternative. If a trade-off must be made, however, preserving the core political values threatened by an independent Taiwan would likely rank higher than the costs arising from military action to subdue Taipei.[62] As a Chinese foreign-affairs specialist in Beijing has observed, "In the Chinese value system,

---

economic benefits associated with proper Sino-U.S. relations by forcing the Taiwan issue. Economic development was China's top priority, according to that view, and U.S. support for that goal was too important for Beijing to risk by forcing the Taiwan issue. As long as Washington and Taipei did not confront Beijing with some egregious loss of face, it was widely believed in the United States, China would not resort to military means to settle the Taiwan issue. After March 1996 such illusions were far less common. Most Americans were more willing to accept Beijing's oft-repeated assertion that no cost was too great to protect 'sovereignty,' meaning the PRC's claim to Taiwan." Garver, p. 148.

61. Lo Ping, pp. 9-11.

62. "...a strategy researcher from the mainland...told the Hong Kong-based Ming Pao Daily News...that though the cost would be huge, Beijing would not care about any negative impact or risks if faced with a Taiwan declaring independence." Lillian Wu, "Beijing Not to Use Force Against Taiwan Rashly: Strategist," Taiwan Central News Agency, October 19, 1999 <http://www.fas.org/news/taiwan/1999/e-10-19-99-24.htm>.

sovereignty, national unification, and preserving the regime have always been higher than peace."[63]

COST/RISK TOLERANCE OF THE CHINESE LEADERSHIP

Elements of the Chinese strategic style indicate that the leadership is inclined toward risk-taking (view of crisis as danger and opportunity, preference for opportunistic behavior, attention to potential gains rather than risks, faith in brilliant stratagems, stress on action over planning, belief that risks can be controlled). However, most past discussions of deterrence do not consider the dilemma for Chinese decision-makers that a Taiwanese declaration of independence would introduce: they could face a choice between two miserable and risky options. This is not a case wherein bowing to U.S. deterrence threats would constitute a "safe" choice in comparison to the costly choice of confronting the United States. The potential cost of allowing Taiwanese independence clearly would be high, as would the potential cost of denying Taiwan independence. The Chinese leadership could have only risky and potentially costly options from which to choose in this case.

Many Cold War deterrence discussions typically failed even to posit this type of dilemma for decision-makers. Rather, they contrasted the Soviet choice of a costly and possible fatal war with the United States with the economically advantageous alternative of avoiding war with the West. The options were thought to be stark: if the Soviet Union were to attack the West, the price would be very dear, perhaps fatal; if the Soviet Union did not attack the West, the consequences could be peaceful coexistence, détente, and the prosperity to be had in good relations with the West. If, in fact, the challenger perceives one course as costly and potentially fatal,

---

63. Richard Bernstein and Ross H. Munro, *The Coming Conflict with China* (New York: Alfred A. Knopf, 1997), p. 162.

and the other course as having only beneficial or benign consequences, it is easy to anticipate that rational decision-makers will choose the beneficial or benign option, and deterrence will "work."

The problem with this convenient conception of deterrence, however, is that international crises frequently do not present decision-makers with a clear choice between fatal or advantageous alternatives. Rather, all alternative courses frequently appear highly costly or even fatal, and yet a choice still must be made. How leaders will respond to this dilemma hardly is so predictable.

As the discussion above suggests, in the case of a Taiwanese declaration of independence the Chinese leadership could be compelled to choose between the risks of war with the United States or the risks Taiwanese independence would pose to personal and regime survival. In such a case the leadership's willingness consciously to accept the level of risk and cost necessary to preclude Taiwanese independence is likely to be very high, because the expected cost of allowing independence is entirely unacceptable. Consequently, given the stakes involved for the Chinese leadership, its cost/risk tolerance is likely to be very high. Indeed, it would be rational, even reasonable to accept great risk and cost to preclude Taiwan's bid for independence.

That the Chinese leadership would be willing to accept the risks and costs of war with the United States in this case appears to be reflected in its private and public discussions. The Chinese leadership almost certainly regards the prospect for war over Taiwan as a risky choice. More miserable and risky, however, is the prospect of a successfully independent Taiwan. PRC officials frequently express their readiness to sacrifice blood and treasure to deny Taiwan independence, even in the face of U.S. military superiority. Chinese Premier Zhu, for example, declared:

> Today, the Chinese people have stood up. So how can it be possible that we will allow Taiwan—which has been a part of China's territory—to be separated from the motherland?

Absolutely, we cannot. Some people have made some calculations about how many aircraft, missiles and warships China possesses and presumed that China dare not and will not use force based on such calculations.... For those people who have made such calculations and who have made such conclusions do not understand and do not know about the Chinese history. The Chinese people are ready to shed blood and sacrifice their lives to defend the sovereignty and territorial integrity of the motherland.[64]

Such unequivocal Chinese statements with regard to Taiwan are fairly commonplace, public and private. As a senior Chinese military official observed, for example, "We told our American friends that we are not Saddam Hussein. But if Taiwan became independent, we simply would have no room to back off and would resort to military force regardless of whether the United States interfered. If the Americans did not come, we would do it. If the Americans came, we would do it."[65] Or, as the president of a prestigious Chinese think tank has explained, "Even when the correlation of military forces is obviously not in our favor China will still go to war over the issue of sovereignty."[66] Xiong Guangkai's statement that China is willing to trade "millions of men" and "entire cities" to prevent Taiwan from breaching the unity of China is illustrative.[67]

---

64. "Full Text of Premier Zhu's Press Conference," accessed at <www.fas.org/news/china/2000>, March 16, 2000, p. 1.

65. Quoted in, Patrick Tyler, "Control of Army is Crucial Issue For China Rulers," *New York Times*, February 23, 1997, p. 1.

66. Comment made in March 1998 to David Finkelstein, former Assistant Defense Intelligence Officer for East Asia and the Pacific. Finkelstein, pp. 99-145.

67. Tyler, "As China Threatens Taiwan, It Makes Sure U.S. Listens," p. 334.

There may be a strong emotional tie to Taiwan reflected in such expressions. Such a tie can be seen in the behavior of Chinese leaders, even in official negotiations. Former National Security Adviser Anthony Lake observed that in negotiations with U.S. representatives PRC officials become noticeably emotional when the discussion turns to Taiwan: "It's more personal. You can hear it in the quality of their voice."[68]

China's history of suffering and surviving grievous losses in wars and domestic upheavals[69] may embolden PRC leaders to discount the salience of cost and risk in a fashion unfamiliar to Washington. (With this history in mind, Mao spoke of China's extraordinary capacity to "eat bitterness.")[70] It may be important to recall in this regard that Maoist atrocities in pursuit of the CCP's particular ideological goals, including the Great Leap Forward (1958-1961), led to the death and murder of 50–70 million Chinese.[71] This is not to suggest that Chinese leaders would be cavalier about the potential for war with the United States, but that they could well be willing to accept costs in this case on a scale far outside U.S. expectations of what is reasonable or even rational.

---

68. Gellman, "U.S. and China Nearly Came to Blows in 1996," pp. A1, A20.

69. Michael Clodfelter, *Warfare and Armed Conflicts*, Vol. 2 (Jefferson, N.C.: McFarland, 1992), pp. 658, 956, 1150, cited in Bates Gill, *The Deterrence Series: Chemical and Biological Weapons and Deterrence Case Study 6— People's Republic of China*, (Alexandria, VA: Chemical and Biological Arms Control Institute, 1998), pp. 9-10, 44; Jasper Becker, *Hungry Ghosts: China's Secret Famine* (London: John Murray, 1996), pp. 266-274.

70. "China, [Mao] would say, with its vast population and its capacity to 'eat bitterness,' could absorb punishment better than any adversary." Tyler, *A Great Wall: Six Presidents and China: An Investigative History*, p. 11.

71. See Stephane Courtois, et al., *The Black Book of Communism: Crimes, Terror, and Repression* (Cambridge: Harvard University Press, 1999), pp. 463-464.

CHINA'S FREEDOM TO CONCILIATE OR PROVOKE

For reasons outlined above, the PRC leadership would have very little freedom to concede to a Taiwanese declaration of independence.[72] This lack of freedom to concede does not, however, necessarily equate to complete license to provoke the United States. The values tradeoff in Chinese decision-making in this case is likely to be shaped significantly by the Chinese leadership's perception of the balance between its perceived lack of freedom to concede on Taiwanese independence, and its perceived level of freedom to provoke the United States. While neither option is likely to be desired, the Chinese leadership in this case ultimately may have to choose one option with its attendant risks and potential costs. If the issue is divided so starkly, will the Chinese leadership perceive greater freedom to concede to

---

72. "The cultivation of nationalism will make it difficult for Beijing to compromise on many important foreign policy issues...For example, owing to succession politics and domestic challenges that threaten the Jiang leadership's legitimacy, the CCP cannot afford to appear to compromise on core issues that involve sovereignty or national prerogative, such as relations with Taiwan and Hong Kong or the status of China's territorial claims in the South China Sea." Montaperto, p. 48.

"For any PRC leader ambitious to secure the 'mandate of heaven'—and incidentally the support of the People's Liberation Army the future of Taiwan is a nonnegotiable issue. Any concession in Taiwan threatens to open the dikes to democracy and regionalism." Porch, p. 28.

"On [the Taiwan] issue, core questions of China's territorial integrity, national honor, and international stature come together in an explosive mix which catapults the military straight to the center of the policymaking arena.

...If Taiwan declares independence, PLA leaders are likely to support military action, despite the dangers. In such situations, particularly over Taiwan, the political and military leaderships will come together in a nationalistic drive to uphold what they see as China's sovereignty." Ellis Joffe, "The Military and China's New Politics: Trends and Counter-Trends," in James C. Mulvenon and Richard Yang, eds., *The People's Liberation Army in the Information Age,* CF-145-CAPP/AF (Santa Monica, Calif.: RAND Corp., 1999), pp. 38, 39.

Taiwanese independence or to provoke the United States with a strong military response?

Interestingly, this examination of how the U.S. should think about post-Cold War deterrence policy leads to the question of how the challenger, in this case China, is likely to view its own capability to deter the United States. The question of how China perceives its own capability to deter the United States is important because following a declaration of independence, China's view of its freedom to provoke the United States probably will be shaped significantly by its expectations of whether it can deter or otherwise prevent Washington from a strong military response that denies Beijing its political objectives.

The nature of the U.S. military response would be critical in this case if, as Defense Department public reports conclude, the PRC ultimately could succeed in a blockade and/or invasion of Taiwan *only if the U.S. does not intervene in strength*. For example, a Chinese blockade of Taiwan—possibly intended to destroy political support for the Taiwanese regime—might succeed if the U.S. did not intervene: "Barring third party intervention, the PLAN's [PLA Navy's] quantitative advantage over Taiwan's Navy in surface and sub-surface assets would probably prove overwhelming over time."[73]

A Chinese missile assault against Taiwan is an option already highlighted by the PRC and feared by Taiwan. Physical damage from conventional missile strikes would be serious, but limited. They could, however, be intended again to undermine support for, or kill leading figures in, the Taiwanese government. They also could be intended to soften up Taiwanese defenses for any subsequent invasion (missile attack and blockade might be a two-

---

73. DoD, *The Security Situation in the Taiwan Strait*, pp. 22-23.

pronged prelude to an amphibious and airborne assault).[74] "Taiwan's most significant vulnerability is its limited capacity to defend against the growing arsenal of Chinese ballistic missiles. [Chinese] missile attacks most likely would involve high-volume, precision strikes against priority military and political targets, including air defense facilities, airfields, Taiwan's C2 [command and control] infrastructure, and naval facilities."[75] Missile strikes could cause economic disruptions and political unrest sufficient to destabilize the Taiwanese government, but these effects are difficult to predict, as is the likely U.S. reaction.

A PRC invasion of Taiwan to compel capitulation likely would be considered only as a last resort, and could easily end in failure. Nevertheless, according to a Pentagon assessment, with sufficient time and military effort, an invasion probably would be successful, *again if the U.S. did not intervene*: "An amphibious invasion of Taiwan by China would be a highly risky and most unlikely option for the PLA, chosen only as a last resort.... Success only would be achieved with a massive commitment of military and civilian assets over a long period of time.... Beijing would have to possess the capability to conduct a multi-faceted campaign, involving air assault, airborne insertion, special operations raids, amphibious landings, maritime area denial operations, air superiority operations, and conventional missile strikes.... Nevertheless, the campaign likely would succeed—barring third party intervention— if Beijing were willing to accept the almost certain political, economic, diplomatic, and military costs that such a course of action would produce."[76] As noted above, Beijing may well be

---

74. See, Hua Di, pp. 7, 10; and, David Shambaugh, "China's Military Views the World," *International Security*, Vol. 24, No. 3 (Winter 1999/2000), p. 60.

75. DoD, *The Security Situation in the Taiwan Strait*, pp. 6, 23.

76. Ibid., pp. 24, 25.

willing to accept those costs, if necessary, given the stakes involved.

A significant potential constraint, in this case, on China's freedom to provoke the U.S., may be the prospect not only of hostilities with the U.S. but of hostilities that ultimately would deny China its goal of controlling Taiwan. In this case at the level of grand strategy, Beijing's goal is to reunify China by subduing Taiwan. At the level of military strategy, Beijing's pivotal goal is to prevent the U.S. from intervening effectively in the PRC-Taiwan conflict. Because the U.S. (the "third party") could thwart a blockade or invasion of Taiwan, keeping the U.S. out might be the key to China's success. If U.S. intervention can be deterred or turned back, China may then feel confident in its capability to bring Taiwan under heel in a number of ways (blockade, missile and air attack, or invasion).

A key question confronting the Chinese then is whether serious U.S. intervention can be prevented. In past Taiwan crises, the U.S. was not deterred from intervening, perhaps because the confrontations were limited and involved relatively low levels of violence. In this postulated crisis, the perceived stakes for the Chinese leadership involve survival, the potential use of force appears greater, and the risks and possible consequences of escalation are much more lethal for the United States. China appears determined to prevent or limit intervention by threatening the U.S. with unacceptable losses. As the Department of Defense's recent report on the subject observes, with obvious reference to the United States as "a third party:"

> If Beijing perceived that war was inevitable, China's [sic] would attempt to contain and limit the conflict, but fight with sufficient force and tactics to achieve a military solution before outside powers could intervene militarily, and before vital trade and foreign investment were disrupted. If a third party were to intervene militarily in a regional conflict involving China, the PLA would employy

all means necessary in the hope of inflicting high casualties and weakening the intervening party's resolve.[77]

This could involve high U.S. combatant casualties resulting from conventional combat or nuclear use in the theater (e.g., August 1999 threat to use "neutron bombs" to destroy aircraft carriers).[78] In extremis, it could involve PRC nuclear missile threats against U.S. and allied cities (e.g., the threat conveyed to Charles Freeman by Xiong Guangkai). A near-explicit threat along these lines, in fact, appeared in an official PLA newspaper:

> On the Taiwan issue, it is very likely that the United States will walk to the point where it injures others while ruining itself.... If the United States chooses to engage in substantial interventions, the US policy makers will be left with no choice but to consider the possible enormous pressure to endure and the possible exorbitant price to pay. China is neither Iraq nor Yugoslavia, but a very special country: On one hand, China is a permanent member of the UN Security Council, on the other hand, it is a country that has certain abilities of launching a strategic counterattack and the capacity of launching a long-distance strike.

---

77. Department of Defense, *Report to Congress, Pursuant to the FY 2000 National Defense Authorization Act*, p. 7, accessed at www.defenselink.mil/news/Jun2000/china, on June 6, 2000.

78. "China wants to be able to put U.S. naval and air forces at credible risk of at least some damage if they intervene in a crisis over Taiwan. By threatening even a few American lives, China believes it may be able to exploit the biggest perceived U.S. vulnerability—weak political will—in order to deter American action." Susan V. Lawrence, "Doctrine of Deterrence," *Far Eastern Economic Review*, Vol. 162 (October 14, 1999), p. 26.

"China's neutron bombs are more than enough to handle aircraft carriers." "USA, Do Not Mix In," *Global Times*, August 19, 1999, cited in Asher Bolande, Agence France Presse, August 19, 1999, Foreign Broadcast Information Service, FTS19990819000118 (*Global Times* is a weekly magazine of the *People's Daily*).

Probably it is not a wise move to be at war with a country such as China.[79]

Another PLA-sponsored publication, the *Haowangjiao Weekly*, reportedly sounded the same theme even more explicitly: "The United States will not sacrifice 200 million Americans for 20 million Taiwanese and eventually they are going to back down."[80] The credibility of this type of threat might be reinforced by prior nuclear use (e.g., an electromagnetic pulse attack, a small number of low-yield detonations) against Taiwan. (Such an attack would be an example of "killing the chicken to warn the monkey,"[81] that is, taking some relatively limited action to lend credibility to a more serious threat.) Chinese threats of high casualties could be directed primarily at Congress and the public in the hope that they, in turn, would pressure the administration to accommodate.

Overall, there appear to be few constraints on PRC deterrent threats. A key question then concerns the *execution* of the types of military actions threatened by China: would PRC leaders be willing to go to war with the United States, in this case to subdue Taiwan and thus safeguard their own political and personal survival? Or, would Chinese leaders choose to accept Taiwanese independence for fear of provoking Washington with the type of

---

79. Zhu Chenghu, "Safeguarding the One-China Policy is the Cornerstone of Peace in the Taiwan Strait—Splitting the Motherland by 'Taiwan Independence' Elements is Bound to Provoke a War," *Jiefangjun Bao*, February 28, 2000, in, Foreign Broadcast Information Service, Document ID CPP20000228000077, February 29, 2000, p. 4.

80. Cited in, Jasper Becker, "PLA Newspaper Details Strategies to 'Liberate' Taiwan," *Hong Kong South China Post* (Internet Version—WWW), March 20, 2000, p. 3, in Foreign Broadcast Information Service translation, CPP20000320000075.

81. "[The Chinese] use a technique for making threats credible that is called—to use their own vernacular—'killing the chicken to warn the monkey' (sha-ji jing-hou), i.e., taking some limited-cost action that validates their willingness to carry out a more substantial threat." Solomon, p. 105.

actions that could be necessary to bring Taiwan under control? Given the perceived stakes involved for the Chinese leadership, it may well consciously choose to subdue Taiwan even at the risk of war with the United States. Such a course surely fits with numerous pronouncements from the Chinese political and military leadership and the stakes involved for China. And if Chinese leaders believe Washington can be deterred from significant intervention by Chinese threats, then the benefits of subduing Taiwan surely would be seen as decisive and the costs manageable.

U.S. VULNERABILITY TO CHINESE DETERRENT THREATS

The Chinese goal of deterring the United States in the event of a Taiwanese declaration of independence and thereby limiting the costs of subduing Taiwan can easily be seen in numerous official Chinese comments on the subject. Chinese officials have warned that the United States would be locked in a "horrendous war" with the PRC if Washington chooses to intervene.[82] Chinese military leaders have warned of costly engagements in the theater, and the potential for intercontinental nuclear war in which some U.S. cities would be destroyed by PRC ICBMs.

PRC officials appear to believe the U.S. would be unwilling to sustain large casualties in this case: Taiwan is viewed as a vital interest for China but not for the United States, and therefore the U.S. would not have the will to fight for Taiwan.[83] Chinese

---

82. "A [PRC] spokesman warned yesterday against U.S. involvement in any future problems with Taiwan, saying [Chinese] troops were not afraid to wage a 'horrendous war' and that Beijing would not back away if Washington intervened." Toni Marshall, "Missile Defense System Proposed," *The Washington Times*, August 18, 1999, p. A11.

83. "The Taiwan issue involves the territorial integrity and national sovereignty of China. It is our vital security interest to prevent Taiwan from drifting toward independence. In contrast, the future of Taiwan does not involve U.S. vital interests. If Beijing copes with the Taiwan issue properly and demonstrates resolve at the crucial moment, Washington will probably keep its

officials say the U.S. will not react militarily if China attacks Taiwan because "we've watched you in Somalia, Haiti, and Bosnia, and you don't have the will" (Xiong Guangkai to Charles Freeman).[84] As Lucian Pye observes, "The Chinese are convinced that, in any military showdown, it is they who would be the more resolute party, while other armies and, more particularly, their political masters are likely to be decadent people with little stomach for blood; thus, they can be counted on to turn tail and run. They regard this as especially true of Americans because they note how U.S. politicians outdo one another in promising not to 'put in harm's way' any American in uniform."[85] A warning to China by the Commander in Chief of the U.S. Pacific Command, Admiral Dennis Blair, that U.S. forces are ready and able to defend Taiwan if it is attacked, reportedly was viewed by some Chinese military leaders, as incredible. U.S. military forces have not, they noted, conducted military exercises with Taiwan for two decades and U.S. warships no longer visit the island to demonstrate support.[86]

If Chinese views are as described above, then the leadership will indeed expect the U.S. to be deterred from serious intervention

---

hands off the issue." PLA senior colonel, in a 1997 interview, quoted in John Wilson Lewis and Xue Litai, "China's Search for a Modern Air Force," pp. 92-93.

84. Barton Gellman, "U.S. and China Nearly Came to Blows in 1996," *The Washington Post*, June 21, 1996, pp. A1, A20. Other Chinese officials made similar remarks to American interlocutors. See, Garver, p. 114.

85. Pye, p. 233. This notion of the capacity of China to absorb damage fits with David Shambaugh's observation with regard to the main lesson the PLA took from NATO operations in Kosovo: "In general, PLA analysts took consolation in Yugoslavia's fortitude against NATO's overwhelming firepower, and they pointed out in interviews that it would be much easier for China to absorb such punishment." Shambaugh, "China's Military Views the World," p. 60.

86. See Bill Gertz, "Military's Top General on way to Beijing for Talks, Maneuvers," *The Washington Times*, October 31, 2000, p. A-3.

in this case, and the perceived advantages of subduing Taiwan would dominate the potential costs in Chinese decision-making. U.S. deterrence threats would, in this case, fail because the Chinese would have confidence in their own capability to deter Washington.

The credibility of a U.S. commitment to prevent the Chinese from resolving the crisis militarily obviously would be critical in this case. There are some factors that should argue for the credibility of such a U.S. commitment. For example:

- The Taiwan Relations Act (1979) specifies that any use of force against Taiwan would be viewed with "grave concern" by the U.S.[87]

- The U.S. has consistently emphasized that the PRC-Taiwan dispute must be settled peacefully, and has warned the PRC that attacks on Taiwan could result in war with the U.S.[88]

- Congressional resolutions express support for Taiwan.[89]

- U.S.-Taiwanese military exchanges have involved planning, training, logistics, air defense, anti-submarine warfare, and command and control.

- The U.S. engaged in shows of force in the 1954, 1958, and 1996 Taiwan Strait crises, including nuclear threats in 1954 and 1958.

---

87. Taiwan Relations Act, Public Law 96-8, Sec. 2(b), April 10, 1979.

88. See Russell Flannery, "U.S. Warns China Not to Attack Taiwan," *The Asia Wall Street Journal,* September 7, 1999, p. 2. See also, Russell Flannery and Eduardo Lachica, "Taiwan Trumpets Presence of U.S. Navy Ships," *The Wall Street Journal,* August 13, 1999, p. A8.

89. "The US also helps to preserve a viable Taiwan in non-military ways. Congressional resolutions regularly express support for the island, and include warnings to China not to attack it." Nancy Bernkopf Tucker, "China-Taiwan: U.S. Debates and Policy Choices," *Survival,* Vol. 40 (Winter 1998-99), p. 158.

- The 1996 case may be particularly important because it showed the U.S., well after the end of the Cold War and the abrogation of the Mutual Defense Treaty, was willing to dispatch two carrier battle groups to aid Taiwan.

Unfortunately, there is also a range of factors that would likely detract from the prospective credibility of the U.S. commitment to Taiwan. For example, given China's nuclear capabilities, the U.S. no longer is able to make nuclear threats against Beijing with impunity. This situation contrasts sharply with the 1954 and 1958 Taiwan Strait crises, and could seriously weaken the credibility of U.S. deterrence threats. Chinese leaders have said as much.

In addition, the difference between U.S. expressions of "grave concern" with regard to Taiwan, as opposed to a U.S. pledge to defend Taiwan militarily surely is not lost on the Chinese leadership. Similarly, the U.S. policy of "strategic ambiguity" with regard to Taiwan may give the U.S. flexibility, but may not convey a sufficiently strong deterrent commitment. [90]

U.S. officials have emphasized this purposeful "ambiguity" with regard to the U.S. commitment to Taiwan. For example, in late 1995, Joseph Nye, then Assistant Secretary of Defense for International Security Affairs, was asked by PRC officials what the U.S. would do if the PLA threatened Taiwan. He replied, "We don't know what we would do, and you don't—because it's going to depend on the circumstances."[91] In addition, reported private

---

90. See Dennis Van Vranken Hickey, "The Taiwan Strait Crisis of 1996: Implications for U.S. Security Policy," *Journal of Contemporary China,* Vol. 7 (November 1998), pp. 405-419; and Jonathan S. Landay, "How Far Would U.S. Go To Protect Taiwan?" *The Christian Science Monitor*, September 3, 1999, p. 3.

91. See, Martin L. Lasater, "A U.S. Perception of a PLA Invasion of Taiwan," in Peter Kien-hong Yu, ed., *The Chinese PLA's Perception of an Invasion of Taiwan* (New York: Contemporary U.S.-Asia Research Institute, 1996), p. 252. See also, Press Briefing by Deputy Press Secretaries Barry Toiv

warnings by U.S. officials and former officials that the U.S. would not defend Taiwan if it declared independence likely undermine perceptions of U.S. credibility.[92]

President Clinton's explicit statement in Shanghai (July 1998) that "our Taiwan policy...is that we don't support independence for Taiwan, or two Chinas, or one Taiwan-one China. And we don't believe that Taiwan should be a member in any organization for which statehood is a requirement" also may undermine U.S. deterrence threats.[93] According to one report, "Chinese officials have told the Pentagon that the People's Liberation Army views

---

and David Leavy, August 13, 1999, transcript released by the Office of the White House Press Secretary <http://www.pub.whitehouse.gov/urires/I2R?urn:pdi://oma.eop.gov.us/1999/13/8.text.1>; and, Press Briefing by National Security Advisor Sandy Berger, National Economic Advisor Gene Sperling, and Press Secretary Joe Lockhart, Sky City Hotel, Auckland, New Zealand, September 11, 1999, transcript released by the Office of the White House Press Secretary <http://www.pub.whitehouse.gov/urires/I2R?urn:pdi://oma.eop.gov.us/1999/9/12/7.text.1>.

92. "On March 11, 1996 [during the Taiwan Strait crisis], [Deputy Presidential National Security Adviser Sandy] Berger and Undersecretary of State Peter Tarnoff summoned Taiwan's National Security Adviser, Ting Mou Shih, to a New York hotel. They told Ting to cool Taiwan's independence drive because U.S. military support was not going to be a blank check." Gellman, "Reappraisal Led to New China Policy," pp. A1, A16.

"...former Secretary of Defense William Perry, who led a so-called Strategic Security Study Group to Beijing and Taipei in January...bluntly warned [Lee Teng-hui] that the US would not defend Taiwan should it declare independence. ...Perry's delegation included Brent Scowcroft, former National Security Adviser; John Shalikashvili, former Chairman of the Joint Chiefs of Staff; and Ronald Hayes, former Commander in Chief, Pacific Command." Tucker, pp. 153-154, 165.

93. Remarks by the President and the First Lady in Discussion on Shaping China for the 21st Century, Shanghai Library, June 30, 1998, transcript released by the Office of the White House Press Secretary <http://www.whitehouse.gov/WH/New/China/speeches.html>.

[this statement] as a green light for military action, if Taipei makes the declaration [of independence]."[94]

Finally, Operation Allied Force (Kosovo) may have served largely to demonstrate the extreme reluctance of U.S. decision-makers to incur casualties in distant conflicts, reinforcing apparently existing Chinese prejudices on the subject and further undermining the credibility of U.S. commitments.

In sum, China appears to view Washington as vulnerable to Chinese deterrent threats with regard to Taiwan, based on the perceptions that the stakes involved are inherently lower for Washington, and correspondingly that the United States would be unwilling to risk significant casualties on behalf of Taiwan.

Further, the U.S. commitment to Taiwan may appear to Chinese leaders as being ambiguous. Indeed, U.S. policy appears designed to convey just such a signal, and as noted above, Chinese leaders pay very close attention to U.S. declaratory policy on the issue of Taiwan. A policy of intentional ambiguity may serve important U.S. purposes, but the problem with this policy in this case is that it likely discourages belief in the credibility of U.S. security commitments. It suggests an exploitable reluctance on the part of the United States to intervene over Taiwan, and may contribute to a Chinese perception that Washington will ultimately bow to Chinese deterrent threats. Chinese comments certainly appear to reflect this perception.

It is not difficult to anticipate that Chinese leaders would discount the U.S. commitment to Taiwan in the context of this scenario, anticipate the effectiveness of their own deterrent threats, and therefore feel themselves at liberty to resolve the crisis militarily. If Washington subsequently responded strongly, the Chinese leaders could easily complain that they could not have anticipated such a U.S. reaction. Argentina's misperception of the

---

94. Gertz, "China's Talk of Forces Buildup Over Taiwan Raises New Fears," p. A3.

British commitment to the Falkland Islands immediately prior to its 1982 invasion of the Falklands may be an apt analogy here.

POSSIBILITIES FOR MISPERCEPTION

Misperception of will, power, intentions, and policies is common in international relations, and flows from numerous factors.[95] In this particular case, there is ample opportunity for misperception on both sides, and ample historical precedents in the Korean War and the Taiwan Strait crises of the 1950s. In each case, Chinese behavior was based on the mistaken belief that America was actively preparing for an attack against China itself; Mao perceived a level of U.S. hostility and imminent military threat that far exceeded the reality.[96]

As noted above, if under the circumstances of this scenario Washington ultimately did pursue a strong military response to Chinese military measures, the Chinese leadership would have misperceived likely U.S. behavior for understandable reasons. Even if Washington revised its current ambiguous orientation, however, there is a strong chance of misperception. U.S. and PRC leaders lack common backgrounds, experiences, and in many cases basic worldviews upon which mutual familiarity and understanding can most easily be based.

In addition, the strong determination of PRC leaders to defeat Taiwanese "separatism" is likely to trigger cognitive defense mechanisms (e.g., denial, bolstering) that limit decision-making and could lead them to self-serving conclusions about U.S. commitments and threats. The PRC leadership appears to be a small, closed group with limited information channels and few

---

95. There is considerable scholarly work on this subject. See, for example, Robert Jervis, *Perception and Misperception in International Politics* (Princeton: Princeton University Press, 1976); and, Stoessinger, *Nations in Darkness*.

96. See, Shu Guang Zhang, pp. 89, 96, 115, 222-224, 265-267.

opportunities for consideration of alternative viewpoints. Strong emotional elements involved in the Taiwan issue may impede a careful assessment of costs and risks. The leadership's emotional and political investment in subduing Taiwan under the postulated circumstances, a determination to "teach a lesson" to the U.S. for meddling in Chinese affairs, and confidence in China's own deterrent could lead Chinese leaders to run seemingly unreasonable risks.

Washington could easily be surprised by the asymmetry of the stakes involved in the crisis, and correspondingly misjudge Chinese determination and cost-risk tolerance. Washington, following from the Cold War deterrence framework, could easily overestimate Chinese susceptibility to U.S. deterrence threats, believing that the Chinese leadership would be deterred by the enormity of U.S. military power, as would any "sane" leadership.

Unfortunately, the avenues for misperception are numerous, including the possible idiosyncratic views of individual leaders. Some of the factors that lead to misperception may be ameliorated by efforts to clarify signals and increase familiarity, but many of them cannot be controlled or possibly even identified in advance.

CHINA'S STRATEGIC PROFILE IN THIS CRISIS AND ITS IMPLICATIONS FOR DETERRENCE

Based on the above examination, it is possible to construct a strategic profile of the Chinese leadership pertinent to this scenario. Although incomplete, this profile should be useful in the elaboration of U.S. deterrence policy concerning China by reducing the margin of error in our efforts to understand the Chinese cost-benefit calculus with regard to Taiwan. The strategic profile for this scenario is drawn from the following summary points:

- PRC leaders are calculating;
- They are willing to take significant risks; .

- Their willingness to absorb costs is high;
- The fate of Taiwan is a survival issue for them;
- There is a political consensus in China for reunification;
- Taiwanese independence is unacceptable to Beijing;
- PRC leaders are ready to use force to protect Chinese territorial integrity in general, and in particular to deny Taiwan independence;
- In the absence of U.S. intervention, China ultimately can subdue Taiwan;
- PRC leaders believe the "stakes" over Taiwan are far less significant for the United States than they are for China, and view the U.S. commitment to Taiwan in this regard as uncertain;
- PRC leaders consider Washington unwilling to absorb significant costs for the purpose of preventing China from subduing Taiwan;
- PRC leaders believe that Washington will be vulnerable to Chinese deterrence threats in a crisis over Taiwan;
- For Beijing, keeping the U.S. out is the key to success.

First, at the most basic level of consideration, the Chinese leadership appears to be fully capable of rational and even predictable decision-making. The CCP has dealt with the same core security issue (the status of Taiwan) in multiple crises over a period of decades, and demonstrated considerable consistency in doing so. Indeed, there appear to be discernible patterns in the conflict behavior of the PRC regime. Emotional factors and various cognitive processes, however, could limit the predictability of Chinese decision-making and behavior and possibly move the leadership toward greater belligerence.

Second, the cost/risk tolerance of PRC leaders with regard to denying Taiwan independence if necessary is likely to be "very high." Doing so would be a survival interest.

Third, subduing Taiwan following a declaration of independence would be the priority value for Chinese decision-making. That is, the issue of Taiwanese independence has a high degree of autonomy in the decision-making of PRC leaders. The possibilities of adverse effects on economic development and/or political relations with other states are judged to have a limited influence on the decision to take military action to end Taiwan's bid for independence.

Fourth, the Chinese leadership's determination to "roll back" Taiwanese independence would be "very high," and its freedom to concede the issue would be "very low." China's freedom to provoke Washington in this case would be high, and particularly so if a U.S. threat of decisive military action were viewed by Chinese leaders as deterrable. There is some evidence to suggest that this, in fact, would be the dominant Chinese view.

Fifth, the Chinese leadership pays close attention to U.S. policies and declarations on the issue of Taiwan. Consequently, in principle, the likelihood that the PRC leadership will recognize and understand U.S. demands and threats is "medium" to "high." In practice, however, the policy of "strategic ambiguity" intentionally clouds the degree of U.S. commitment, reducing to "medium" to "low" the likelihood that Beijing would anticipate strong U.S. military action. If and when U.S. forces were committed to Taiwan's defense, "strategic ambiguity" would evaporate, but this could be too late to usefully promote the credibility of U.S. deterrence policies.

Sixth, the credibility of U.S. deterrent threats, from the perspective of the PRC leadership, would likely be "medium," that is, uncertain until demonstrated through strong U.S. military action. And, given the stakes involved for China's leadership, it is quite possible that even a strong U.S. deterrent threat judged to be largely credible would not be sufficient to deter China from attempting to subdue Taiwan in this case.

Seventh, in theory, China is vulnerable to U.S. deterrent threats in cross-Strait crises. As suggested above, however, in the particular case of a declaration of independence by Taipei, China's leadership may not be deterrable. China may not be susceptible to U.S. deterrence threats, regardless of their severity, largely because denying Taiwan independence is a near- absolute goal for the Chinese leadership. It may see "one China, one Taiwan" as an outcome that would lead to its own downfall, the collapse of the CCP regime, and the breakup of China. Consequently, Chinese leaders would not have the option to concede. China's apparent belief in the fragility of American will to enforce deterrence threats would likely reinforce this Chinese rigidity.

The chart below contrasts a notional challenger who should be highly susceptible to deterrence threats with the Chinese leadership in this case study. The conclusion illustrated by this comparison is that the Chinese leadership in this case would be unlikely to share many of the characteristics that contribute to a foe who is highly deterrable in principle.

Notional Highly-Deterrable Foe Compared with PRC Leadership		
	Notional Highly-Deterrable Adversary	China In This Scenario
Predictability	Very High	High
Determination	Very Low	Very High
Cost/Risk Tolerance	Very Low	Very High
Influence of Other Issues	Very High	Very Low
Freedom to Conciliate	Very High	Very Low
Freedom to Provoke	Very Low	Very High
Understanding of U.S. Demands/Threats	Very High	Medium
Credibility of U.S. Threats	Very High	Medium

If the U.S. is to have any logical prospect of deterring military action by the PRC in this situation, its deterrent threat would have to hold out the promise of costs judged in Beijing to be at least as dear and probable as the costs that would attend Taiwan's independence. The possibility that no U.S. deterrent policy would be viewed by China as sufficiently lethal and credible to "work" in this case leads to the real potential that rational and informed Chinese leaders could not be deterred by Washington.

Those who continue to have enormous confidence in the Cold War deterrence framework typically show great skepticism toward such a conclusion, or that any "rational" leadership could prove undeterrable in the face of preponderant U.S. nuclear capabilities. They suggest that only "irrational" leaders could be undeterrable, and because no leader on the horizon appears to be functionally irrational, continuing high confidence in deterrence is warranted.[97] However, consistent with numerous actual historical cases, this case suggests strongly that leaders can be rational, and in practice, undeterrable because they judge the potential cost of inaction on their part to be intolerable and the cost of action to be acceptable, or subject to some possible control or limitation. Chinese leaders do not need to suffer from any form of psychopathy or cognitive distortion to be undeterrable over Taiwan.

Deterrence can fail or fail to apply because leaders: are very highly motivated and willing to absorb great cost; unwilling/unable to count the expected cost; dubious or ignorant of their opponent's commitment; or a myriad of other factors frequently found in the real-world behavior of leaders under stress. In this case of a crisis over Taiwanese independence, Washington's capacity to deter

---

97. George Lewis, Lisbeth Gronlund, and David Wright, "National Missile Defense: An Indefensible System," *Foreign Policy* (Winter 1999-2000), pp. 128-129. See also, Stephen Walt, "Rush to Failure," *Harvard Magazine*, Vol. 102, No. 5 (May-June 2000), p. 35.

China may be undermined by several of these factors operating simultaneously.

The U.S. is unlikely to deter military action by Beijing at the outset of the crisis because PRC leaders are very highly motivated to prevent Taiwan's independence. The stakes are higher for China, and PRC leaders in this case are likely to be more cost- and risk-tolerant and, most importantly, view themselves as such. In addition, Beijing will wield its own nuclear deterrent threat as an "asymmetric response" to U.S. conventional superiority; indeed, Chinese leaders appear to view nuclear weapons as extremely valuable for deterring U.S. intervention or escalation in just such a conflict. This is critical in this case because, as noted above, the U.S. objectives of protecting the U.S. homeland, forward-deployed forces, and allies may well take precedence over defending Taiwanese independence and avoiding the decrease in U.S. international status that a Chinese victory over Taiwan would yield for Washington.

Consequently, to conclude that Chinese leaders, in this case, simply may not be deterrable in practice is not to question Chinese rationality. It is a conclusion logically derived from an attempt to understand the basic features of the Chinese (and U.S.) cost-benefit and risk calculus in a specific context.

Chapter 7

THE NEW DETERRENCE FRAMEWORK, EVIDENCE AND MISPLACED CONFIDENCE

The framework for thinking about post-Cold War deterrence policy suggested here leads to less confidence in the predictability of deterrence than generally has prevailed in Washington, including in discussions of the prospects for U.S. deterrence of China. The difference between the conclusions offered here and those drawn from the Cold War deterrence framework are stark.

For example, Joseph Nye, as Assistant Secretary of Defense for International Security Affairs, confidently claimed, "I know how to deter" Chinese missiles. The basis of Nye's confidence? "If deterrence prevented 10,000 Soviet missiles from reaching the United States, it baffles me as to why it wouldn't prevent 20 Chinese missiles from reaching Alaska."[1] Assuming for the moment that deterrence, in fact, prevented attack by "10,000 Soviet missiles," Nye's Cold War-derived confidence in deterrence ignores the fact that dramatically different players and contexts are likely to have a similarly dramatic effect on how deterrence operates, or if it can operate at all.

More recently, the Clinton White House claimed that the modernization of the Chinese strategic nuclear arsenal is not a serious U.S. concern because, "We believe that we have a clearly

---

1.   Remarks to the Defense Writers Group, October 18, 1995, Washington, D.C., quoted in "Word for Word," *Defense News*, October 23-29, 1995, p. 26.

superior nuclear force" (i.e., because the U.S. dominates the nuclear balance with China, deterrence will work).[2]

A Center for Naval Analysis (CNA) summary report on deterrence in Sino-U.S. relations similarly records continuing confidence in Cold War-style nuclear deterrence: "The United States must not forget that we still have overwhelming nuclear superiority vis-à-vis China. What is wrong with relying on 'old fashioned' nuclear deterrence in dealing with China?"[3]

This case study, however, suggests that U.S. nuclear superiority may not be decisive, and Chinese strategic nuclear weapons are worthy of considerable concern because they could be essential to China's confidence in its own capacity to deter Washington. And, with Washington deterred, the Chinese may easily see victory over Taiwan as practicable at a cost that is preferable to the wholly intolerable consequences of successful Taiwanese independence.

What may be "wrong" with "old fashioned nuclear deterrence" in this case is precisely the fact that, as these White House and CNA quotes illustrate, it tends to equate a rational opponent and a lethal U.S. threat with the certainty of deterrence effectiveness: U.S. nuclear superiority is expected to "ensure" an effective U.S. deterrence policy. Yet this study demonstrates that in this case at least, U.S. nuclear superiority may well not equate to "ensuring" deterrence. Of greater possible significance are the apparent Chinese beliefs that: the stakes involved over Taiwan are much greater for China, and China is more able and willing to absorb cost and run risks to subdue Taiwan than is the United States to prevent China from doing so. The fact that these Chinese beliefs may accurately reflect Chinese and U.S. values and will regarding

---

2. The White House, Office of the Press Secretary, Press Briefing by Joe Lockhart, December 6, 1999.

3. *China And National Missile Defense: Workshop Number 2*, Center for Naval Analysis, Compiled by Michael McDevitt, December 14, 1999, p. 5.

Taiwan suggests strongly that "old fashioned deterrence," even with U.S. nuclear superiority, is far from certain.[4]

Finally, Bates Gill and Michael O'Hanlon of the Brookings Institution claim that "the logic of deterrence and the overwhelming power of the American nuclear arsenal" will prevent Chinese nuclear attack against the United States in the event of war over Taiwan.[5] Perhaps, but there can be no certainty here; and, what about strikes against U.S. overseas forces, bases, territories, and allies? At what point in the midst of an acute crisis will this "logic of deterrence" become decisive in Chinese behavior, if in fact it does? If denying Taiwan independence is a survival issue for Chinese leaders, it is not clear that they will not willingly run enormous risks, and/or as desperate leaders, discount in a self-serving fashion the risks of nuclear brinkmanship. In any event, they are very likely to accept a level of cost and risk that would be shocking to Washington because it would appear so unreasonable.

If the Chinese leadership confronts two miserable options, the risk of war with the U.S., or accepting Taiwanese independence, it may consider regime survival to be at risk in either case; it is not clear which option would appear the more intolerable. One hopes that sensible Chinese leaders would never choose to initiate nuclear

---

4. Fifty-two percent of the U.S. public disagrees with the statement, "The United States should come to the defense of Taiwan with military force, if it is attacked by China." Only 35 percent agree (June 1999 public opinion survey). National sample of 1,200 Americans interviewed in a telephone survey by Opinion Dynamic Corporation between June 16 and 28, 1999. Cited in William Watts, *Americans Look at Asia: A Potomac Associates* Perspective (New York: Henry Luce Foundation, October 1999) <http://www.hluce.org/images/usasia_report_1099.pdf>, p. 29. Sixty-three percent of the public would oppose defending Taiwan if war with China would ensue (August 1999 public opinion survey). National sample of 1,017 Americans interviewed in a telephone survey by ICR-International Communications Research between August 25 and 29, 1999. Cited in Daniel Merkle, "Should U.S. Defend Taiwan?" ABCNEWS.com, September 1, 1999.

5. Quoted in, "China's Military, Take 3," *National Interest*, No. 58 (Winter 1999/2000), p. 119.

war. Expecting rational, reasonable, well-informed, and dispassionate decisions in such a context, however, is to ignore how humans frequently behave. Expressions of certainty that "the logic of deterrence" will control a desperate Chinese leadership are based more on continuing faith in the deterrence tautology than the available evidence about leadership behavior under stress and in acute crises.

Perhaps more importantly, it is clear that in this case the "logic of deterrence" and U.S. nuclear superiority would not prevent China from making nuclear threats against the United States; as noted above, such threats already have been issued. And, in a serious contest of wills involving mutual nuclear threats, the likely asymmetries in the stakes, willingness to absorb cost, and to run risks are all to China's advantage. These factors will likely be of much greater significance to the outcome of U.S. and Chinese deterrence threats than is the difference in the number of U.S. and Chinese nuclear weapons.

As noted above, desperate domestic political imperatives can limit rational decision-making and encourage a leadership toward high-risk brinkmanship. Once a leadership, driven by an internal or external imperative, has committed itself to the course of high-risk brinkmanship, objective realities that should cause it to revise its position may be ignored or distorted to be compatible with the prior decision. Leaders who must confront a severe domestic peril that appears to necessitate a military initiative may be so limited in their cognitive skills that even severe and credible threats will not reliably deter them. Against a highly determined challenger, such as China in this case, historical evidence again suggests that to establish a credible U.S. commitment for deterrence purposes may well require, "a policy of retaliation, escalation, and war. The willingness to go to war is the ultimate test of resolve...the dilemma for leaders is that acting tough may require going to war, which is costly immediately and only may have [deterrence] payoffs in the future."[6] Years of circumspect U.S. support for Taiwan and a conscious policy of "ambiguity" are very unlikely to have communicated firm U.S. resolve to Chinese leaders, who in any event are likely to be predisposed to see softness in the U.S. commitment because they want to see softness.

Indeed, historical case studies suggest specifically that the fear of domestic political fragility that would likely drive Chinese decision-making in this case is one of the most powerful motivations to aggressive policies and the potential for the self-serving distortion of reality in decision-making.[7] Chinese leaders appear to accept the popular notion that U.S. sensitivity to casualties renders Washington vulnerable to deterrence in general, and that the asymmetry in stakes in a crisis over Taiwan will further encourage U.S. disengagement. And, to be sure, significant elements of the Congress, elite, and public opinion would vocally contend that the future of Taiwan is not a vital U.S. interest worth war with China. It is difficult realistically to conceive how Washington could be seen by Chinese leaders in this case as having sufficient interests at stake in Taiwan to compete with them in a severe contest of wills headed toward "horrendous war" and nuclear threats. That Chinese leaders might discount U.S. will in a self-serving fashion because doing so would ease their decision-making significantly can only add to the uncertainty of U.S. deterrence efforts in this case.

If the significance of the Chinese domestic political imperative in this case is underestimated or ignored entirely, U.S. superiority

---

6. See, Elli Lieberman, *Deterrence Theory: Success or Failure in Arab-Israeli Wars?* McNair Paper 45 (Washington, D.C.: National Defense University, October 1995), p. 64. See also, Kenneth Watman and Dean Wilkening, *U.S. Regional Deterrence Strategies* (Santa Monica, CA: RAND, 1995), pp. 62-64.

7. Richard Ned Lebow, "The Deterrence Deadlock: Is There a Way Out?" in *Psychology and Deterrence*, by Robert Jervis, Richard Ned Lebow, and Janice Stein (Baltimore, MD: Johns Hopkins University Press, 1985), p. 186.

in nuclear and conventional arms could wrongly lead U.S. decision-makers to confidence in their capability to deter China. "Mirror-imaging" an opponent washes out precisely those types of factors, such as unique domestic political imperatives, that can confound expectations about how deterrence "should" operate between sensible leaders.

"All other things being equal," Washington should be able to deter virtually any adversary given its superiority in nuclear and conventional arms. This essentially is the calculation of the Cold War deterrence framework, which simply assumes "all other things" to be equal. As this case illustrates, however, non-military factors very important to deterrence frequently are not equal. Unfortunately, the Chinese leadership is likely to see itself in a desperate political condition upon a Taiwanese declaration of independence. And a domestic political imperative, such as the one shaping Chinese decision-making regarding Taiwan, is very likely to encourage Chinese brinkmanship over the issue.

This case study, based on a new deterrence framework, concludes that at least some U.S. deterrence goals would be highly uncertain and perhaps wholly impracticable given the assumed circumstances. This conclusion stands in stark contrast to the relatively easy confidence in deterrence that is derived from the Cold War deterrence framework. And, it should be noted, the assumed circumstances in this case are not farfetched; they are indeed plausible.

Consideration of deterrence derived from a relatively close examination of the challenger and context, as is proposed here, admittedly may be faulty. This case study suggests, however, that such an approach can help to avoid some of the basic errors that beset the Cold War deterrence framework. In particular, it can reduce the chance that gross misinterpretation of an opponent's will, goals, and values will lead to false confidence about the likely outcome of a deterrence policy.

SUGGESTED U.S. DETERRENCE OPTIONS

The stark conclusion that deterrence of a Chinese military initiative is likely to be very difficult or impossible in the event of a Taiwanese declaration of independence may be accurate, but it also is unsatisfying. The question that emerges is: given this assessment of Chinese interests what might be a preferred U.S. approach to deterrence under the described circumstances?

Any such effort must be speculative and under the conditions of this case there appears to be very little room for U.S. confidence in deterrence. But a starting place is to identify plausible U.S. threats that, at least in principle, could be seen by Beijing as involving a level of cost comparable to, or greater than, the "loss" of Taiwan—that is, a U.S. policy of deterrence based on a manifest threat to the survival of the Beijing leadership.

One option that would appear to satisfy this requirement in principle would be for the United States to commit itself fully to the defeat of any Chinese effort to subdue Taiwan militarily or through military coercion. If a threat to do so were executed successfully, the cost to the Chinese leadership of being defeated militarily could magnify the cost of losing Taiwan. For an authoritarian leadership increasingly dependent on nationalism, the potential loss of Taiwan compounded by military defeat might be perceived as a severe survival threat. In a potentially analogous case, Argentina's military junta responsible for the 1982 loss to Britain fell as a result of military defeat; members subsequently were prosecuted for "gross negligence," dismissed from the armed forces, and sentenced to varying prison terms.

This proposed deterrent threat would be significantly different from the types of threats often associated with Cold War policies. Those threats, at least as discussed publicly, typically focused on punishing Moscow severely in the event of war. Views on how the threatened punishment should be defined varied throughout the Cold War, with differing emphasis placed on the types of targets to be threatened: Secretary of Defense McNamara spoke publicly of destroying population and industry, "assured destruction;" Secretary of Defense Schlesinger spoke publicly of destroying the Soviet capability for economic recovery; subsequently, Secretary of Defense Brown spoke of directly threatening the lives of the Soviet leadership and their instruments of political and military power.[8] In each case, however, the declared U.S. deterrence threat, if executed, would likely not have spared America from annihilating Soviet nuclear strikes. Consequently, whether the U.S. declared threats involved the "assured destruction" of Soviet population and industry or political and military power, actually carrying out the threat would have been strategically meaningless for the United States.

The deterrent threat suggested here is "punitive" in the sense of intending to present Chinese leaders with the expectation of overwhelming cost in the event of conflict. That expected "cost" to the CCP leadership, however, could only follow from a manifest U.S. capability to defeat the PLA militarily, deny China its military objectives regarding Taiwan, and do so at a *prospective cost acceptable* to U.S. leaders. Such a military and foreign policy defeat for China would be the immediate instrument to threaten CCP survival: the extended cost to the CCP, to be exploited for U.S. deterrence purposes, would be the expected domestic political repercussions for the CCP of losing Taiwan through military defeat. In this case, deterrent effect would reside in the fear of Chinese leaders that military defeat and the enforced loss of Taiwan would precipitate the CCP's political collapse, i.e., a threat to CCP regime survival.

In a departure from much official Cold War rhetoric about nuclear deterrence, the U.S. policy discussed here would focus on a

---

8.   See the discussion in Keith B. Payne, *Nuclear Deterrence in U.S.-Soviet Relations* (Boulder, CO: Westview Press, 1982); and Payne, *Deterrence in the Second Nuclear Age* (Lexington, KY: University Press of Kentucky, 1996), pp. 60-78.

military threat and capability intended to deter, but a threat based on specific and meaningful military objectives. To establish a deterrence policy on the capability to achieve meaningful military goals, the United States would have to make blatantly clear both its will and capability to defeat Chinese conventional and weapons of mass destruction (WMD) attacks against Taiwan at a tolerable cost in terms of potential U.S. military, civilian, and allied losses. This would require the manifest capability to project sizable and suitable forces to the theater to demonstrate and, if necessary, enforce the U.S. commitment to Taiwan, and to deny China any hope for a fait accompli. The U.S. would need to be, and to be seen as being, capable of preventing China from subduing Taiwan before U.S. forces could be brought to bear. Measures helpful in this regard would be U.S. military assistance to Taiwan that extended the period of time the island could hold out without direct intervention by U.S. combat forces, and measures that would reduce the time required to deploy sizable U.S. forces in defense of Taiwan.

If U.S. deterrence policy failed, and China initiated hostilities against Taiwan, the U.S. would have to decide if it was then willing to execute its threat of defeating China in a regional war over the status of Taiwan. If Washington chose not to wage a war to defeat China, its credibility throughout Asia as an alliance partner and leader would likely suffer significantly. Clearly, Washington would have to weigh this potential cost against the risks of serious intervention.

The question here probably is not whether Chinese leaders would, in principle, perceive the loss of Taiwan and China's military defeat in this crisis as costly, and therefore constitute an exploitable U.S. deterrent threat. The question is whether any Chinese leadership would judge such a U.S. deterrent threat as sufficiently real, in practice, to be decisive in its decision-making. As suggested above, Chinese leaders may self-servingly conclude that the United States would lack the will and/or the capability to execute this threat, particularly if they could plausibly threaten significant U.S. military and civilian losses. Clearly, Beijing would work hard to undermine U.S. will by threatening great losses. Correspondingly, Chinese leaders already have promised Washington a "horrendous" war if events unfold as described above.

The Clinton Administration's policy of "strategic ambiguity" is hardly likely to highlight U.S. will and determination with regard to Taiwan. Indeed, it was not designed to do so. Consequently, a conclusion suggested by this discussion is that under the circumstances of this crisis, "strategic ambiguity" would be unhelpful for deterrence purposes, and, if deterrence is the priority goal, should be replaced with a policy likely to be seen as strongly committing the U.S. to countering military attacks against Taiwan.

Shifting the U.S. policy of "strategic ambiguity" to one of greater commitment in the midst of a crisis, however, may not be useful for U.S. deterrence purposes. Case studies indicate that the perceptions of commitment that most contribute to deterrence are shaped less by in-crisis adjustments and declarations than by a history of demonstrated commitment and manifest national interest, particularly including military demonstrations of commitment.[9] To strengthen U.S. deterrence options for times of crisis, the U.S. probably would need to revise its policy of ambiguity well in advance of a crisis, and take highly visible military steps compatible with a new policy of explicit commitment.

There are various factors, in addition to domestic opposition, that would likely limit the attractiveness of U.S. moves intended to strengthen the U.S. deterrence position. For example, U.S. leaders could fear that a stronger political and military commitment to Taiwan would encourage it toward independence, triggering the crisis in question. In addition, U.S. Asian allies may be expected to

---

9.   See, Watman and Wilkening, *U.S. Regional Deterrence Strategies*, pp. 62-64.

encourage U.S. restraint for fear that a war with China would draw them in.

Perhaps the most limiting factor, however, is the obvious fact that U.S. intervention against Chinese efforts to subduc Taiwan would risk escalation to a large-scale theater war, possibly including Chinese regional nuclear use, and nuclear threats against the U.S. homeland. Preserving the credibility of U.S. deterrence commitments in such circumstances would require Chinese leaders to believe that Washington would commit considerable force to the defense of Taiwan despite China's own intercontinental nuclear threats and possible regional nuclear use. That is, Chinese leaders would need to believe to some degree that the U.S. would be willing to project power against China, on behalf of Taiwan, with the attendant risk of a large-scale war, possibly including a nuclear war.

As noted above, there are obvious and virtually inherent asymmetries in stakes and cost/risk tolerance in a crisis over Taiwan. It is difficult to conceive of a route to credibility for Washington's deterrence threats in this context unless Washington is able to bring into balance the manifest risks and benefits involved in a regional war. Because the asymmetry in the stakes in this crisis probably is beyond predictable manipulation, the U.S. could attempt to find a more believable balance between risk and benefit by driving its prospective losses in terms of military and civilian casualties down to a level more compatible with its stakes.

To align U.S. risks and stakes by limiting potential U.S. costs for the purposes of deterrence, or indeed for carrying out U.S. threats in the event deterrence failed, key U.S. military capabilities would need to include those that promise to limit prospective U.S. military and civilian losses, while also defeating China militarily. Such a military posture would require a combination of offensive and defensive capabilities.

For example, as in Operations Allied Force (Kosovo, 1999), Deliberate Force (Bosnia, 1995), and Desert Storm (Iraq, 1991), the heavy use of airpower could help limit potential U.S. military casualties in a war with China. As Zhang Xingli, a defense analyst at the Chinese Academy of Social Sciences noted, "[In Kosovo], it was not face-to-face warfare. NATO attacked from a distance. It suffered no losses. [That] makes China think." [10]   Long-range, manned combat aircraft, or manned aircraft with long-range standoff weapons, could be deployed at "sanctuary" bases beyond the striking distance of many PRC ballistic missiles. Stealthy manned aircraft, unmanned combat air vehicles, and long-range missiles would further reduce the exposure of U.S. military personnel to Chinese attack.

In addition, Chinese ballistic missiles constitute a "pocket of excellence" in the capabilities of the PLA, and could be used to strike at U.S. bases in East Asia and also at U.S. naval forces in the region.[11] PRC missile attacks would greatly increase the costs of U.S. intervention, and the threat to the United States posed by PRC nuclear-armed ICBMs is intended by Beijing to inhibit U.S. intervention altogether. Consequently, U.S. sensors, weapons, platforms, and command, control, and communications systems that facilitate the destruction of PRC missile launchers, missiles, and supporting infrastructure could help make this Chinese cudgel less effective for deterring or defeating U.S. intervention.

---

10. Susan Lawrence, "Doctrine of Deterrence," *Far Eastern Economic Review*, 162 (October 14, 1999), p. 26.

11. With regard to the vulnerability of naval forces to ballistic missile attack, see Douglas Porch, "The Taiwan Strait Crisis of 1996: Strategic Implications for the United States Navy," *Naval War College Review*, 52 (Summer 1999), p. 31. See also Mark Stokes, *China's Strategic Modernization: Implications for the United States* (Carlisle, PA: Strategic Studies Institute, Army War College, September 1999), pp. 142, 146; John Garver, *Face Off: China, the United States, and Taiwan's Democratization* (Seattle: University of Washington Press, 1997), pp. 128-129; and Harlan Jencks, "Wild Speculations on the Military Balance in the Taiwan Strait," in *Crisis in the Taiwan Strait*, James Lilley and Chuck Downs, eds. (Washington, D.C.: NDU Press, 1997), pp. 156-159.

Depending on the circumstances, the U.S. might exploit nonnuclear and/or nuclear capabilities for attacking silo-based and mobile missiles. Unless the Chinese employed WMD against U.S. targets, however, the U.S. National Command Authorities almost certainly would be highly reluctant to authorize preventive nuclear strikes against such targets. And, even with improved U.S. attack capabilities, China's theater ballistic missiles would be difficult to destroy on the ground. All PRC short-, medium-, and intermediate-range ballistic missiles are mobile, making them easier to hide and harder to find.[12] Consequently, offensive operations against Chinese ballistic missiles would need to be complemented by ballistic missile defense (BMD), and other active and passive defenses for U.S. forward-deployed forces, including air defenses against combat aircraft and cruise missiles and protective measures against WMD.

Missile defense for the United States itself clearly would be needed to diminish the salience of Chinese ICBM threats to U.S. cities, a key to China's potential capability to coerce Washington. The future Chinese deployment of mobile ICBMs "will provide China's strategic nuclear forces improved mobility [and] survivability,"[13] reducing the likely effectiveness of U.S. offensive operations against Chinese missiles. China's often-expressed opposition to U.S. BMD suggests the PRC leadership believes that such a defense could undermine the deterrent value of the Chinese ICBM force, including its role in preventing U.S. intervention in a PRC-Taiwan conflict. Instead of undermining deterrence, as is the

---

12. House Select Committee on U.S. National Security and Military/Commercial Concerns with the People's Republic of China, *Report Volume* I (Washington, D.C.: U.S. Government Printing Office, 1999), pp. 180-181, 187-188.

13. Department of Defense, *Selected Military Capabilities of the People's Republic of China*, Report to Congress Pursuant to Section 1305 of the FY 97 National Defense Authorization Act (Washington, D.C.: Department of Defense, April 2, 1997), p. 4.

charge against BMD derived from the Cold War deterrence framework, in this case it could be essential to the credibility of the U.S. deterrence commitment.

In sum, this study employs a methodology far different from that of the Cold War deterrence framework and reaches far different conclusions. It first identifies very specific characteristics of the Chinese leadership, suggests reasons why Washington should not attribute confidence to nuclear deterrence "working" predictably in this case despite U.S. nuclear superiority, and then proposes exploitation of a putative Chinese political vulnerability. Because the Chinese leadership would be very highly motivated to deny Taiwanese independence for fear of its own survival, the same fear might be exploited for U.S. deterrence purposes. A U.S. deterrence policy that promises the military defeat of China in any attempt to subdue Taiwan could speak to this very specific political vulnerability of the Chinese leadership—the same vulnerability that is likely to render the Chinese leadership very difficult or impossible to deter in such a crisis. In this case, U.S. deterrence policy would be built on a military threat that would be meaningful if executed and on striking a credible balance between U.S. risk and benefit by significantly limiting U.S. civilian and military vulnerabilities.

The approach described here would by no means "ensure" an effective policy of deterrence in the assumed crisis. Even if the United States established a deterrent threat based on its manifest will and capability to defeat China's efforts to subdue Taiwan at an acceptable price, deterrence could fail for any of the reasons discussed above. It is not possible to "ensure deterrence" in any case, Cold War promises notwithstanding, and in this crisis over Taiwan, deterrence is likely to be particularly fragile no matter how well-informed the U.S. position.

Indeed, confidence in this suggested deterrence strategy should not be high. It is difficult to envisage any practicable, high-confidence U.S. deterrence strategy under the circumstances of this case. Nevertheless, the deterrence policy posited here represents an attempt to recognize its fragility, tailor a policy specifically to the opponent and context, and to identify a potentially meaningful path in the event deterrence fails and Washington decides to move to a military solution. The methodology and results stand in sharp contrast to those of the Cold War framework.

Chapter 8

LESSONS OF THIS CASE STUDY

From the Specific to the General

At least four significant "lessons" can be drawn from this analysis of deterrence and the China case study. Each is discussed below.

A NEW AND STRESSING ROLE FOR DETERRENCE: DETERRING THEIR DETERRENT

First, the China case illustrates well the unprecedented mission for U.S. deterrence policy in the post-Cold War period: deterring a regional challenger's WMD escalation while conventionally defeating that challenger on or near its own territory, i.e., "deterring their deterrent."

NATO's Cold War deterrence strategy was built on the assumption that the Soviet leadership would never be confident that it could employ its conventional force superiority against Western Europe without triggering Western nuclear retaliation. Although it generally was conceded that the Soviet Union could use its conventional force advantages to conquer Western Europe in relatively short order, and NATO nuclear escalation could have been suicidal, Soviet fear of escalation nevertheless was expected to deter any sizable westward projection of Soviet power.

In the future, Washington will want results from its deterrence policy that it said were not possible for the Soviet Union vis-à-vis NATO during the Cold War: confidence that it can deter an opponent's threat of WMD escalation even while projecting power and defeating that opponent on or near its own soil. The China case study illustrates how difficult it may be to "deter their deterrent" with confidence even when Washington has conventional force superiority and an enormous numerical advantage in nuclear weapons.

A question for the post-Cold War period is: in an intense contest of wills why should a power such as China attribute credibility to U.S. deterrence threats when the stakes involved for Washington are relatively modest and the risks high? By what logical calculation should Washington be able to register a challenger's nuclear escalation threat, be confident of deterring that threat, and move against the challenger? What profound advantage would Washington have in such a case that Moscow lacked during the Cold War when it was believed that the Soviet Union could not confidently deter NATO's threat of escalation?

Unfortunately, there is no current answer to these questions. As the China case illustrates, U.S. leaders are unlikely to be more cost/risk tolerant in terms of prospective military and/or civilian losses than would be the regional aggressor; the reverse probably is true. And, as the China case again illustrates, the stakes involved in a regional conflict frequently may be less for the U.S. than for the regional aggressor because it is likely to see its own survival at risk.

There is no existing basis for believing that U.S. leaders will be any more willing to persist in the context of nuclear threats to U.S. cities than we believed Soviet leaders would be willing to provoke NATO's nuclear threat during the Cold War. Indeed, U.S. efforts to deter and coerce will likely be at a great disadvantage in terms of the costs, benefits, and the interests involved in prospective regional crises when American cities are vulnerable to WMD escalation.

Clearly, Washington will want its deterrence policy to accomplish the task of "deterring their deterrent" when its will and capability to project power would otherwise be undermined by a regional aggressor's threat of WMD escalation. This is an enormous and virtually unprecedented deterrence challenge for the United States.

U.S. REGIONAL DETERRENCE POLICIES: REDUCING RISKS

The second "lesson" of this case study follows from the first. Because American leaders will want U.S. conventional force superiority to serve deterrence purposes in at least some regional crises, Washington will have to work to bring into credible balance the prospective risks and benefits of regional force projection. If U.S. leaders believe that projecting force into, for example, Asia or the Middle East, carries a serious risk of WMD use against unprotected U.S. cities, it is difficult to conceive of their willingness to intervene, and the credibility of U.S. threats to do so will likely be limited. In such cases, as in the Chinese case described above, to safeguard both the credibility of the U.S. deterrent and the U.S. will to intervene if necessary will require defensive capabilities to limit the risk to U.S. cities and expeditionary forces.

Such damage-limitation capabilities could include the entire spectrum of: offensive capabilities for counterforce strikes; active defenses such as air and ballistic missile defenses; and passive defenses such as physical protection and preparation for biological attacks. In instances where the stakes of an acute crisis are significantly and manifestly less for Washington than for the challenger, such as in the crisis over Taiwan, effective protection for civilians and power projection forces may be necessary to bring U.S. interests and risks into balance. In the absence of such a balance, the credibility of U.S. deterrence policy may well be discounted sharply by any attentive challenger, and particularly so by a challenger motivated by an internal or external imperative to discount U.S. threats.

This conclusion obviously has significant implications for U.S. missile defense programs. For example, American and European critics of missile defense frequently charge that those programs reflect a dangerous "Fortress America" mentality. In fact, in the post-Cold War era, missile defense in concert with other defensive capabilities may be necessary for the U.S. freedom of action long taken for granted in Washington, including the freedom to project force into distant theaters and to make related deterrence threats in defense of American and allied interests.

This "lesson" illustrates the dichotomy between the Cold War deterrence framework and the conclusions drawn from this study. As noted above, the Cold War deterrence framework leads to the conclusion that capabilities for protection, particularly including ballistic missile defense and offensive counterforce capabilities, undermine deterrence; they are "destabilizing." And, under the Clinton Administration, U.S. officials and defense commentators, continuing to be guided by this Cold War deterrence framework, correspondingly sought to reassure China that U.S. missile defense programs would not undermine China's nuclear missile threat to the United States. In contrast, this study demonstrates that offensive and defensive damage-limitation capabilities are likely to be essential elements undergirding U.S. deterrence policy, including with regard to the prospective deterrence of China over Taiwan.

THE VALUE OF A MORE EMPIRICAL FRAMEWORK FOR DETERRENCE

Third, this study demonstrates the potential value of a more empirical deterrence framework. For the purposes of post-Cold War deterrence, it is important to know the opponent to the extent feasible, acknowledge that which is not known, and to establish deterrence policies informed by what can be known about the specific opponent's beliefs and modes of thought. From the 1960s to the present, the debate about deterrence has focused almost exclusively on "how much is enough?" in terms of warheads and launchers. In the future, the question of "how much do we know?"

about an opponent and context should precede any debate about "how much is enough?"

In the absence of a close examination of the opponent and context, it will be impossible to appreciate the thinking and motivations underlying a challenger's prospective behavior and how these might affect deterrence. The China case illustrates the importance of such an examination. How else, for example, could U.S. leaders anticipate that a severe domestic political imperative could lead a potential opponent like China to a ready willingness to accept great risks and costs, and possibly to discount U.S. resolve and capability in a self-serving fashion? A challenger's perceptions, goals, resolve, will, concept of national honor, and cost/risk tolerance will be keys to its behavior under threat; and those qualities cannot be known via the Cold War framework's assumption that challengers will be rational, reasonable, pragmatic, and predictable in familiar terms.

Recognition of the hollowness of confident, blanket predictions about the behavior of diverse challengers, particularly challengers under the stress of a security crisis, leads inevitably to recognition of the fragility of confident, blanket statements about the future effectiveness of deterrence. Continued uncritical acceptance of the deterrence tautology will, over time, lead to a disaster.

When the United States was relatively invulnerable to foreign powers, courtesy of two great oceans and power, folly and sloppiness in anticipating an opponent's behavior had few immediate repercussions for most Americans. But Washington now confronts a future with numerous unfamiliar regional challengers, some armed with weapons of mass destruction and emerging long-range delivery capabilities, and the risks involved in being surprised will mount. In this post-Cold War context, convenient ignorance of a challenger's particular thought and beliefs, and foolish notions that only "stupid" or "irrational" foes could reason far differently than we, will exacerbate the potential for deadly surprises. The unanticipated failure of deterrence becomes more likely, and a single surprise could lead to hundreds of thousands, even millions, of American civilian casualties, particularly if no preparation has been made for deterrence failure.

Expectations that a challenger's decision-making will be pragmatic, rational, and reasonable may prove accurate on occasion; such expectations also may be completely misleading. In the future, it will be critically important to understand which is more likely when orchestrating U.S. deterrence policy. Such discernment may be possible only following a study of a challenger's perceptions, goals, resolve, will, concept of national honor, cost/risk tolerance, etc. Knowledge of an opponent in this sense can never be complete, but a dedicated effort may narrow the margin of ignorance, improving the basis for anticipating behavior and thus the prospects for deterrence.

A recommendation that follows from this point is for the establishment of a formal process dedicated to the detailed examination of challengers and potential challengers for the purpose of informing U.S. deterrence policies. Such a process could bring together a multidisciplinary team to address, in a much more rigorous and comprehensive fashion than undertaken here, the series of questions and issues pertinent to the deterrence of challengers and potential challengers. Having mature, systematic work on the subject of how deterrence may operate vis-à-vis a specific challenger and context—as opposed to impromptu efforts, presumption, ad hoc impressions and images—could be very helpful in the context of an emerging crisis. It could also help provide a more thoughtful basis for answering the question "how much is enough?" for deterrence, as opposed to the Cold War framework's parochial assumption that rationality, pragmatism, and reasonableness, as defined in Washington, are universal.

Because its findings could range far outside the lines of policy in Washington, any agency responsible for this process would require a significant degree of independence. The danger of not being so independent is illustrated by the political storm that followed the CIA's reportedly unflattering characterization of

Haitian leader Jean-Bertrand Aristide at a time when the Clinton Administration greatly favored Aristide.[1]

Recognition that deterrence requirements, and indeed the relevance of deterrence, can vary markedly depending upon the character of the challenger and the context carries significant implications. For example, in the absence of serious study covering a wide spectrum of challengers, potential challengers, and plausible flashpoints, it is the height of hubris to state confidently that "The possibility of even a few nuclear detonations in populated areas provides ample deterrence,"[2] or "Effective deterrence of potential nuclear adversaries can be maintained at the reduced levels envisioned by START III and beyond."[3] The factors significant to the functioning of deterrence are sufficiently variable that the authors of such statements cannot possibly know what they so confidently claim.

Some future foes may indeed be deterred by very modest U.S. nuclear capabilities, or by none at all. Others, highly motivated and cost/risk tolerant, may be deterrable only by severe nuclear threats involving robust capabilities. And, in some cases, policies of deterrence simply may not be applicable at any level of nuclear capability. Confidently claiming that all future crises will reflect the first and most benign of these possibilities amounts to little more than baseless fortune telling and should be treated as such.

Recent suggestions that the United States pursue "maximally verifiable and irreversible" deep nuclear force reductions, and

---

1. Thomas Omestad, "Psychology and the CIA: Leaders on the Couch," *Foreign Policy*, No. 95 (Summer 1994), pp. 105-112.

2. McGeorge Bundy, William Crowe Jr., and Sidney Drell, *Reducing Nuclear Danger* (New York: Council on Foreign Relations Press, 1993), p. 95.

3. National Defense Panel, *Transforming Defense: National Security in the 21st Century* (December 1997), p. ii.

"lock in" dramatic reductions in nuclear capabilities,[4] make no sense when it is recognized that future deterrence requirements are ambiguous at best. Deep nuclear force reductions may well be compatible with current U.S. deterrence requirements; whether such a benign situation will prevail in the future, however, is wholly unknown. What is known is that the strategic environment has shifted dramatically over the past two decades, and the future appears no less fluid. Washington does not know today whether Russia, China, or various rogue states will be neutral, friend, foe, or part of a hostile alliance in the future. It cannot therefore be sensible now to "lock in" the character and quantity of U.S. nuclear forces intended for deterrence based on the assumption of a continuing benign strategic environment.

The reduction of U.S. nuclear forces, even deep reductions, is not the problem here per se. A comprehensive review of opponents and deterrence requirements may conclude that such reductions are now appropriate. If so, the U.S. should adjust its force structure accordingly. The problem is continuing in the Cold War approach to strategic arms control that focuses on mechanistically codifying force ceilings that could severely limit the U.S. flexibility necessary to adapt its nuclear capabilities to levels compatible with future deterrence requirements. The U.S. political culture typically does not permit Washington to seek withdrawal or even serious revision of established and codified strategic arms control treaties, even when the strategic environment has changed dramatically and affected treaties contain formal provisions for revision and withdrawal. Strategic arms control treaties become their own justification, all but impossible for Washington to redefine or revise. The technical and legal contortions to which successive Republican and Democratic Administrations have gone to

---

4.   As recommended in, The Committee on Nuclear Policy, *Jump-START: Retaking the Initiative to Reduce Post-Cold War Nuclear Dangers* (Washington, D.C.: The Henry Stimson Center, February 25, 1999), pp. 7, 11.

simultaneously comply with, and seek relief from, the ABM Treaty illustrate the point. The United States has been locked into the treaty by a domestic norm that views strategic arms control agreements as sacrosanct. Agreements become highly resistant to redefinition, let alone rejection, even as dramatically different security conditions arise. Future U.S. arms control initiatives must take into account that the U.S. flexibility necessary to adapt to rapidly shifting conditions and requirements may be a key to post-Cold War deterrence, but contrary to perpetuation of the Cold War strategic arms control process.

The past deterrence framework, and the approach to arms control derived from it, are wholly ill-suited to the fluidity of the post-Cold War era. To perpetuate the existing mechanistic and legalistic strategic arms control process when we know so little about future challengers and crises, and hence potential deterrence requirements, would be to continue embracing the falsehood that we can confidently identify and codify the level of nuclear capabilities that will be effective for deterrence "stability" now and in the future.

DETERRENCE IS INHERENTLY UNRELIABLE: PREPARE FOR ITS FAILURE

Finally, regardless of how well-informed U.S. deterrence policy may be, it is important to acknowledge that deterrence can fail unpredictably for the variety of potential reasons noted above: desperate leaders driven by an internal or external imperative may distort reality in a self-serving fashion; they may be inattentive, drugged, foolish, or simply so cost/risk tolerant in pursuit of an absolute goal that U.S. deterrence policy is impracticable. The notion that U.S. nuclear weapons, or any particular type of threat, can "ensure" deterrence and that nuclear deterrence is "existential" is a dangerous myth.

Deterrence is inherently unreliable because challengers, including rational decision-makers, are not wholly predictable or controllable under any circumstances, and under conditions of great stress may often be beyond predictable reason and practicable control. This problem is certain to be exacerbated by Washington's lack of familiarity with, and the unpredictability of, regional rogue powers.

Stating these facts as such often is perceived as a rejection of all deterrence theory and policy. That is neither my intention nor an implication of this study. Deterrence can be a valuable tool of U.S. foreign policy. Nevertheless, when considering deterrence for the post-Cold War era, it is essential that the limits of deterrence theory and policy be recognized. In the past, the U.S. has been surprised when coercion or deterrence failed to perform as hoped, and Washington subsequently chose to, or was compelled to, wage war, as with Japan in 1941 and Iraq fifty years later. In both of these cases, the U.S. succeeded at a cost modest by many historical comparisons.

In the future, however, a variety of regional foes assuredly will be armed with WMD and long-range delivery capabilities. In these circumstances, to misunderstand deterrence–that is, to believe that it can be "ensured," and so not to prepare for its failure–could lead to unprecedented catastrophe.

As in the China case described above, the same force structure and threats that back U.S. deterrence policy may need to have military utility and significantly limit U.S. vulnerability as a hedge against potential deterrence failure, an event that will remain unpredictable under the best of circumstances. This conclusion points to the importance of deterrence by "denial" threats, deterrence threats that are based on the will and capability to defeat an opponent's military objectives and minimize potential U.S. losses. Again, to the extent that U.S. deterrence threats can proceed from the same capabilities that would be called upon to project forces successfully *at tolerable cost*, the U.S. may both reinforce its will for deterrence purposes and hedge its bets against inherently unreliable policies of deterrence.

This conclusion is a direct challenge to the integrity of the Cold War deterrence framework and to the continuing confidence in deterrence inspired by that framework. It suggests that, to the extent possible, the United States should prepare for deterrence failure even as it strives to deter. Such preparation could again involve the entire spectrum of active and passive defenses for U.S. expeditionary forces abroad and civilians at home. For example, as the proliferation of missiles, including long-range missiles, continues apace, the absence of any homeland ballistic missile defense to protect against rogue missile threats constitutes a particularly egregious vulnerability.

When the inherent limitations of deterrence predictability are recognized, the folly of extending the Cold War formula for deterrence to China and others, becomes apparent. Defense against ballistic missiles, and other forms of defense that have been rejected in the past on the basis of overriding confidence in deterrence, should now be seen as potentially contributing to deterrence in some cases, and, perhaps more importantly, as wise insurance against the near-certainty that at some future point deterrence will unexpectedly fail. Continuing assertions that the United States does not need defenses because deterrence will work reliably is an extension of the Cold War deterrence tautology; it is an obscurant and high-risk proposition in the post-Cold War era.

Noted British historian A.J.P. Taylor was perhaps optimistic in his comment on the effectiveness of deterrence: "A deterrent may work ninety-nine times out of a hundred. On the hundredth occasion it produces catastrophe."[5] I suspect that deterrence does not "work ninety-nine times out of a hundred." But, even if Taylor's estimate is accurate, in a world increasingly armed with weapons of mass destruction, on that "hundredth occasion," U.S.

---

5. A.J.P. Taylor, *War By Time-Table* (London: MacDonald & Co., 1969), p. 121.

preparation for deterrence failure may literally save millions of lives that otherwise would be lost, and preserve the continuing viability of the U.S. government.

SELECTED WORKS CITED

Abrams, Elliot, ed. *Honor Among Nations*. Washington D.C.: Ethics and Public Policy Center, 1996.

Allen, Kenneth W. and Eric A. McVadon. *China's Foreign Military Relations*, Report No. 32. Washington, D.C.: Henry L. Stimson Center, October 1999.

Archibald, Kathleen, ed. *Strategic Interaction and Conflict: Original Papers and Discussion*. Berkeley, CA: Institute of International Studies, University of California, Berkeley, 1966.

Beach, Lee Roy. *Psychology: Core Concepts and Special Topics*. New York: Holt, Rinehart and Winston, 1973.

Becker, Jasper. *Hungry Ghosts: China's Secret Famine*. London: John Murray, 1996.

Bennet, James. "Clinton Calls Tests Mistake and Announces Sanctions Against India." *New York Times*, May 14, 1998.

Bernstein, Richard and Ross H. Munro. *The Coming Conflict With China*. New York: Alfred A. Knopf, 1997.

Bertsch, Gary and Suzette Grillot, eds. *Russell Symposium Proceedings, U.S. Security Interests in the 1990s*. Athens, GA: University of Georgia, 1993.

Betts, Richard. *Surprise Attack*. Washington, D.C.: Brookings Institution, 1982.

Bill, James A. "Iran and the Crisis of '78." *Foreign Affairs*, Vol. 57, Winter 1978/79.

Binnendijk, Hans, and Ronald N. Montaperto, eds. *Strategic Trends in China*. Washington, D.C.: National Defense University Press, 1998.

Blight, James, et al. *Cuba on the Brink: Castro, the Missile Crisis, and the Soviet Collapse*. New York: Pantheon Books, 1993.

Bosworth, Stephen. "Dealing with North Korea: Ambassador Stephen W. Bosworth." *The Nuclear Roundtable, Meeting Summary*. Washington, D.C.: Henry L. Stimson Center, May 31, 1996.

Boyne, Sean. "Taiwan's Troubles: National Defence Report Highlights Chinese Threat." *Jane's Intelligence Review*, Vol. 10, September 1998.

Bozeman, Adda. "War and the Clash of Ideas." *Orbis*, Vol. 20, No. 1, Spring 1976.

Brecher, Michael, and Jonathan Wilkenfeld. *A Study of Crisis*. Ann Arbor, MI.: University of Michigan Press, 1997.

Bullock, Alan. *Hitler, A Study in Tyranny*. New York: Harper and Row, 1962.

Bundy, McGeorge. "To Cap the Volcano." *Foreign Affairs*, Vol. 48, No. 1, October 1969.

Bundy, McGeorge, and William Crowe Jr., and Sidney Drell. *Reducing Nuclear Danger*. New York: Council on Foreign Relations Press, 1993.

Burleigh, Michael. *The Third Reich: A New History*. New York: Hill and Wang, 2000.

Bush, Richard. "The United States Role in the Taiwan Straits Issue." Speech at the University of Illinois at Carbondale. December 7, 1998. <http://www.taiwansecurity.org/IS-Bush.htm>.

Cameron, Normai, and R.H Stevens, translators. *Hitler's Secret Conversations, 1941-1944*. New York: Farrar, Straus, and Young, 1953.

Campbell, Kurt. Testimony. U.S. House. Committee on International Relations. Hearings. September 15, 1999.

Carnesale, Albert, and Joseph Nye. "Defusing The Nuclear Menace." *Washington Post*, September 4, 1988.

Carter, Ashton B., and William J. Perry. *Preventive Defense: A New Security Strategy for America.* Washington, D.C.: Brookings Institution Press, 1999.

Chan, Steve. "Chinese Conflict Calculus and Behavior: Assessment from a Perspective of Conflict Management." *World Politics*, Vol. 30, April 1978.

Chang, Gordon H. *Friends and Enemies: The United States, China, and the Soviet Union, 1948-1972*. Stanford, CA: Stanford University Press, 1990.

Chiles, Hank. Testimony. U.S. Senate. Committee on Armed Services. *Nominations Before the Senate Armed Services Committee*. DC: U.S. Government Printing Office, 1994.

Christensen, Thomas J. "Chinese Realpolitik." *Foreign Affairs*, Vol. 75, September-October 1996.

_____. "Threats, Assurances, and the Last Chance for Peace." *International Security*, Vol. 17, No. 1, Summer 1992.

_____. *Useful Adversaries: Grand Strategy, Domestic Mobilization, and Sino-American Conflict, 1947-1958.* Princeton, N.J.: Princeton University Press, 1996.

Chzanowski, Paul L. "Transition to Deterrence Based on Strategic Defense." *Energy and Technology Review* (January-February 1987).

CIA: The Pike Report. Nottingham, England: Spokesman Books, 1977.

Commission to Asses the Ballistic Missile Threat to the United States (Rumsfeld Commission). *Executive Summary of the Report of the Commission to Assess the Ballistic Missile Threat to the United States.* July 15, 1998.

Craig, Gordon and Alexander George. *Force and Statecraft*, Third Edition. New York: Oxford University Press, 1995.

Craven, Wesley Frank, and James Lea Cate, eds. *The Army Air Forces in World War II, Volume III, Europe: Argument To V-E Day.* Washington, D.C.: Office of Air Force History, 1983.

Crawford, Neta. "The Passion of World Politics." *International Security*, Vol. 24, No. 4, Spring 2000.

Davis, Richard. Testimony. U.S. Senate. Select Committee on Intelligence. *Foreign Missile Threats: Analytic Soundness of National Intelligence Estimate 95-19.* Hearings. December 4, 1996.

December, William N., and James J. Jenkins. *General Psychology: Modeling Behavior and Experience.* Englewood Cliffs, NJ: Prentice-Hall, 1970.

Derbyshire, John. "Hitting the Great Wall of China." *Weekly Standard*, June 5, 2000.

Deutch, John. Testimony. U.S. House, Committee on Foreign Affairs. *U.S. Nuclear Policy.* Hearings. Washington, D.C.: U.S. Government Printing Office, 1995.

Deutsche Welle Radio. "Interview with Lee Teng-hui, President of the Republic of China (Taiwan)." July 9, 1999. Transcript. <http://www.dwelle.de/english/interview.html>.

"Documentation: ABM Treaty 'Talking Points,'" *Comparative Strategy*, Vol. 19, No. 4, October-December 2000.

Domarus, Max. *Hitler: Speeches and Proclamations 1932-1945, The Chronicle Of A Dictatorship, Vol. III, 1939-1940*. Wauconda, IL: Bolchazy-Carducci Publishers, 1997.

Dreyer, Edward L., and June Teufel Dreyer. "The Chinese People's Liberation Army's Perception of an Invasion of Taiwan." In *The Chinese PLA's Perception of an Invasion of Taiwan*, edited by Peter Kien-hong Yu. New York: Contemporary U.S.-Asia Research Institute, 1996.

Earle, Edward Mead. "Hitler: The Nazi Concept of War." In *Makers of Modern Strategy: Military Thought from Machiavelli to Hitler*, edited by Edward Mead Earle. Princeton, NJ: Princeton University Press, 1961.

Ensor, R.C.K., *Herr Hitler's Self-Disclosure in Mein Kampf*, Oxford Pamphlets on World Affairs, No. 3. Oxford: Clarendon Press, July 6, 1939.

_____. *Who Hitler Is*, Oxford Pamphlets on World Affairs, No. 20. Oxford: Clarendon Press, 1939.

Enthoven, Alain, and K. Wayne Smith. *How Much Is Enough?* New York: Harper and Row, 1971.

"Excerpts From Gore's Remarks on Bush, the Presidential Race and the Issues," *New York Times*, June 14, 2000.

Fallaci, Oriana. "Galtieri: No Regrets, No Going Back." *Times* (London), June 12, 1982.

Feigenbaum, Evan A. "China's Military Posture and the New Economic Geopolitics." *Survival*, Vol. 41, No. 2, Summer 1999.

Finkelstein, David M. "China's National Military Strategy." In *The People's Liberation Army in the Information Age*, CF-145-CAPP/AF, edited by James C. Mulvenon and Richard Yang. Santa Monica, CA: RAND Corp., 1999.

Flannery, Russell. "U.S. Warns China Not to Attack Taiwan." *The Asian Wall Street Journal*, September 7, 1999.

Flannery, Russell, and Eduardo Lachica. "Taiwan Trumpets Presence of U.S. Navy Ships." *The Wall Street Journal*, August 13, 1999.

Foreign Broadcast Information Service (translation). Hsiao Peng. "Beidaihe Meeting Maintains that United States Supports Taiwan Independence." *Sing Tao Ji Pao*, August 5, 1999. FTS19990805000247.

_____. "Belarus: Russia's Rocket Troops Chief Views Cooperation, Astrology." *Vo Slavu Rodiny*. February 26, 1998. FTS19980226000115.

_____. Lo Ping. "Political Bureau Studies New Strategy Against Taiwan." *Cheng Ming*. August 1, 1999. FTS19990807000271.

_____. "'Strength' Cannot Save Li Teng-hui—On the 'Four Cards' Behind the 'Two-State Theory.'" *Liberation Army Daily*. August 18, 1999. FTS19990818000354.

_____. Sha Lin. "Two Senior Colonels and 'No-Limit Warfare.'" *Zhongguao Qingnian Bao*, June 28, 1999. FTS19990728000697.

_____. Liang Qiao, and Wang Xiangsui. *Unrestricted Warfare: Assumptions on War and Tactics in the Age of Globalization.* Beijing: PLA Literature and Arts Publishing House, February 1, 1999. FTS1999122100136Z.

_____. "USA, Do Not Mix In." *Global Times*, August 19, 1999. Cited in Asher Bolande, Agence France-Presse. August 19, 1999. FTS19990819000118.

Foreman, William. "Taiwan Backs China Reforms." Associated Press, October 9, 1999. <http://www.taiwansecurity.org/AP/ AP-991009-Taiwan-Backs-China-Reforms.htm>.

Förster, Jürgen, et al. "Hitler's Decision In Favor of War Against the Soviet Union." *Germany and the Second World War, Vol. IV: The Attack on the Soviet Union.* New York: Oxford University Press, 1998.

Fursenko, Aleksandr, and Timothy Naftali. *One Hell of a Gamble.* New York: W.W. Norton, 1997.

Galbraith, John Kenneth. *A Life In Our Times.* Boston: Houghton Mifflin Company, 1981.

Garver, John W. *Face Off: China, the United States, and Taiwan's Democratization.* Seattle, WA: University of Washington Press, 1997.

Gates, Robert. Testimony. U.S. Senate. Select Committee On Intelligence. *Intelligence Analysis Of The Long Range Missile Threat To The United*

States. Hearings. Washington, D.C.: U.S. Government Printing Office, 1997.

Gellman, Barton. "Reappraisal Led to New China Policy." *The Washington Post*, June 22, 1998.

_____. "U.S. and China Nearly Came to Blows in 1996." *The Washington Post*, June 21, 1996.

George, Alexander. *Bridging the Gap: Theory and Practice in Foreign Policy*. Washington, D.C.: United States Institute of Peace Press, 1993.

_____. *Forceful Persuasion*. Washington, D.C.: U.S. Institute of Peace, 1991.

_____. *The "Operational Code": A Neglected Approach To the Study of Political Leaders and Decision-Making*. Santa Monica, CA: RAND, September 1967.

George, Alexander, and Richard Smoke. *Deterrence in American Foreign Policy: Theory and Practice*. New York: Columbia University Press, 1974.

Gertz, Bill. *Betrayal: How the Clinton Administration Undermined American Security*. Washington, D.C.: Regnery Publishing, Inc., 1999.

_____. "China's Talk of Forces Buildup Over Taiwan Raises New Fears." *Washington Times*, August 10, 1999.

_____. "Military's Top General on Way to Beijing for Talks, Maneuvers." *Washington Times*, October 31, 2000.

_____. "Perry: Missile Defense Unnecessary." *Washington Times*, April 26, 1996.

Gill, Bates. *The Deterrence Series: Chemical and Biological Weapons and Deterrence Case Study 6—People's Republic of China*. Alexandria, VA: Chemical and Biological Arms Control Institute, 1998.

Gill, Bates, and Michael O'Hanlon "China's Military, Take 3." *National Interest*, No. 58, Winter 1999/2000.

Gonen, Jay. *The Roots of Nazi Psychology*. Lexington, KY: University Press of Kentucky, 2000.

Goodrick-Clarke, Nicholas. *The Occult Roots of Nazism*. New York: NYU Press, 1992.

Gould-Davies, Nigel. "Rethinking the Role of Ideology in International Politics During the Cold War." *Journal of Cold War Studies*, Vol. 1, No. 1, Winter 1999.

Gray, Colin S. *Nuclear Strategy and Strategic Planning.* Philadelphia: Foreign Policy Research Institute, 1984.

Green, Phillip. *Deadly Logic: The Theory of Nuclear Deterrence.* Columbus, OH: Ohio State University Press, 1966.

Group for the Advancement of Psychiatry, Committee on Social Issues. *Psychiatric Aspects of the Prevention of Nuclear War*, Report No. 57. September, 1964.

Habiger, Eugene E. Testimony. U.S. Senate. Committee on Armed Services. *Department of Defense Authorization For Appropriations For Fiscal Year 1999 And The Future Years Defense Program.* Hearings. Washington D.C.: U.S. Government Printing Office, 1998.

_____. Testimony. U.S. Senate, Committee on Armed Services. *Statement of General Eugene E. Habiger.* Hearings. March 13, 1997 (mimeo).

Haffner, Sebastian. *The Meaning of Hitler.* Cambridge, MA: Harvard University Press, 1979.

Haig, Alexander M. *Caveat.* New York: MacMillan, 1984.

Halle, Louis. "Does War Have A Future?" *Foreign Affairs*, Vol. 52, No. 1. October 1973.

Halloran, Richard. "China a Long Shot in Taiwan Attack." *Washington Times*, September 3, 1999.

Harris, Whitney. *Tyranny on Trial.* Dallas: Southern Methodist University Press, 1999.

Harrison, David and Damien McElroy. "China's Military Plots 'Dirty War' Against the West." *London Sunday Telegraph*, October 17, 1999.

Hasting, Max, and Simon Jenkins. *The Battle for the Falklands.* New York: Norton, 1983.

Heuser, Beatrice. "Warsaw Pact Military Doctrines in the 1970s and 1980s: Findings in the East German Archives." *Comparative Strategy*, Vol. 12, No. 4, Winter 1994.

Hitler, Adolf. *Hitler's Secret Book.* New York: Bramhall House, 1986.

_____. *Mein Kampf.* Boston: Houghton Mifflin, 1943.

Howard, Sir Michael. "Lessons of the Cold War." *Survival,* Vol. 43, No. 4, Winter 1994-1995.

Hua Di. *China's Security Dilemma to the Year 2010.* Stanford, CA.: Center for International Security and Arms Control, October 1997.

Hybel, Alex. *Power Over Rationality.* Albany: State University of New York Press, 1993.

Iklé, Fred Charles. "Can Nuclear Deterrence Last Out the Century?" *Foreign Affairs*, Vol. 51, No. 2, January 1973.

_____. *Possible Consequences of a Future Spread of Nuclear Weapons.* January 2, 1965. Committee on Nuclear Proliferation, Committee File, NSF, Boxes 6-7, LBJ Library.

_____. "Nuclear Strategy: Can There Be A Happy Ending?" *Foreign Affairs*, Vol. 63, No. 4, Spring 1985.

"India's Nuclear Irresponsibility," *The Washington Post,* May 13, 1998.

Information Office of the State Council of the People's Republic of China. *China's National Defense.* July 1998. <http://www.china.org.cn/WhitePapers/NationalDefense/NationalDefense-2.html>.

Jäckel, Eberhard. *Hitler in History.* Hanover: Brandeis University Press and University Press of New England, 1984.

_____. *Hitler's Weltanschauung: A Blueprint for Power.* Middletown, CT: Wesleyan University Press, 1973.

James, Daniel. *Che Guevara.* New York: Stein and Day Publishers, 1969.

Jencks, Harlan W. "China's 'Punitive' War on Vietnam: A Military Assessment." *Asian Survey*, Vol. 19, August 1979.

_____. "Wild Speculations on the Military Balance in the Taiwan Strait." In *Crisis in the Taiwan Strait*, edited by James R. Lilley and Chuck Downs. Washington, D.C.: National Defense University Press, 1997.

Jeremiah, David. News Conference, CIA Headquarters, June 2, 1998 (mimeo).

Jervis, Robert. "The Political Effects of Nuclear Weapons: A Comment." *International Security*, Vol. 13, No. 2, Fall 1988.

Joffe, Ellis. "The Military and China's New Politics: Trends and Counter-Trends." In *The People's Liberation Army in the Information Age*, CF-145-CAPP/AF edited by James C. Mulvenon and Richard Yang, Santa Monica, CA: RAND Corp., 1999.

Joffee, Josef. "A Peacenik Goes to War." *New York Times Magazine*, May 30, 1999, *The New York Times on the Web*, "Archives."

Johnston, Alastair Iain. "China's Militarized Interstate Dispute Behavior, 1949-1992: A First Cut at the Data." *The China Quarterly*, No. 153, March 1998

_____. "China's New 'Old Thinking': The Concept of Limited Deterrence." *International Security*, Vol. 20, No. 3, Winter 1995/96.

_____. "Prospects for Chinese Nuclear Force Modernization: Limited Deterrence Versus Multilateral Arms Control." *The China Quarterly*, No. 146, June 1996.

Josephus, *The Works of Josephus*. Translated by William Whiston. Peabody, MA: Hendrickson Publishers, 1987.

Kagan, Donald. "Honor, Interest, and the Nation State." In *Honor Among Nations*, edited by Elliot Abrams, Washington D.C.: Ethics and Public Policy Center, 1996.

_____. *On The Origins Of War*. New York: Doubleday, 1995.

Kaplan, Fred. *The Wizards of Armageddon*. New York: Simon and Schuster, 1983.

Karsten, Peter, Peter D. Howell and Artis Frances Allen. *Military Threats: A Systematic Historical Analysis of the Determinants of Success*. Westport, CT: Greenwood Press, 1984.

Kaufman, William. "Limited Warfare." In *Military Policy and National Security*, edited by William Kaufman, Princeton, NJ: Princeton University Press, 1956.

Keeny, Spurgeon. "Inventing an Enemy." *New York Times,* June 18, 1994.

_____."The New Missile 'Threat' Gap*." Arms Control Today*, June/July 1998.

Kent, Glenn A., Randall J. DeValk, and David E. Thaler. *A Calculus of First-Strike Stability (A Criterion for Evaluating Strategic Forces),* A RAND Note, N-2526-AF, June 1988.

Kent, Sherman. "A Crucial Estimate Relived." In *Sherman Kent and the Board of National Estimates, Collected Essays*, Washington, D.C.: Center for the Study of Intelligence, Central Intelligence Agency, 1994.

Kim Myong Chol. *North Korea Makes Public Threat to Blow Up US Mainland.* <www.kimsoft.com/1997>, March 3, 2000.

_____."North Korea prepared to fight to the end as Kim Jong-il has his own version of *The Art of War*," *Asia Times*, April 10, 1996.

Kissinger, Henry. *Years of Upheaval*. Boston: Little Brown & Co., 1982.

Kolkowicz, Roman. "Strategic Elites and Politics of Superpower." *Journal of International Affairs*, Vol. 26, No. 1, 1972.

_____. "Strategic Parity and Beyond: Soviet Perspectives." *World Politics*, Vol. 23, No. 3, April 1971.

_____. *The Soviet Union and Arms Control: A Superpower Dilemma*. Baltimore: Johns Hopkins University Press, 1970.

Krauze, Enrique. "The Return of Che Guevara." *The New Republic*, Vol. 218, No. 6, February 9, 1998.

Kuhns, Woodrow J., ed. *Assessing Soviet Threat: The Early Cold War Years*. Center for the Study of Intelligence, Central Intelligence Agency, 1997.

Laffin, John. *Hitler Warned Us*. New York: Barnes & Noble Books, 1998.

Landay, Jonathan S. "How Far Would US Go To Protect Taiwan?" *The Christian Science Monitor*, September 3, 1999.

_____. "Risks in a Chinese Invasion of Taiwan." *The Christian Science Monitor*, September 9, 1999.

Langer, Walter. *The Mind of Adolf Hitler: The Secret Wartime Report*. New York: Basic Books, 1972.

Laris, Michael. "Chinese Web Warriors." *Washington Post*, September 11, 1999.

Laris, Michael, and Steven Mufson. "China Mulls Use of Force Off Taiwan, Experts Say." *Washington Post*, August 13, 1999.

Lasater, Martin L. "A U.S. Perception of a PLA Invasion of Taiwan." In *The Chinese PLA's Perception of an Invasion of Taiwan*, edited by Peter Kienhong Yu, New York: Contemporary U.S.-Asia Research Institute, 1996.

Lautenbacker, Conrad C., and Lowell, Paul M. Testimony. U.S. Committee on Armed Services. Seapower Subcommittee. *Department of Defense Authorization for Appropriations for Fiscal Year 2000 and the Future Years Defense Program, Part 2.* Hearings. Washington, D.C.: U.S. Government Printing Office, 1999.

Lawrence, Susan V. "Doctrine of Deterrence." *Far Eastern Economic Review*, Vol. 162, October 14, 1999.

Lawrence, Susan V., and Bruce Gilley. "Rising Star." *Far Eastern Economic Review*, Vol. 162, October 7, 1999.

Lebow, Richard Ned. *Between Peace and War.* Baltimore, MD: Johns Hopkins University Press, 1981.

_____. "Miscalculation in the South Atlantic: The Origins of the Falklands War." In *Psychology and Deterrence*, by Robert Jervis, Richard Ned Lebow, Janice Stein, Baltimore, MD: Johns Hopkins University Press, 1985.

_____. "The Deterrence Deadlock: Is There A Way Out?" In *Psychology and Deterrence*, by Robert Jervis, Richard Ned Lebow, Janice Stein, Baltimore, MD: Johns Hopkins University Press, 1985.

Lebow, Richard Ned, and Janice Gross Stein, *When Does Deterrence Succeed And How Do We Know.* Occasional Paper, No. 8. Ottawa, Canadian Institute for International Peace and Security, February 1990.

Leites, Nathan. *A Study of Bolshevism.* Glencoe, IL: Free Press, 1953.

_____. *The Operational Code of the Politburo.* New York: McGraw-Hill, 1951.

Lewis, George, Lisbeth Gronlund, and David Wright. "National Missile Defense: An Indefensible System." *Foreign Policy*, No. 117, Winter 1999-2000.

Lewis, John Wilson, and Xue Litai. *China Builds the Bomb.* Stanford, CA: Stanford University Press, 1988.

_____."China's Search for a Modern Air Force." *International Security*, Vol. 24, No. 1, Summer 1999.

_____. *China's Strategic Seapower: The Politics of Force Modernization in the Nuclear Age*. Stanford, CA: Stanford University Press, 1994.

Li, Rex. "The Taiwan Strait Crisis and the Future of China-Taiwan Relations." *Security Dialogue*, Vol. 27, No. 4, December 1996.

Li Zhisui. *The Private Life of Chairman Mao*. New York: Random House, 1994.

Lieberman, Elli. *Deterrence Theory: Success or Failure in Arab-Israeli Wars?* McNair Paper 45. Washington, D.C.: National Defense University, October 1995.

Lippman, Thomas W. "Nuclear Powers Condemn Tests, Urge Restraint on India, Pakistan." *Washington Post*, June 5, 1998.

Lippmann, Walter. *Public Opinion*. New York: The MacMillian Co., 1927.

Lukacs, John. *The Hitler Of History*. New York: Knopf, 1997.

MacEachin, Douglas. *The Tradecraft of Analysis: Challenge and Change in the CIA*. Washington, D.C.: Consortium for the Study of Intelligence, 1994.

Mann, James. *About Face: A History of America's Curious Relationship with China, from Nixon to Clinton*. New York: Alfred A. Knopf, 1999.

_____. "U.S. Has Secretly Expanded Military Ties With Taiwan." *Los Angeles Times*, July 24, 1999.

Mansourov, Alexandre. "Stalin, Mao, Kim, and China's Decision to Enter the Korean War, September 16-October 15, 1950: New Evidence from the Russian Archives." *Cold War International History Project Bulletin*, Nos. 6-7 (Winter 1995-1996).

Marshall, Toni. "Missile Defense System Proposed." *Washington Times*, August 18, 1999.

Maurer, John. *The Outbreak of the First World War*. Westport, CT: Praeger, 1995.

Maxwell, Stephen. *Rationality in Deterrence*, Adelphi Papers, No. 50. London: Institute for Strategic Studies, August 1968.

McCullough, David. *Truman*. New York: Simon and Schuster, 1992.

McDevitt, Michael (compiled by). *China And National Missile Defense: Workshop Number 2*, Center for Naval Analysis, December 14, 1999.

McKinney, Cynthia. "Should the U.S. Have a Missile Defense System?" *American Legion Magazine,* Vol. 148, No. 1. January 2000.

McLaughlin, John E. Testimony. U.S. Senate. Select Committee on Intelligence. *Emerging Missile Threats to North America During the Next 15 Years*. Hearings. December 4, 1996.

McMillan, Joseph. "Talking to the Enemy: Negotiations in Wartime." *Comparative Strategy*, Vol. 11, No. 4. Philadelphia: Taylor and Francis, October-December 1992.

McVadon, Eric A. "Systems Integration in China's People's Liberation Army." In *The People's Liberation Army in the Information Age*, CF-145-CAPP/AF, edited by James C. Mulvenon and Richard Yang, Santa Monica, CA: RAND Corp., 1999.

Merkle, Daniel. "Should U.S. Defend Taiwan?" ABCNEWS.com, September 1, 1999. <http://nbcnews.com>.

Montaperto, Ronald. "China." In *1997 Strategic Assessment: Flashpoints and Force Structure*, edited by Hans A. Binnendijk and Patrick L. Clawson, Washington, D.C.: National Defense University Press, 1997.

Morton, Louis. "Japan's Decision for War." *Command Decisions*, New York: Harcourt, Brace, 1959.

Mueller, John. "The Search for the 'Breaking Point' in Vietnam." *International Studies Quarterly*, Vol. 24, No. 4, December 1980.

Murdock, Deroy. "A Hero Who Taught the World." *Washington Times*, August 27, 2000.

Myers, Steven Lee and Jane Perlez, "Documents Detail U.S. Plan to Alter '72 Missile Treaty." *New York Times*, April 28, 2000.

Nan Li. "The PLA's Evolving Campaign Doctrine and Strategies." In *The People's Liberation Army in the Information Age*, CF-145-CAPP/AF, edited by James C. Mulvenon and Richard Yang, Santa Monica, CA: RAND Corp., 1999.

_____. "The PLA's Evolving Warfighting Doctrine, Strategy and Tactics, 1985-95: A Chinese Perspective." *The China Quarterly*, No. 146, June 1996.

Naroll, Raoul, Vern L. Bullogh, Frada Naroll. *Military Deterrence In History: A Pilot Cross-Historical Survey*. Albany, N.Y.: State University of New York Press, 1974.

National Defense Panel. *Transforming Defense: National Security in the 21st Century*. December 1997.

National Intelligence Council. *Foreign Missile Developments and the Ballistic Missile Threat to the United States Through 2015*. September 1999.

Noland, Robert. "Presidential Disability and the Proposed Constitutional Amendment." *American Psychologist,* No. 21, March 1966.

Nuland, Sherwin. "The Final Pollution." *The New Republic*, June 14, 1999.

Oakly, Phyllis. Address at the National Defense University, Center for Counterproliferation Research, *Symposium on Deterrence*, October 28, 1998.

Oberdorfer, Don. "Glaspie Says Saddam Is Guilty of Deception." *Washington Post,* March 21, 1991.

_____. "Missed Signals in the Middle East." *Washington Post Magazine,* March 17, 1991.

Odom, William E. *The Collapse of the Soviet Military*. New Haven: Yale University Press, 1998.

Office of Naval Intelligence, *Chinese Exercise Strait 961: 8-25 March 1996*, Executive Summary. Washington, D.C.: Office of Naval Intelligence, May 1996 (in National Security Archive, *China and the United States: From Hostility to Engagement, 1960-1998*, Electronic Briefing Book, Document 14 <http://www.gwu.edu/~nsarchiv/NSAEBB/NSAEBB19/14-01.htm>).

Omestad, Thomas. "Psychology and the CIA: Leaders on the Couch." *Foreign Policy*, No. 95, Summer 1994.

O'Neill, Robert. "The Use of Military Force: Constant Factors and New Trends." *The Changing Strategic Landscape*. In Adelphi Papers, No. 236, London: International Institute For Strategic Studies, 1989.

Park, Bert, M.D. *Ailing, Aging, Addicted*. Lexington, KY: University Press of Kentucky, 1993.

Payne, Keith B. *Deterrence In The Second Nuclear Age*. Lexington, KY: The University Press of Kentucky, 1996.

_____. *Nuclear Deterrence in U.S.-Soviet Relations*. Boulder: Westview Press, 1982.

Payne, Keith B., and Lawrence Fink. "Deterrence Without Defense: Gambling on Perfection." *Strategic Review*, Vol. 16, No. 1, Winter 1989.

Perlez, Jane. "China and U.S. Are Reported To Trade Threats on Taiwan." *New York Times*, August 13, 1999.

Perry, William. *Remarks at The Washington Institute for Near East Policy*. Federal News Service transcript, February 6, 1996.

Pillsbury, Michael. *Chinese Perceptions of the Soviet-American Military Balance*, SPC 534. Arlington, VA: System Planning Corp., March 1980.

_____. "Chinese Views of Future Warfare: Implications for the Intelligence Community." U.S. Senate Select Committee on Intelligence. Hearings. September 18, 1998.

_____. *Dangerous Chinese Misperceptions: The Implications for DOD*. Washington, D.C.: DoD Office of Net Assessment, 1998.

Pipes, Richard. "Why the Soviet Union Thinks It Could Fight and Win a Nuclear War." *Commentary*, Vol. 64, No. 1, July 1977.

Pomfret, John. "China Ponders New Rules of 'Unrestricted War.'" *Washington Post*, August 8, 1999.

_____. "Taiwan May Get Antimissile Technology." *Washington Post*, July 9, 2000.

Pomfret, John, and Steven Mufson, "China, Taiwan Step Up Sorties Over Strait." *Washington Post*, August 3, 1999.

Porch, Douglas. "The Taiwan Strait Crisis of 1996: Strategic Implications for the United States Navy." *Naval War College Review*, Vol. 52, Summer 1999.

Post, Jerrold, M.D., and Robert Robins. *When Illness Strikes The Leader*. New Haven: Yale University Press, 1993.

Powell, Colin. *My American Journey*. New York: Random House, 1995.

Pry, Peter. *War Scare*. Westport, CT: Praeger, 1999.

Pye, Lucian W. "Understanding Chinese Negotiating Behavior: The Roles of Nationalism and Pragmatism." In *Between Diplomacy and Deterrence: Strategies for U.S. Relations with China*, edited by Kim R. Holmes and James J. Przystup, Washington, D.C.: Heritage Foundation, 1997.

Raum, Tom. "Envoy Threatens Force to Resolve Row with Taiwan." *Washington Times*, August 20, 1999.

Rauschning, Hermann. *Hitler Speaks*. London: Thornton Butterworth, 1939.

Record, Jeffrey. "Defeating Desert Storm (and Why Saddam Didn't)." *Comparative Strategy*, Vol. 12, No. 2, April-June 1993.

Regan, Donald T. *For The Record*. New York: Harcourt Brace, 1988.

Remarks to the Defense Writers Group. Washington, D.C.: October 18, 1995. Quoted in "Word for Word," *Defense News*, October 23-29, 1995.

Robert McNamara, "Misreading the Enemy." *New York Times*, April 21, 1999.

Roberts, Jonathan M. *Decision-Making during International Crises*. New York: St. Martin's Press, 1988.

Rühl, Lothar. "Angriffskrieger Markus Wolf." *Die Welt*, August 9, 1991.

_____. "Noch 1990 Zielte die NVA Richtung Westdeutschland und Benelux." *Die Welt*, July 31, 1991.

_____. "Offensive Defence in the Warsaw Pact." *Survival*, Vol. 33, No. 5, September–October 1991.

Sagan, Scott. "The Origins of the Pacific War." *Journal of Interdisciplinary History*, Vol. 18, No. 4, Spring 1988.

Sammon, Bill. "Clinton Misread Yugoslav Resolve." *Washington Times*, June 21, 1999.

Sammon, Bill, and David R. Sands, "Beijing's Anger Over Taiwan Worries U.S." *Washington Times*, August 14, 1999.

Scarborough, Rowan. "It's Not 'Star Wars' II, Republicans Say In Fighting Missile Defense." *Washington Times*, January 23, 1995.

Scrowcroft, Brent, John Deutch, and R. James Woolsey. "A Small, Survivable, Mobile ICBM." *Washington Post*, December 26, 1986.

Semykin, Col. Viktor. Interviewed for, "The Missiles of October: What the World Didn't Know." *ABC News*, Journal Graphics transcript no. ABC-40, October 17, 1992.

Shambaugh, David. "Containment or Engagement of China? Calculating Beijing's Response." *International Security*, Vol. 21, No. 2, Fall 1996.

Shryock, Richard W. "The Intelligence Community Post Mortem Program, 1973-1975." *Studies in Intelligence*, Fall 1977.

Shu Guang Zhang. *Deterrence and Strategic Culture: Chinese-American Confrontations, 1949-1958*. Ithaca, NY: Cornell University Press, 1992.

Shubik, Martin. "Terrorism, Technology, and the Socioeconomic of Death." *Comparative Strategy*, Vol. 16, No. 4. October-December 1997.

Sklar, Dusty. *Gods and Beasts: The Nazis and the Occult.* New York: Thomas Crowell, 1977.

Slocombe, Walter B. Testimony. U.S. Senate. Committee on Governmental Affairs. Subcommittee on International Security. *The Future of Nuclear Deterrence.* Hearings. Washington, D.C.: U.S. Government Printing Office, 1997.

Smith, R. Jeffrey. "India Sets Off Nuclear Devices." *Washington Post*, May 12, 1998.

Snyder, Glen. *Deterrence and Defense: Toward a Theory of National Security.* Princeton, NJ: Princeton University Press, 1961.

Solomon, Richard H. *Chinese Negotiating Behavior: Pursuing Interests Through 'Old Friends.'* Washington, D.C.: United States Institute of Peace Press, 1999.

Sorley, Lewis. *Thunderbolt: General Creighton Abrams and the Army of His Times.* New York: Simon and Schuster, 1992.

Statements by Gen. Wafic al Samarrai. *Frontline.* "The Gulf War, Parts I and II," January 9-10, 1996. Transcript.

Statements by Tariq Aziz. *Frontline.* "The Gulf War, Part I," January 9, 1996. Transcript.

Stoessinger, John G. *Nations in Darkness*. New York: Random House, 1971.

_____. *Why Nations Go to War*. New York: St. Martin's Press, 1993.

Stokes, Mark A. *China's Strategic Modernization: Implications for the United States*. Carlisle, PA: Strategic Studies Institute, Army War College, September 1999.

Sun-tzu. translation by Ralph D. Sawyer. *The Art of War*. New York: Barnes and Noble, 1994.

Swaine, Michael D. *The Role of the Chinese Military in National Security Policymaking*, revised edition, MR-782-1-OSD. Santa Monica, CA: RAND Corp., 1998.

"Syrian official protected Italy's troops over love for Italian actress." *Washington Times*, January 3, 1998.

Tai Ming Cheung. "Chinese Military Preparations Against Taiwan Over the Next 10 Years." In James R. Lilley and Chuck Downs, eds., *Crisis in the Taiwan Strait*. Washington, D.C.: National Defense University Press, 1997.

"Taiwan's High-Stakes Game," *The Economist*, Vol. 352 (August 21, 1999).

Tajima, Takashi. *China and South-east Asia: Strategic Interests and Policy Prospects*. Adelphi Paper, No. 172. London: International Institute for Strategic Studies, 1981.

Taylor, A.J.P. *War By Time-Table*. London: MacDonald & Co., 1969.

Tenet, George J. Testimony. U.S. Senate. Committee on Armed Services. Hearings. February 2, 1999. <http://www.odci.gov/cia/public_affairs/speeches/ps020299.html>.

_____. Testimony. U.S. Senate Committee on Foreign Relations. *The Worldwide Threat in 2000: Global Realities of Our National Security*. Hearings. March 21, 2000.

The Committee on Nuclear Policy. *Jump-START: Retaking the Initiative to Reduce Post-Cold War Nuclear Dangers*. Washington, D.C.: The Henry Stimson Center, February 25, 1999.

The President's NMD Decision and U.S. Foreign Policy. Conference on International Reactions to U.S. National and Theater Missile Defense Deployments. Stanford University, March 3, 2000.

The White House. *A National Security Strategy for a New Century.* Washington, D.C.: The White House, October 1998.

_____. Press briefing by Deputy Press Secretaries Barry Toiv and David Leavy. Office of the White House Press Secretary, August 13, 1999. <http://www.pub.whitehouse.gov/uri-res/I2R?urn:pdi://oma.eop. gov.us/1999/8/13/8.text.1 >.

_____. Press Briefing by Joe Lockhart. Office of the White House Press Secretary, December 6, 1999.

_____. Press briefing by National Security Advisor Sandy Berger, National Economic Advisor Gene Sperling, and Press Secretary Joe Lockhart. Sky City Hotel, Auckland, New Zealand. Office of the White House Press Secretary, September 11, 1999. <http://www.pub. whitehouse.gov/uri-res/I2R?urn:pdi://oma.eop.gov.us/1999/9/ 12/7.text.1>.

_____. Remarks by the President and the First Lady in Discussion on Shaping China for the 21st Century. Shanghai Library. Office of the White House Press Secretary, June 30, 1998. <http://www.whitehouse.gov/WH/New/ China/speeches.html>.

Thies, Wallace. *When Governments Collide: Coercion and Diplomacy in the Vietnam Conflict 1964-1968.* Berkeley, CA: University of California Press, 1980.

Tilelli, John. "The Far East, Know Thine Enemy." *Air Force Times*, December 20, 1999.

Trevan, Tim. *Saddam's Secrets*. New York: Harper Collins Publishers, 1999.

Trevor-Roper, H.R. "The Mind of Adolf Hitler." In Normai Cameron and R.H Stevens, translators. *Adolf Hitler, Hitler's Secret Conversations, 1941-1944*. New York: Farrar, Straus, and Young, 1953.

Tucker, Nancy Bernkopf. "China-Taiwan: US Debates and Policy Choices." *Survival*, Vol. 40, No. 4, Winter 1998-99.

Tucker, Robert. "The Dictator and Totalitarianism." In Fred Greenstein and Michael Lerner, eds. *A Source Book for the Study of Personality and Politics*. 1971.

Tyler, Patrick E. *A Great Wall: Six Presidents and China: An Investigative History*. New York: Public Affairs, 1999.

_____. "As China Threatens Taiwan, It Makes Sure U.S. Listens." *New York Times*, January 24, 1996.

U.S. Air Force. *Gulf War Air Power Survey, Vol. I, Planning and Command and Control. Volume I. Gulf War Air Power Survey.* Washington, D.C.: U.S. Government Printing Office, 1993.

U.S. Commission on National Security. *New World Coming: American Security in the 21st Century.* September 15, 1999.

U.S. Defense Intelligence Agency. *China's International Defense-Industrial Organizations.* Defense Intelligence Reference Document DI-1921-60-98 (Washington, D.C.: Defense Intelligence Agency, 1998) (unclassified).

_____. "General Chi Haotian." Biographic sketch, October 1995 (sanitized and declassified). In National Security Archive, *China and the United States: From Hostility to Engagement, 1960-1998*, Electronic Briefing Book, Document 13 <http://www.gwu.edu/~nsarchiv/ NSAEBB/ NSAEBB19/13-01.htm>.

_____. "Lieutenant General Xiong Guangkai." Biographic sketch, October 1996 (sanitized and declassified). In National Security Archive, *China and the United States: From Hostility to Engagement, 1960-1998*, Electronic Briefing Book, Document 15 <http://www.gwu.edu/~nsarchiv/ NSAEBB/NSAEBB19/15-01.htm>.

U.S. Department of Defense. *Department of Defense Annual Report Fiscal Year 1980.* Washington, D.C.: U.S. Government Printing Office, January 25, 1979.

_____. *Future Military Capabilities and Strategy of the People's Republic of China.* Report to Congress Pursuant to Section 1226 of the FY 98 National Defense Authorization Act. Washington, D.C.: Department of Defense, July 9, 1998.

_____. *Nuclear Deterrence.* Office of the Under Secretary of Defense For Acquisition & Technology, Report of the Defense Science Board Task Force. October 1998.

_____. *Selected Military Capabilities of the People's Republic of China.* Report to Congress Pursuant to Section 1305 of the FY 97 National Defense Authorization Act. Washington, D.C.: Department of Defense, April 2, 1997.

_____. *The Security Situation in the Taiwan Strait.* Report to Congress Pursuant to the FY 99 Appropriations Bill. Washington, D.C.: Department of Defense, February 1, 1999.

_____. *The United States Security Strategy for the East-Asia Pacific Region—1998.* Washington, D.C.: Office of International Security Affairs, Department of Defense, November 1998.

U.S. Department of State. *Foreign Relations of the United States, 1964-1968,* Vol. XXXIX, *Korea.* <http://www.state.gov/www.about_state/history/Vol_XXXIX/index.html>.

_____. Joint press conference by Secretary of State Madeleine K. Albright and PRC Foreign Minister Tang Jiaxuan. Waldorf-Astoria Hotel, New York City, September 23, 1999. Transcript. <http://www.usia.gov/products/pdq/pdq.htm>.

_____. International Information Programs, Washington File, On The Record Press Briefing. *Transcript: Adm. Blair Briefing on Korea, India-Pakistan, China-Taiwan.* April 5, 2000. <http://usinfo.state.gov>.

U.S. House. Select Committee on U.S. National Security and Military/Commercial Concerns with the People's Republic of China. *Report, Volume I.* Washington, D.C.: U.S. Government Printing Office, 1999.

Van Vranken Hickey, Dennis. "The Taiwan Strait Crisis of 1996: Implications for US Security Policy." *Journal of Contemporary China,* Vol. 7, November 1998.

Waite, Robert. "Afterward." In *The Mind of Adolf Hitler* by Walter Langer, New York: Basic Books, 1972.

_____. *The Psychopathic God.* New York: Da Capo Press, 1993.

Waldron, Arthur. "The Art of *Shi.*" *The New Republic,* Vol. 216, June 23, 1997.

Walker, Tony, and Stephen Fidler, "China Builds Up Missile Threat." *The Financial Times,* February 10, 1999.

Walpole, Robert D. "North Korea's Taepo Dong Launch and Some Implications on the Ballistic Missile Threat to the United States." In speech at the Center for Strategic and International Studies, December 8, 1998. <http://www.odci.gov/cia/public_affairs/speeches/walpole_speech_120898.html>.

_____. Speech at the Carnegie Endowment for International Peace. September 17, 1998. <http://www.odci.gov/cia/public_affairs/speeches/archives/1998/walpole_speech_091798.html>.

Walt, Stephen. "Rush to Failure." *Harvard Magazine*, Vol. 102, No. 5, May-June 2000.

Watts, William. *Americans Look at Asia: A Potomac Associates Perspective.* New York, NY: Henry Luce Foundation, October 1999. <http://www.hluce.org/images/usasia_report_1099.pdf>.

Weinberg, Gerhard. *Germany, Hitler & World War II.* New York: Cambridge University Press, 1996.

Weiner, Tim. "CIA Chief Defends Secrecy, in Spending and Spying, to Senate." *New York Times*, February 23, 1996.

_____. "U.S. Blundered On Intelligence, Officials Admit." *New York Times*, May 13, 1998.

Weisner, Jerome. Testimony. U.S. Senate, Committee on Foreign Relations. Subcommittee on International Organization and Disarmament. *Strategic and Foreign Policy Implications of ABM Systems.* Part II, Hearings. Washington, D.C.: U.S. Government Printing Office, 1969.

Whiting, Allen S. *The Chinese Calculus of Deterrence: India and Indochina.* Ann Arbor, MI: University of Michigan Press, 1975.

_____. "The PLA and China's Threat Perceptions." *The China Quarterly*, No. 146, June 1996.

Wilkening, Dean, Kenneth Watman. *Strategic Defenses and First-Strike Stability*, R-3412-FF/RC. Santa Monica, CA: The RAND Corporation, November 1986.

Witte, Count Sergei. Ed. and translated by Abraham Yarmolinsky. *The Memoirs of Count Witte*. Garden City, NY: Doubleday, Page, 1921.

Wohlforth, William. "A Certain Idea of Science: How International Relations Theory Avoids the New Cold War History." *Journal of Cold War Studies*, Vol. 1, No. 2, Spring 1999.

Wolf, Barry. *When the Weak Attack the Strong: Failures of Deterrence*, A RAND Note, N-3261-A. Santa Monica, CA: RAND, 1991.

Wu, Lilian. "Beijing Not to Use Force Against Taiwan Rashly: Strategist." Taiwan Central News Agency, October 19, 1999. <http://www.fas.org/news/taiwan/1999/e-10-19-99-24.htm>.

Yan Xuetong. "Take China's War Warnings Seriously." *The Asian Wall Street Journal*, September 3-4, 1999.

Zagare, Frank. "Rationality and Deterrence." *World Politics*, Vol. 42, No. 2, January 1990.

Zentner, Christian, and Freidemann Bedurftig. *The Encyclopedia of the Third Reich*. New York: De Capo Press, 1997.

Zimmerman, Peter. *Missile Defense And American Security*. Progressive Policy Institute Defense Working Paper, No. 2, May 1996.

Index